Study Guide & Working Papers

for

College Accounting
Chapters 1-14

Second Edition

John J. Wild
University of Wisconsin – Madison

Vernon Richardson
University of Arkansas

Ken W. Shaw
University of Missouri – Columbia

Study Guide & Working Papers for
COLLEGE ACCOUNTING
John J. Wild, Vernon Richardson, and Ken W. Shaw

Published by McGraw-Hill/Irwin, an imprint of The McGraw-Hill Companies, Inc., 1221 Avenue of the
Americas, New York, NY 10020. Copyright © 2011, 2008 by The McGraw-Hill Companies, Inc. All rights reserved.

1 2 3 4 5 6 7 8 9 0 WDQ/WDQ 0

ISBN: 978-0-07-726885-5
MHID: 0-07-726885-7

www.mhhe.com

TABLE OF CONTENTS

©*The McGraw-Hill Companies, Inc., 2011*

College Accounting, 2nd Edition

TO THE STUDENT

This study guide is provided as a learning tool for your study of *College Accounting, 2nd Edition* by John J. Wild, Vernon J. Richardson, and Ken W. Shaw. You should understand that the material provided is not intended to substitute for your textbook. Instead, the objectives of this guide are as follows:

1. To summarize important information that is explained in the text. For example, the **chapter outline** of each chapter identifies important topics in the chapter. In reading the outline, you should ask yourself whether or not you understand each of the topics listed. If not, you should return to the appropriate chapter in *College Accounting, 2e* and read carefully the portions that explain the specific outlined topics about which you are unclear.

2. To provide you with copies of **visuals** that your instructor may use in class to introduce selected topics. Even if not used in class, these visuals serve as useful study tools.

3. To provide you with a quick means of testing your knowledge of the chapter. If you are unable to correctly answer the **problems** that follow the chapter outline, you should again return to the appropriate chapter in *College Accounting, 2e* and review the sections about which you are unclear.

Your best approach to the use of this booklet out of class is:

- **First,** read the learning objectives and the related summary paragraphs. Then, ask whether your understanding of the chapter seems adequate for you to accomplish the objectives.

- **Second,** review the chapter outline, taking time to think through (describing to your self) the explanations that would be required to expand the outline. Use the notes column to indicate your questions or weaknesses. Return to *College Accounting, 2e* to answer questions and cover areas of weakness.

- **Third,** review visuals if provided in the chapter. These will reinforce major concepts of the chapter.

- **Fourth,** answer the requirements of the problems that follow the chapter outline. Then, check your answers against the solutions that are provided after the problems.

- **Fifth,** return to *College Accounting, 2e* for further study of any material you have not fully mastered.

You may also find it helpful to **bring outlines and visuals to class**. In class you can use a highlighter to mark areas your instructor emphasizes. Use the note section for additional notes and/or to indicate the numbers of relevant quick studies or exercises from the text that were worked in a notebook or on working papers during class. You can then refer back to these when studying with the outline later.

The next page is provided to recommend an **overall approach to succeeding** in an accounting course.

HOW TO SUCCEED IN YOUR ACCOUNTING COURSE

A.   **Stay Up-To-Date**

Accounting is a unique discipline in that learning takes place in "building blocks." The best analogy is that it is almost impossible to learn to read without learning the sounds of the letters in the alphabet. It is almost impossible for you to learn topics in accounting without having a level of understanding of the previously addressed topic. Accounting is the language of business, and like any language, it is learned through a developmental process.

Staying up-to-date includes completing all assignments on a timely basis. This allows you to take full advantage of classroom assignment check. The best insurance for staying up-to-date is to use good time management skills. This means plan a regular study schedule for the week—and stick to it! Staying up-to-date will give you the foundations to learn and **_succeed!_**

B.   **Know How to Use Your Textbook**

   1.   Overview the chapter

      a.   Preview the learning objectives and mark those that the instructor has listed in the course outline or mentioned in class.

      b.   Read title page which provide a very brief look at chapter contents, as well as a look back and ahead. This allows you to see the links or building blocks you will put in place.

      c.   Read the Summary of Learning Objectives found at the end of the chapter as well as in this study guide. This first pass on summaries is just to get a broad perspective of the contents. Do not expect to understand all that you read at this point.

   2.   Read the chapter

      a.   Using a highlighter as you read will keep you mentally alert. Writing is a proven vehicle for learning. Use the wide text margins to note key concepts as well as your questions. This will clarify your thoughts as you read.

      b.   Use How You Doin'. These are brief questions interspersed throughout the chapter. Use them to check whether you are grasping essential concepts. Guidance answers are found at the end of the chapter.

      c.   Reread the Summary of Learning Objectives. Make sure you thoroughly understand those specified by the instructor.

   3.   Use the demonstration problems

Don't miss these! Students find these most helpful in learning how to solve accounting problems. They address all major topics of the chapter. An approach to planning the solution is offered. Complete solutions are also provided.

C.   **Get Involved**

   1.   The more actively involved you are in the learning process, the more you will understand and retain. Ask questions that arose while you were reading the chapter. Fully participate in all classroom activities.

   2.   Form a study group or a learning team. Meet regularly outside class. Support each other's learning. Teaching others is proven to be the most effective way of reinforcing your learning and increasing your retention. All students benefit from collaborating in the learning process.

College Accounting, 2ⁿᵈ Edition

Part One:
Study Guide

CHAPTER 1
INTRODUCTION TO ACCOUNTING

Learning Objective 1:

Explain the purpose and importance of accounting in the information age.

Summary

Accounting is an information and measurement system that aims to identify, record, and communicate relevant, reliable, and comparable information about business activities. It helps assess opportunities, products, investments, and social and community responsibilities.

Learning Objective 2:

Identify users and uses of accounting.

Summary

Users of accounting are both internal and external. Some users and uses of accounting include: (a) management for controlling, monitoring, and planning; (b) lenders for measuring the risk and repayment of loans; (c) shareholders for assessing the return and risk of stock; (d) directors for overseeing management; and (e) employees for judging employment opportunities.

Learning Objective 3:

Identify career opportunities in accounting and related fields.

Summary

Opportunities in accounting include financial, managerial, and tax accounting. They also include accounting-related fields such as lending, consulting, managing, and planning.

Learning Objective 4:

Explain why ethics are crucial to accounting.

Summary

The goal of accounting is to provide useful information for decision making. For information to be useful, it must be trusted. This demands ethical behavior in accounting.

Learning Objective 5:

Explain the meaning of generally accepted accounting principles.

Summary

Generally accepted accounting principles are a common set of standards applied by accountants. Accounting principles aid in producing relevant, reliable and comparable information.

Learning Objective 6:

Identify the groups that establish generally accepted accounting principles.

Summary

Generally accepted accounting principles (GAAP) are established by two main groups in the United States: The Financial Accounting Standards Board (FASB) and the Securities and Exchange Commission (SEC). The FASB is a private entity that sets financial accounting principles. The SEC is the governmental entity that establishes financial reporting requirements for companies that issue stock to the public.

Learning Objective 7:

Identify the three types of ownership structures.

Summary

Proprietorships, partnerships, and corporations are the three main types of ownership structures. A proprietorship is a business owned by one person, while a partnership is owned by two or more partners. Proprietorships and partnerships are not separate legal entities from their owners. Corporations are separate legal entities from their owners, who are called shareholders.

| **Chapter Outline** | **Notes** |

Chapter Outline

I.   **Importance of Accounting**—it provides information about what businesses own, what they owe, and how they perform. Information is essential for decision makers.

  A. Accounting Activities

   Accounting is an information and measurement system that identifies, records and communicates relevant, reliable, and comparable information about an organization's business activities.

  B. Users of Accounting Information

   1. External Information Users—those not directly involved with running the company. Examples: shareholders (investors), lenders, customers, suppliers, regulators, lawyers, brokers, the press.

    a. Financial Accounting—area of accounting aimed at serving external users by providing them with *general-purpose financial statements*.

    b. General-Purpose Financial Statement—statements that have broad range of purposes which external users rely on.

   2. Internal Information Users—those directly involved in managing and operating an organization. Examples: research and development managers, purchasing managers, human resource managers, distribution managers, marketing managers, internal auditors.

    a. Managerial Accounting—is the area of accounting that serves the decision-making needs of internal users.

    b. Internal Reports—not subject to same rules as external reports. They are designed with special needs of internal users in mind.

  C. Opportunities in Accounting

   1. Four broad areas of opportunities are financial, managerial, taxation, and accounting related.

    a. Private accounting offers the most opportunities.

    b. Public accounting offers the next largest number of opportunities.

    c. Government (and not-for-profit) agencies, including business regulation and investigation of law violations also offer opportunities.

   2. Certifications—Demand for accounting professionals is very high. Certifications will increase marketability for professional accountants.

    a. Certified Public Accountant (CPA)

    b. Certified Management Accountant (CMA)

    c. Certified Internal Auditor (CIA)

    d. Certified Fraud Examiner (CFE)

    e. Certified Bookkeeper (CB)

II. **Fundamentals of Accounting**—accounting is guided by principles, standards, concepts, and assumptions.

    A. Ethics—a key concept. Ethics are beliefs that distinguish right from wrong.

        1. Guidelines for Ethical Decision Making

            a. Identify ethical concerns

            b. Analyze options

            c. Make ethical decisions

        2. Sources of Ethical Guidance

            a. AICPA Code of Professional Ethics

            b. Sarbanes-Oxley Act

    B. Generally Accepted Accounting Principles (GAAP)—concepts and rules that govern financial accounting. Purpose of GAAP is to make information in accounting statements relevant, reliable and comparable.

        1. Setting Accounting Principles

            a. U.S. major rule-setting bodies are the Securities and Exchange Commission (SEC) and the Financial Accounting Standards Board (FASB).

            b. The International Accounting Standards Board (IASB) issues standards that identifies preferred accounting practices in the global economy and hopes to create harmony among accounting practices in different countries.

        2. Rules-Based versus Principles-Based

            a. U.S. accounting practices are rules-based.

            b. Principles-based system would develop and apply broad, fundamental concepts for reporting.

    C. Ownership Structures—the business entity assumption requires a business to be accounted for separately from other businesses and its owners.

        1. Types of Ownership Structures

            a. Proprietorships are owned by one person.

            b. Partnerships are owned by two or more partners.

            c. Corporations are businesses separate from their owners, called shareholders.

        2. Types of Businesses

            a. Service businesses provide services to customers.

            b. Merchandisers buy products and resell them to consumers.

            c. Manufacturers make products to sell to merchandisers and consumers.

Alternate Demonstration Problem
Chapter One

Reggie Bush has always liked riding bicycles. Recently, he has decided to open a retail shop, Trojan Bikes, to sell and repair bikes. Reggie has asked your advice on how he should set up his accounting system and who will likely need to see the financial reports he generates.

Required:

Describe the basic process for setting up an accounting system. List four potential external or internal users of Trojan Bikes' financial statements. Explain how they might use these statements.

Planning the Solution:

Think about the necessary components for an adequate accounting system.

Look back at the list of possible external and internal users and think about how each might use Trojan Bikes' financial statements.

Consider any user that might use and need Trojan Bikes' financial statements.

Solution to Alternate Demonstration Problem:

Reggie should consider hiring a professional accountant to set up his accounting system. At a minimum, he will need to have a computer and accounting software to record and summarize all transactions of his business. The system should also include a printer for printing invoices to customers, checks to vendors and employees, and monthly and annual financial reports for interested parties.

Interested users would include:

1. Reggie Bush, owner and internal user. Reggie will use the financial reports to help him manage his business. His reports will tell him which products are the most profitable as well as where his money is going. He can also use the information for planning future operations.

2. Internal Revenue Service, external user. All companies are required to report the results of their operations to the Federal Government and pay any applicable taxes. The government uses the information to ensure compliance with tax regulations and to report economic data to the public.

3. Lenders (Banks), external users. Frequently, business owners borrow money to finance their operations in order to buy inventory and/or expand their operations. Banks who loan money to businesses want financial information to assess the financial strength of the company and monitor their operations.

4. Suppliers (Creditors), external user. Suppliers of bicycles and bicycle accessories may want financial information in order to assess the ability of the Company to pay for them. They will use the information to establish an appropriate level of credit to extent to the bike shop.

Problem I

The following statements are either true or false. Place a (T) in the parentheses before each true statement and an (F) before each false statement.

1. ( ) Accounting is an information system that communicates information about an organization's activities.

2. ( ) Recordkeeping is the same as accounting.

3. ( ) External users of accounting are not directly involved in the business.

4. ( ) Regulators do not have any legal authority over any aspect of a business.

5. ( ) A CPA is a highly regarded accounting specialist.

Problem II

You are given several words, phrases, or numbers to choose from in completing each of the following statements or in answering the following questions. In each case select the one that best completes the statement, or answers the question, and place its letter in the answer space provided.

_____ 1. The board that currently has the primary authority to identify generally accepted accounting principles is the:

    a. APB.

    b. FASB.

    c. FEI.

    d. ASB.

    e. AICPA.

_____ 2. Which of the following are included as an external user?

    a. Lenders.

    b. Shareholders.

    c. Labor unions.

    d. Regulators.

    e. All of the above.

_____ 3. Which of the following are not included as an internal user?

    a. Officers.

    b. Managers.

    c. Controllers.

    d. Governments.

    e. Budget officers.

_____ 4. Guidelines for making ethical decisions include:

    a. Identify ethical concerns.

    b. Analyze options.

    c. Consider all consequences.

    d. Choose best option.

    e. All of the above.

Problem III

Many of the important ideas and concepts discussed in Chapter 1 are reflected in the following list of key terms. Test your understanding of these terms by matching the appropriate definitions with the terms. Record the number identifying the most appropriate definition in the blank space next to each term.

_____ Accounting

_____ Auditors

_____ Bookkeeping

_____ Ethics

_____ External users

_____ Financial accounting

_____ Financial Accounting Standards Board (FASB)

_____ Generally Accepted Accounting Principles (GAAP)

_____ Internal users

_____ International Accounting Standards Board (IASB)

_____ Managerial accounting

_____ Recordkeeping

_____ Securities and Exchange Commission (SEC)

_____ Shareholders

1. An information and measurement system that identifies, records, and communicates relevant information about a company's business activities.
2. The rules that specify acceptable accounting practice.
3. Persons using accounting information who are not directly involved in running the organization.
4. The federal agency created by Congress in 1934 to regulate securities markets, including the flow of information from companies to the public.
5. The recording of financial transactions and events, either manually or electronically (also called bookkeeping).
6. Those who examine financial statements to verify that they are prepared according to generally accepted accounting principles.
7. Codes or conduct by which actions are judged as right or wrong, fair or unfair, honest or dishonest.
8. Persons using accounting information who are directly involved in managing and operation an organization; examples include managers and officers.
9. A board that identifies preferred accounting practices and encouraging their worldwide acceptance.
10. The area of accounting aimed at serving the decision-making needs of internal users.
11. The area of accounting aimed at serving external users.
12. A part of accounting that involves recording transactions and events, either electronically or manually (also called recordkeeping).

13. An independent group of seven full-time members who are currently responsible for setting accounting rules.

14. The owners of a corporation (also called stockholders).

Problem IV

Complete the following by filling in the blanks.

1. _____ is an information and measurement systems that identifies, records, and communicates information about an organization's business activities.

2. _____ _____ of accounting information are not directly involved in running the organization.

3. Financial statements provided to external users are referred to as _____-_____ _____ _____.

4. Users who are directly involved in managing and operating an organization are called _____ _____.

5. The _____ and _____ _____ is a government group that establishes reporting requirements for companies that issue stock to the public.

6. Beliefs that distinguish right from wrong are called _____.

7. A _____-_____ system develops and applies broad, fundamental concepts for reporting.

Solutions for Chapter 1

Problem I

1. T
2. F
3. T
4. F
5. T

Problem II

1. B   3. D
2. E   4. E

Problem III

1	Accounting	2	Generally Accepted Accounting Principles (GAAP)
6	Auditors	8	Internal users
12	Bookkeeping	9	International Accounting Standards Board (IASB)
7	Ethics	10	Managerial accounting
3	External users	5	Recordkeeping
11	Financial accounting	4	Securities and Exchange Commission (SEC)
13	Financial Accounting Standards Board (FASB)	14	Shareholders

Problem IV

1. Accounting
2. External users
3. general-purpose financial statements
4. internal users
5. Securities and Exchange Commission
6. ethics
7. principles-based

CHAPTER 2
ACCOUNTING FOR BUSINESS TRANSACTIONS

Learning Objective 1:

Define the accounting equation and each of its components.

Summary

The accounting equation is Assets = Liabilities + Equity. Assets are resources owned by a company. Liabilities are creditors' claims on assets. Equity is the owner's claim on assets *(the residual)*. The expanded accounting equation is Assets = Liabilities + [Owner Capital – Owner Withdrawals + Revenues – Expenses].

Learning Objective 2:

Analyze business transactions using the accounting equation.

Summary

A *transaction* is an exchange of value between two parties. Examples include exchange of products, services, money and rights to collect money. Transactions always have at least two effects on one or more components of the accounting equation. This equation is always in balance.

Learning Objective 3:

Identify and prepare basic financial statements and explain how they interrelate.

Summary

Three basic financial statements report on an organization's activities: balance sheet, income statement, and statement of owner's equity.

I. **Transaction Analysis and the Accounting Equation**

   A. Accounting equation (Assets = Liabilities + Equity)—elements of the equation include:

      1. Assets—resources owned or controlled by a company. (e.g. cash, supplies, equipment and land)

      2. Liabilities—creditors' claims on assets. These claims reflect obligations to transfer assets or provide products or services to others.

      3. Equity—owner's claim on assets. Also called *net assets* or *residual equity*.

         a. Investments—assets an owner puts into the company result in an increase in equity. Recorded under the title *Owner, Capital.*

         b. Revenues—gross increases in equity resulting from a company's earning activities.

         c. Owner's withdrawals—assets an owner takes from the company for personal use (results in decrease in equity).

         d. Expenses—cost of assets or services used to earn revenues (results in decrease in equity).

         e. Expanded Accounting Equation: Assets = Liabilities + Owner's Capital – Owner's Withdrawal + Revenues – Expenses

         f. Net Income = Revenue – Expenses

   B. Transaction and the Accounting Equation—each transaction and event always leaves the equation in balance. (Assets = Liabilities + Equity)

      1. Transaction types

         a. External value exchanges between two entities.

         b. Internal exchanges within an entity.

      2. Accounts are used to record transactions and events.

      3. Transaction Analysis Illustration

         a. Investment by owner
            + Asset (Cash) = + Owner's Equity (Owner, Capital)
                                    reason: investment
            Increase on both sides of equation keeps equation in balance

         b. Purchased supplies for cash
            + Asset (Supplies) = – Asset (Cash)
            Increase and decrease on one side of the equation keeps the equation in balance.

c. Purchase equipment for cash
    + Asset (Equipment) = − Asset (Cash)
    Increase and decrease on one side of the equation keeps
    the equation in balance.

d. Purchase supplies on credit
    + Asset (Supplies) = + Liability (Account Payable)
    Increase on both sides of equation keeps equation in
    balance.

e. Provided services for cash
    + Asset (Cash) = + Owner's Equity (reason: revenue earned)
    Increase on both sides of equation keeps equation in
    balance.

f. Payment of expense in cash (salaries, rent etc.)
    − Asset (Cash) = − Owner's Equity (reason: expense
    incurred)
    Decrease on both sides of equation keeps equation in
    balance.

g. Payment of expense in cash (salaries, rent etc.)
    − Asset (Cash) = − Owner's Equity (reason: expense
    incurred)
    Decrease on both sides of equation keeps equation in
    balance.

h. Provided services and facilities for credit
    + Asset (Accts Receivable) = + Owner's Equity (reason:
    revenue earned)

    Increase on both sides of equation keeps equation in
    balance.

i. Receipt of cash from account receivable
    + Asset (Cash) = − Asset (Accounts Receivable)
    Increase and decrease on one side of the equation keeps
    the equation in balance.

j. Payment of accounts payable
    −Asset (Cash) = − Liability (Accounts Payable)
    Decrease on both sides of equation keeps equation in
    balance.

k. Withdrawal of cash by owner
    −Asset (Cash) = − Owner's Equity (reason: owner's
    withdrawal)
    Decrease on both sides of equation keeps equation in
    balance.

II. **Financial Statements**

   A. The basic financial statements and their purposes are:

     1. *Income Statement*—describes a company's revenues and expenses along with the resulting net income or loss over a period of time. (Net income occurs when revenues exceed expenses. Net loss occurs when expenses exceed revenues.)

     2. *Statement of Owner's Equity*—explains changes in equity from net income (or loss) and from owner investment and withdrawals over a period of time.

     3. *Balance Sheet*—describes a company's financial position (types and amounts of assets, liabilities, and equity) at a point in time

WARNING: <u>NO MATTER WHAT HAPPENS</u> ALWAYS KEEP THIS SCALE IN BALANCE

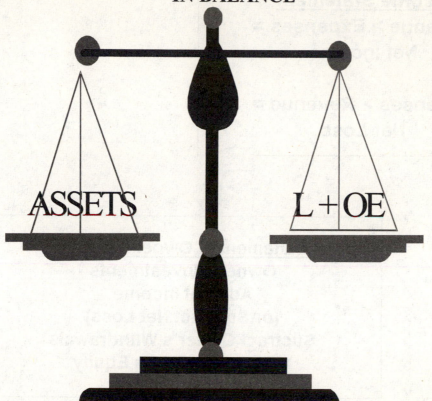

Basic Accounting Equation

ASSETS = LIABILITIES + OWNER'S EQUITY

TRANSACTION ANALYSIS RULES

1) Every transaction affects at least two items.
2) Every transaction must result in a balanced equation.

TRANSACTION ANALYSIS POSSIBILITIES:				
A	=	L	+	OE
(1) +	and		+	
or (2) –	and		–	
or (3) + and –	and	No change		
or (4) No change	and	+ and –		

Income Statement
Revenue > Expenses =
Net Income

Expenses > Revenue =
Net Loss

Statement of Owner's Equity
Owner's Investments
Add Net Income
(or Subtract Net Loss)
Subtract Owner's Withdrawals
= Ending Owner's Equity

Balance Sheet
Assets
=
Liabilities +
Owners Equity

Alternate Demonstration Problem
Chapter Two

One summer, Bill Smith decided to earn money as a lawn service professional. He solicited business in the neighborhood and obtained enough lawn servicing jobs that he thought he could be successful. On the basis of these commitments, Bill went to the bank, withdrew $2,000 of his savings and deposited the funds in a business bank account. At the end of the summer, Bill tried to figure out how well he had done. He examined his business bank account checkbook and noted the following:

- Deposits, all from customer collections, totaled $11,400.

- Checks written:

  - Truck and equipment rental, $1,800

  - Gas, oil, and lubrication, $880

  - Miscellaneous supplies used, $90

  - Helpers, $4,700; including payroll taxes, $500

  - Insurance, $175

  - Telephone, $100

- Transfer from business bank account to his personal savings account, $2,000.

Bill also had records that showed:

- Customers still owed him $600 for services that were performed.

- He still owed another $100 to a vendor for gas and oil.

Required:

1. Show the effect of each transaction on the accounting equation.

2. Prepare an income statement for Bill for his summer business.

3. Prepare a statement of owner's equity for Bill for his summer business.

4. Prepare a balance sheet for Bill at the end of the summer.

Solution: Alternate Demonstration Problem
Chapter Two

1.

	Item		Assets	=	Liabilities	+	Equity
a.	Cash investment	+	$ 2,000			+	$ 2,000
b.	Revenue received	+	11,400			+	11,400
c.	Truck and equipment rental	−	1,800			−	1,800
d.	Truck expenses	−	880			−	880
e.	Miscellaneous supplies used	−	90			−	90
f.	Helpers	−	4,700			−	4,700
g.	Payroll taxes	−	500			−	500
h.	Insurance	−	175			−	175
i.	Telephone	−	100			−	100
j.	Withdrawal	−	2,000			−	2,000
k.	Revenue earned-not collected	+	600			+	600
l.	Oil and gas bill not yet paid			+	$100	−	100
			$3,755		$100		$3,655

2.

BILL SMITH'S LAWN SERVICE CO.
Income Statement
For the period from June 1 through August 31 20XX

Total revenue ($11,400 + $600)..		$12,000
Expenses:		
Truck expenses ($880 + $100).................................	$ 980	
Truck and equipment rental	1,800	
Supplies	90	
Helpers..	4,700	
Payroll taxes	500	
Insurance	175	
Telephone	100	
Total expenses		8,345
Net income		$ 3,655

3.

BILL SMITH'S LAWN SERVICE CO.
Statement of Owner's Equity
For the period from June 1 through August 31 20XX

W. Smith, Capital – June 1	$ 0
Add: Investments by Owner	2,000
Net Income	3,655
Less: Owner Withdrawals	(2,000)
W. Smith, Capital – August 31, 20XX	$ 3,655

4.

BILL SMITH'S LAWN SERVICE CO.
Balance Sheet
August 31, 20XX

Assets		Liabilities and Owner's Equity	
Cash	$3,155	Accounts payable	$ 100
Accounts receivable	600	Bill Smith, Capital...............	3,655
		Total liabilities and	
Total assets	$3,755	owner's equity	$3,755

Problem I

The following statements are either true or false. Place a (T) in the parentheses before each true statement and an (F) before each false statement.

1. ( ) The return on assets ratio is calculated by dividing average total assets by net income.

2. ( ) Equity equals liabilities minus assets.

3. ( ) Internal transactions are exchanges within an organization.

4. ( ) An arrangement to purchase office supplies on credit is referred to as an account receivable.

5. ( ) Net income + Owner investments - Owner withdrawals = the increase in owner's equity during the year.

Problem II

You are given several words, phrases, or numbers to choose from in completing each of the following statements or in answering the following questions. In each case select the one that best completes the statement, or answers the question, and place its letter in the answer space provided.

_____ 1. Financial statement information about Boom Company is as follows:

December 31, 2009:

    Assets $42,000

    Liabilities 17,000

December 31, 2010:

    Assets 47,000

    Liabilities 14,800

During 2010:

    Net income 18,000

    Owner investments..?

    Owner withdrawals 10,800

The amount of owner investments during 2010 is:

a. $ 7,200.

b. $14,400.

c. $25,000.

d. $ 0.

e. Some other amount.

_____ 2.   Properties owned by a business are called:

    a. Dividends.

    b. Assets.

    c. Retained earnings.

    d. Revenues.

    e. Owner's equity.

_____ 3.   If a business rendered services for a customer in exchange for $175 cash, what would be the effects on its accounting equation?

    a. Assets, $175 increase; Liabilities, no effect; Owner's Equity, $175 increase.

    b. Assets, no effect; Liabilities, $175 decrease; Owner's Equity, $175 increase.

    c. Assets, $175 increase; Liabilities, $175 increase; Owner's Equity, no effect.

    d. Assets, $175 increase; Liabilities, $175 decrease; Owner's Equity, $350 increase.

    e. There is no effect on the accounting equation.

_____ 4.   Properties owned by a business are called:

    a. Dividends.

    b. Assets.

    c. Retained earnings.

    d. Revenues.

    e. Owner's equity.

Problem III

Many of the important ideas and concepts discussed in Chapter 2 are reflected in the following list of key terms. Test your understanding of these terms by matching the appropriate definitions with the terms. Record the number identifying the most appropriate definition in the blank space next to each term.

_____ Account	_____ Internal transactions	
_____ Accounting equation	_____ Liabilities	
_____ Assets	_____ Net income	
_____ Balance sheet	_____ Net loss	
_____ Equity	_____ Owner capital	
_____ Events	_____ Owner investment	
_____ Expanded accounting equation	_____ Owner withdrawal	
_____ Expenses	_____ Return on assets	
_____ External transactions	_____ Revenues	
_____ Income statement	_____ Statement of owner's equity	

1. A financial statement that lists the types and dollar amounts of assets, liabilities, and equity as of a specific date; also called the *statement of financial position*.

2. A generic account which includes owner investments, revenues, owner withdrawals, and expenses.

3. A record within an accounting system in which increases and decreases are entered and stored.

4. Arises when expenses are more than sales.

5. Resources expected to produce future benefits.

6. Creditor's claims on an organization's assets.

7. The owner's claims on an organization's assets.

8. The equality where Assets = Liabilities + Owner's Equity.

9. The financial statement that subtracts expenses from revenues to yield a net income or loss over a specified period of time.

10. A report of changes in equity over a period of time; adjusted for increases (owner investment and net income) and for decreases (withdrawals and net loss).

11. The amount a business earns after subtracting all expenses necessary for its sales.

12. A ratio serving as an indicator of operating efficiency; defined as net income divided by average total assets.

13. The costs incurred to earn sales.

14. The amounts earned from selling products or services (also called sales).

15. Happenings that both affect an organization's financial position and can be reliably measured.

16. Exchanges within an organization that can also affect the accounting equation.

17. Exchanges of economic consideration between one entity and another.

18. Assets = Liabilities + Equity where Equity equals [Owner capital – Owner withdrawals + Revenues – Expenses].

19. Assets put into the business by the owner.

20. Assets an owner takes from the company for personal use.

Problem IV

Complete the following by filling in the blanks.

1. Assets created by selling goods and services on credit are called _____. Liabilities created by buying goods and services on credit are called _____.

2. Equity on a balance sheet is the difference between a company's _____ and its _____.

3. The statement of owners' equity discloses all changes in equity during the period including _____, _____, and _____.

4. The balance sheet equation is _____ equals _____ plus _____. It is also called the _____ equation.

5. Creditor's claims on assets are called _____.

6. An excess of revenues over expenses for a period results in a _____. An excess of expenses over revenues results in a _____. The financial statement that lists revenues and expenses is the _____.

7. A balance sheet prepared for a business shows its financial position as of a specific _____. Financial position is shown by listing the _____ of the business, its _____, and its _____.

Problem V

The assets, liabilities, and owner's equity of Linda Cornell's law practice are shown on the first line in the equation in the table on the following page. Below you will find eight transactions completed by Ms. Cornell. Show by additions and subtractions in the spaces provided in the table, the effects of each transaction on the items of the equation. Show new totals after each transaction as in Exhibit 1-9, page 17 in the text.

1. Paid the rent for three months in advance on the law office, $3,000.
2. Paid cash to purchase a new typewriter for the office, $900.
3. Completed legal work for Ray Holland and immediately collected the full payment of $2,500 in cash.
4. Purchased law books on credit, $700.
5. Completed $1,500 of legal work for Julie Landon on credit, and immediately entered in the accounting records both the right to collect and the revenue earned.
6. Paid for the law books purchased in Transaction 4.
7. Received $1,500 from Julie Landon for the legal work in Transaction 5.
8. Paid the weekly salary of the office secretary, $575.

Refer to your completed equation table and fill in the blanks:

a. Did each transaction affect two items of the equation? _____.

b. Did the equation remain in balance after the effects of each transaction were entered? _____.

c. If the equation had not remained in balance after the effects of each transaction were entered, this would have indicated that

_____.

d. Ms. Cornell earned $2,500 of revenue upon the completion of Transaction 3, and the asset that flowed into the business as a result of this transaction was in the form of _____.

e. Ms. Cornell earned $1,500 of revenue upon the completion of Transaction 5, and the asset that flowed into the business upon the completion of this transaction was

_____.

f. The right to collect $1,500 from Julie Landon was converted into _____ in Transaction 7. Nevertheless, the revenue was earned upon the completion of the _____ in Transaction 5.

Problem V Table

#	ASSETS						=	LIABILITIES	+	EQUITY				
	Cash	+	Accounts Receivable	+	Prepaid Rent	+	Law Library	+	Office Equipment	=	Accounts Payable	+	L Cornell, Capital	−	L. Cornell, Withdrawals	+	Revenues	−	Expenses
	$4,000							$12,000		$3,250		$19,250		$19,250					
1																			
2																			
3																			
4																			
5																			
6																			
7																			
8																			

Solutions for Chapter 2

Problem I

1. F
2. F
3. T
4. F
5. T

Problem II

1. D
2. B

3. A
4. A

Problem III

3	Account		16	Internal transactions
8	Accounting equation		6	Liabilities
5	Assets		11	Net income
1	Balance sheet		4	Net loss
7	Equity		2	Owner capital
15	Events		19	Owner investment
18	Expanded accounting equation		20	Owner withdrawal
13	Expenses		12	Return on assets
17	External transactions		14	Revenues
9	Income statement		10	Statement of owner's equity

Problem IV

1. accounts receivable; accounts payable
2. assets; liabilities
3. net income or net loss; new investments by the owner; withdrawals
4. Assets; Liabilities; Owner's Equity; accounting
5. liabilities
6. net income (profit); net loss; income statement
7. date; assets; liabilities; equity

Problem V

	Cash +	Accounts Receivable +	Prepaid Rent +	Law Library +	Office Equipment =	Accounts Payable +	L. Cornell, Capital +	L. Cornell, – Withdrawals +	Revenues –	Expenses
	$4,000			$12,000	$3,250		$19,250			
1.	–3,000		+3,000							
	$1,000		$3,000	$12,000	$3,250		$19,250			
2.	–900				+900					
	$ 100		$3,000	$12,000	$4,150		$19,250			
3.	+2,500								+$2,500	
	$2,600		$3,000	$12,000	$ 4150		$19,250		$2,500	
4.				+700		+700				
	$2,600		$3,000	$12,700	$4,150	$ 700	$19,250		$2,500	
5.		+1,500							1,500	
	$2,600	$1,500	$3,000	$12,700	$4,150	$ 700	$19,250		$4,000	
6.	–700					–700				
	$1,900	$1,500	$3,000	$12,700	$4,150	$ 0	$19,250		$4,000	
7.	+1,500	–1,500								
	$3,400	$ 0	$3,000	$12,700	$4,150	$ 0	$19,250		$4,000	
8.	–575									575
	$2,825+	$ 0+	$3,000+	$12,700+	$4,150=	$ 0+	$19,250–	$0 +	$4,000–	$575

a. Yes
b. Yes
c. an error had been made
d. cash
e. an account receivable
f. cash; legal work

CHAPTER 3
APPLYING DOUBLE-ENTRY ACCOUNTING

Learning Objective 1:

Describe a T-account and its use in recording transactions.

Summary

A T-account is a tool to show the effects of transactions and events on accounts. A T-account has both a left (debit) and right (credit) side.

Learning Objective 2:

Define debits and credits and explain their role in double-entry accounting.

Summary

Debit refers to left, and credit refers to right. Debits increase assets, withdrawals, and expenses, while credits decrease them. Credits increase liabilities, owner capital and revenues; debits decrease them. Double-entry accounting means each transaction affects at least two accounts and has at least one debit and one credit. The system for recording debits and credits follows from the accounting equation. The left side of an account is the normal balance for assets, withdrawals, and expenses, and the right side is the normal balance for liabilities, capital and revenues.

Learning Objective 3:

Post transactions in T-accounts.

Summary

We analyze transactions using the concepts of double-entry accounting. This analysis is performed by determining a transaction's effects on accounts. These effects are recorded in journals and posted to ledgers. Posting is the process of entering dollar amounts for transactions in the appropriate debit or credit side of the affected T-accounts.

Learning Objective 4:

Prepare and explain the use of a trial balance.

Summary

A trial balance is a list of accounts from the ledger showing their debit or credit balances in separate columns. The trial balance is a summary of the ledger's contents and is useful in preparing financial statements and revealing recordkeeping errors.

Learning Objective 5:

Prepare financial statements from a trial balance.

Summary

The balance sheet, the statement of owner's equity and the income statement use data from the trial balance for their preparation.

I. **Analyzing and Processing Transactions**

    a. The T-Account

        i. Accounts—record increases and decreases in specific items in the accounting equation

        ii. The T-account is a tool to represent the accounts that appear in the accounting system

    b. Debits and Credits

        i. Debits on the left

        ii. Credits on the right

    c. Double-Entry Accounting

        i. Debits must equal credits for each transaction

        ii. Debits increase Assets, Drawing and Expenses

        iii. Debits decrease Liabilities, Capital and Revenue

        iv. Credits increase Liabilities, Capital and Revenue

        v. Credits decrease Assets, Drawing and Expenses

        vi. Normal balance—side of an account on which increases are recorded

    d. Analyzing Transactions—TAP Process

        i. <u>T</u>ransaction—determine accounts affected

        ii. <u>A</u>nalysis—use accounting equation

        iii. <u>P</u>ost—make entries to T-accounts

    e. Analyzing Transactions an Illustration

        i. Investment by the Owner—Dr. Cash, Cr. Capital

        ii. Purchase Supplies for Cash—Dr. Supplies, Cr. Cash

        iii. Purchase Equipment for Cash—Dr. Equipment, Cr. Cash

        iv. Purchase Supplies on Credit—Dr. Supplies, Cr. Accounts Payable

        v. Provide Services for Cash—Dr. Cash, Cr. Consulting Revenue

        vi. Payment of Expense with Cash—Dr. Expense (Rent), Cr. Cash

        vii. Payment of Expense with Cash—Dr. Expense (Salaries), Cr. Cash

        viii. Provide Consulting and Rental Services on Credit— Dr. Accounts Receivable, Cr. Consulting Revenue, Cr. Rental Revenue

        ix. Receipt of Cash on Account—Dr. Cash, Cr. Accounts Receivable

      x. Partial Payment of Accounts Payable—Dr. Accounts Payable, Cr. Cash

     xi. Withdrawal of Cash by Owner—Dr. Withdrawals, Cr. Cash

    xii. Receipt of Cash for Future Services – Dr. Cash, Cr. Unearned Consulting Revenue

   xiii. Pay Cash for Future Insurance Coverage – Dr. Prepaid Insurance, Cr. Cash

   xiv. Purchase Supplies for Cash – Dr. Supplies, Cr. Cash

    xv. Payment of Expense with Cash – Dr. Expenses (Utilities), Cr. Cash

   xvi. Payment of Expense with Cash – Dr. Expenses (Salaries), Cr. Cash

f. Accounting Equation Analysis

     i. Balance all T-accounts—total the debits and credits for each account and compute a net total (balance) for each account

    ii. Assets must equal Liabilities and Equity

g. Trial Balance—a list of all accounts and their corresponding balances with separate columns for debit and credit amounts

     i. Preparing a Trial Balance

        1. Prepare a heading which includes the name of the company, the name of the schedule (Trial Balance) and the date of the balances.

        2. List the account title for all accounts in the first column

        3. Insert the debit amounts in the debit column

        4. Insert the credit amounts in the credit column

        5. Total debits and credits to match

        6. Investigate discrepancies

h. Using a Trial Balance to Prepare Financial Statements

     i. Income Statement—Includes all Revenue and Expenses over an accounting period

    ii. Statement of Owner's Equity—Includes Net Income (Loss), Additional Capital contributions, Owner's withdrawals over an accounting period

   iii. Balance Sheet—Assets, Liabilities and Owners Capital at the end of an accounting period

The Rules of Debit and Credit

	Increase	Decrease
Assets	Debit	Credit
Liabilities	Credit	Debit
Equity	Credit	Debit
Revenue	Credit	Debit
Expenses	Debit	Credit

Matthew Leinart decided to open a business teaching people ballroom dancing. The following transactions occurred during the month of January, 2010:

    a.   Leinart invested $5,000 into a new checking account in the name of the business, The Dancing Quarterback.

    b.   Paid rent on a studio for the month of January, $500

    c.   Paid $600 for Liability insurance for one year.

    d.   Bought electronic equipment and music CD's on credit in the amount of $1,200

    e.   Received and paid a bill for advertising, $250.

    f.   Collected $650 for dancing lessons for the first half of the month.

    g.   Received and paid the utility bill for the month of January, $200

    h.   Sent a bill to 'Active Seniors' for dancing lessons given but not collected, $350

    i.   Made a payment to creditor for equipment purchased in c above, $200.

    j.   Bought supplies on account for $150.

    k.   Collected $1,300 for dancing lessons for the second half of the month.

    l.   Paid salaries to dance instructors for January, $800.

    m.   Leinart withdrew cash for personal use, $500.

Required:

1.   Apply the rules of Debit and Credit to each transaction.

2.   Record the transactions in T-accounts, set up accounts for Cash, Accounts Receivable, Prepaid Insurance, Supplies, Equipment, Accounts Payable, Leinart - Capital, Leinart - Drawing, Dancing Lesson Revenue, Rent Expense, Utilities, Expense, Advertising Expense, Salaries Expense.

3. **Calculate totals in all T-accounts and prepare a trial balance.**

4. **Prepare an income statement for The Dancing Quarterback for the month ended January 31, 2010.**

5. **Prepare a statement of owner's equity for The Dancing Quarterback for the month ended January 31, 2010.**

6. **Prepare a balance sheet for The Dancing Quarterback at January 31, 2010.**

Solution – Alternative Demonstration Problem

The Dancing Quarterback
Alternate Demonstration Problem – Chapter 3

	Cash					Accounts Payable					Dancing Lesson Revenue	
a	5000	500	b	i	200	1200	d				650	f
f	650	600	c			150	j				350	h
k	1300	250	e			1150					1300	k
		200	g								2300	
		200	i		**Leinart, Capital**							
		800	l			5000	a			**Salary Expense**		
		500	m					l		800		
	3900				**Leinart, Drawing**							
				m	500					**Rent Expense**		
	Accounts Receivable							b		500		
h	350											
										Utilities Expense		
	Supplies							g		200		
j	150											
										Advertising Expense		
	Prepaid Insurance							e		250		
c	600											
	Equipment											
d	1200											

The Dancing Quarter Back
Trial Balance
31-Jan-10

	Debits	Credits
Cash	$ 3,900	
Accounts Receivable	350	
Supplies	150	
Prepaid Insurance	600	
Equipment	1,200	
Accounts Payable		$ 1,150
Leinart, Capital		5,000
Leinart, Withdrawal	500	
Dancing Lesson Revenue		2,300
Salary Expense	800	
Rent Expense	500	
Utilities Expense	200	
Advertising Expense	250	
	$ 8,450	$ 8,450

The Dancing Quarter Back	
Income Statement	
For the month ended January 31, 2010	

Revenue:		
Dancing Lesson Revenue		$ 2,300
Expenses:		
Salary Expense	800	
Rent Expense	500	
Utilities Expense	200	
Advertising Expense	250	
Total Expenses		1,750
Net Income		$ 550

The Dancing Quarter Back		
Balance Sheet		
As of January 31, 2010		
Assets:		
Cash		$ 3,900
Accounts Receivable		350
Supplies		150
Prepaid Insurance		600
Equipment		1,200
Total Assets		$ 6,200
Liabilities:		
Accounts Payable		$ 1,150
Owner's Equity:		
Leinart, Capital		5,050
Total Liabilities and Equity		$ 6,200

The Dancing Quarter Back	
Statement of Owner's Equity	
For the month ended January 31, 2010	
Leinart, Capital-January 1, 2010	$---
Add: Contributions	5,000
Add: Net Income	550
Less: Leinert, Withdrawals	(500)
Leinart, Capital-January 31, 2010	$ 5,050

Problem I

The following statements are either true or false. Place a (T) in the parentheses before each true statement and an (F) before each false statement.

1. ( ) Debits are used to record increases in assets, withdrawals, and expenses.

2. ( ) In double-entry accounting, the total amount debited does not need to equal the total amount credited.

3. ( ) The cost of renting an office during the current period is an expense; however, the cost of renting an office six periods in advance is an asset.

4. ( ) Expenses decrease Owner's Equity.

5. ( ) The general ledger is a record containing all accounts used by a company.

Problem II

You are given several words, phrases, or numbers to choose from in completing each of the following statements or in answering the following questions. In each case select the one that best completes the statement or answers the question and place its letter in the answer space provided.

_____ 1. Hans Hammer's company had a capital balance of $12,300 on June 30 and $23,800 on July 31. Net income for the month of July was $14,000. How much did Hammer withdraw from the business during July?

      a. $22,100
      b. $25,500
      c. $2,500
      d. $11,500
      e. $0

_____ 2. Which of the following transactions does not affect the equity in a proprietorship?

      a. Investments by the owner.
      b. Withdrawals of cash by the owner.
      c. Cash receipts for revenues.
      d. Cash receipts for unearned revenues.
      e. Cash payments for expenses.

_____ 3. The following transactions occurred during the month of October:

Paid $1,500 cash for store equipment.

Paid $1,000 in partial payment for supplies purchased 30 days previously.

Paid October's utility bill of $600.

Paid $1,200 to owner of business for his personal use.

Paid $1,400 salary of office employee for October.

What was the total amount of expenses during October?

      a. $3,000
      b. $4,500
      c. $2,000
      d. $3,500
      e. $5,700

_____ 4. Prepaid accounts (also called prepaid expenses) are:

      a. assets.
      b. expenses.
      c. liabilities.
      d. revenue.
      e. capital.

_____ 5. A debit will:

      a. increase a liability account.
      b. increase an asset account.
      c. decrease an asset account.
      d. increase a revenue account.
      e. increase a capital account.

Problem III

Following are the first 10 transactions completed by P. L. Wheeler's new business called Wheeler's Repair Shop:

    a.   Started the business with a cash deposit of $1,800 to a bank account in the name of the business.

    b.   Paid three months' rent in advance on the shop space, $675.

    c.   Purchased repair equipment for cash, $700.

    d.   Completed repair work for customers and collected cash, $1,005.50.

    e.   Purchased additional repair equipment on credit from Comet Company, $415.50.

    f.   Completed repair work on credit for Fred Baca, $175.

    g.   Paid Comet Company $290.50 of the amount owed from transaction (e).

    h.   Paid the local radio station $75 for an announcement of the shop opening.

    i.   Fred Baca paid for the work completed in transaction (f).

    j.   Withdrew $350 cash from the bank for P. L. Wheeler to pay personal expenses.

Required

1.   Record the transactions directly in the T-accounts that follow. Use the transaction letters to identify the amounts in the accounts.

2.   Prepare a trial balance as of the current date using the form that follows.

Cash	Accounts Payable

	P. L. Wheeler, Capital

Accounts Receivable	P. L. Wheeler, Withdrawals

Prepaid Rent	Repair Services Revenue

Repair Equipment	Advertising Expense

WHEELER'S REPAIR SHOP

Trial Balance

_____ , 20 ____

Problem IV

Using the Trial Balance below, prepare the Income Statement, Statement of Owner's Equity and the Balance Sheet for Landen Landscaping for the month of May.

LANDEN LANDSCAPING

Trial Balance

May 31, 20XX

		Debit				Credit			
Cash		$	3	0 0 0					
Accounts receivable				2 0 0					
Supplies				1 4 0					
Accounts Payable						$		3 1 0	
A. Landen, Capital, May 1							1	8 0 0	
A. Landen, Withdrawals				8 0 0					
Landscaping revenue							4	3 3 0	
Wages expense			1	5 0 0					
Rent expense				8 0 0					
Totals		$	6	4 4 0		$	6	4 4 0	

LANDEN LANDSCAPING
Income Statement
For Month Ended _____ , 20 ____

						$	
		$					
						$	

LANDEN LANDSCAPING
Statement of Owner's Equity
For Month Ended _____ , 20 ____

		$					
						$	
						$	

LANDEN LANDSCAPING
Balance Sheet
_____ , 20 ____

			$				$	
			$				$	

Problem V

Many of the important ideas and concepts discussed in Chapter 3 are reflected in the following list of key terms. Test your understanding of these terms by matching the appropriate definition with the terms. Record the number identifying the most appropriate definition in the blank space next to each term.

_____	Account	_____	Ledger
_____	Account balance	_____	Owner's capital
_____	Credit	_____	Owner withdrawals
_____	Creditor	_____	Posting
_____	Debit	_____	T-account
_____	Double-entry accounting	_____	Trial balance
_____	Footing	_____	Unearned revenues

1. Liabilities created by advance cash payments from customers for products or services; revenues are earned when the products or services are delivered in the future.

2. A list of accounts and their balances at a point in time; total debt balances equal total credit balances.

3. A location within an accounting system where increases and decreases in a specific asset, liability, equity, revenue, or expense are recorded and stored.

4. An account form used as a tool to show the effects of transactions and events on specific accounts.

5. Recorded on the left side; an entry that increases asset and expense accounts, and decreases liability, equity, and revenue accounts.

6. The difference between the increases (including the beginning balance) and decreases in an account.

7. Individuals or organizations entitled to receive payments from a company.

8. The total of a column of numbers.

9. Recorded on the right side; an entry that decreases asset and expense accounts, or increases liability, equity, and revenue accounts.

10. Account showing the owner's claim on company assets; equals owner investments plus net income (or less net losses) minus owner withdrawals since the company's inception; also referred to as *equity*.

11. Record containing all accounts of a business.

12. The process of transferring journal entry information to the ledger.

13. An accounting system in which each transaction affects at least two accounts and has at least one debit and one credit.

14. Payment of cash or other assets from a business to its owner(s).

Problem VI

Complete the following by filling in the blanks.

1. The process of recording transactions in a journal is called _____. The process of transferring journal entry information to the ledger is called _____.

2. The _____ creates a link between a journal entry and the ledger accounts by providing a cross-reference for tracing the entry from one record to the other.

3. Notes receivable and prepaid insurance are examples of a(n) _____ account. Unearned revenues and interest payable are examples of a(n) _____ account.

4. Balances of _____ and _____ accounts flow into the income statement. Then, net income from the income statement and balances from _____ and _____ accounts flow into the statement of changes in equity.

5. a. The normal balance of an asset account is a _____.

   b. The normal balance of a liability account is a _____.

   c. The normal balance of the capital account is a _____.

   d. The normal balance of the withdrawals account is _____.

   e. The normal balance of a revenue account is a _____.

   f. The normal balance of an expense account is a _____.

6. The steps in preparing a trial balance are:

   _____.

   _____.

   _____.

   _____.

   _____.

7. A trial balance that fails to balance is proof that _____ either in journalizing, in posting, or in preparing the trial balance.

8. A trial balance that balances is not absolute proof that no errors were made because

   _____.

Solutions for Chapter 3

Problem I

1. T
2. F
3. T
4. T
5. T

Problem II

1. C
2. D
3. C
4. A
5. B

Problem III

	Ca	sh		
(a)	1,800.00	(b)	675.00	
(d)	1,005.50	(c)	700.00	
(i)	175.00	(g)	290.50	
		(h)	75.00	
		(j)	350.00	

	Repair Equipment	
(c)	700.00	
(e)	415.50	

	P.L. Wheeler, Withdrawals	
(j)	350.00	

	Accounts Receivable		
(f)	175.00	(i)	175.00

	Accounts Payable		
(g)	290.50	(e)	415.50

	Repair Services Revenue		
		(d)	1,005.50
		(f)	175.00

	Prepaid Rent	
(b)	675.00	

	P.L. Wheeler, Capital	
	(a)	1,800.00

	Advertising Expense	
(h)	75.00	

WHEELER'S REPAIR SHOP
Trial Balance
(Current Date)

Cash	$ 890.00	
Prepaid rent	675.00	
Repair equipment	1,115.50	
Accounts payable		$ 125.00
P.L. Wheeler, Capital		1,800.00
P.L. Wheeler, Withdrawals	350.00	
Repair services revenue		1,180.50
Advertising expense	75.00	
Totals	$3,105.50	$3,105.50

Problem IV

LANDEN LANDSCAPING
Income Statement
For Month Ended May 31, 20XX

Revenues						
Landscaping revenue					$ 4 3 3 0	
Operating expenses						
Wages expense	$ 1 5 0 0					
Rent expense	8 0 0					
Total operating expenses					2 3 0 0	
Net income					$ 2 0 3 0	

LANDEN LANDSCAPING
Statement of Owner's Equity
For Month Ended May 31, 20XX

A. Landen, Capital, May 1	$ 1 8 0 0				
Plus: Net income	2 0 3 0				
			$ 3 8 3 0		
Less: Withdrawals by owner			8 0 0		
A. Landen, Capital, May 31			$ 3 0 3 0		

LANDEN LANDSCAPING
Balance Sheet
May 31, 20XX

Assets				Liabilities			
Cash	$ 3 0 0 0			Accounts payable	$ 3 1 0		
Accounts receivable	2 0 0			**Equity**			
Supplies	1 4 0			A. Landen, Capital, May 31	3 0 3 0		
Total Assets	$ 3 3 4 0			Total liabilities and equity	$ 3 3 4 0		

©The McGraw-Hill Companies, Inc., 2011

Problem V

3	Account	11	Ledger
6	Account balance	10	Owner's capital
9	Credit	14	Owner withdrawals
7	Creditor	12	Posting
5	Debit	4	T-account
13	Double-entry accounting	2	Trial balance
8	Footing	1	Unearned revenues

Problem VI

1. journalizing, posting

2. Posting reference (PR) column

3. asset, liability

4. revenue, expense; capital, withdrawals

5. (a) debit; (b) credit; (c) credit; (d) debit; (e) credit; (f) debit

6. (1) Determine the balance of each account; (2) List in their ledger order the accounts having balances, with the debit balances in one column and the credit balances in another; (3) Add the debit balances; (4) Add the credit balances; (5) Compare the two totals for equality.

7. at least one error has been made

8. some types of errors do not create unequal debits and credits

CHAPTER 4
PREPARING THE GENERAL JOURNAL AND GENERAL LEDGER

Learning Objective 1:

Explain the steps in processing transactions.

Summary

The accounting process identifies business transactions and events, analyzes and records their effects, and summarizes and prepares information useful in making decisions. Transactions and events are the starting points in the accounting process. Source documents help in their analysis. The effects of transactions and events are recorded in journals. Posting along with a trial balance help summarize and classify these effects.

Learning Objective 2:

Describe source documents and their purpose.

Summary

Source documents identify and describe transactions and events. Examples are sales tickets, checks, purchase orders, bills, and bank statements. Source documents provide objective and reliable evidence, making information more useful.

Learning Objective 3:

Describe a chart of accounts.

Summary

The chart of accounts is a list of all accounts and usually includes an identification number assigned to each account.

Learning Objective 4:

Record transactions in a general journal.

Summary

Transactions are recorded in a journal. The journal includes columns for dates, account titles and explanations, debit amounts, credit amounts, and a posting reference column.

Learning Objective 5:

Post entries to a general ledger.

Summary

Each entry in a journal is posted to a ledger. The ledger provides information that is used to produce financial statements. Balance column accounts are widely used and include columns for debits, credits, and the account balance. A posting reference column provides a link between the ledger and the entry in the journal.

Learning Objective 6:

Prepare financial statements from a trial balance.

Summary

A trial balance is prepared from the general ledger, and then used to prepare the income statement, statement of owner/s equity, and the balance sheet.

Learning Objective 7:

Explain how to correct errors in the general journal and general ledger.

Summary

If an error in a journal entry is discovered before the error is posted, it can be corrected by drawing a line through the incorrect information. If an error in a journal entry is not discovered until after it is posted, correct this error with a *correcting entry* that removes the amount from the erroneous accounts and records it to the correct accounts.

Chapter Outline

I. **Analyzing and Recording Process**—identifies business transactions and events, analyzes and records their effects, and provides the information for financial statements.

   a. Accounting books

      i. Journal—where entries are recorded

      ii. Ledger—complete collection of all accounts

   b. Source documents

      i. Sales invoices to customers

      ii. Purchase invoices from vendors

      iii. Checks received from customers

      iv. Checks issued to vendors or employees

   c. Chart of Accounts—list of all accounts a company uses, including identification numbers

      i. Asset accounts start with 1

      ii. Liability accounts start with 2

      iii. Equity accounts start with 3

      iv. Revenue accounts start with 4

      v. Expense accounts start with 5

   d. Journalizing Transactions to the General Journal

      i. Date of the transaction

      ii. Account(s) debited and amount

      iii. Account(s) credited and amount

      iv. Record a description of the transaction

   e. Posting Transactions to the General Ledger

      i. Record the debits in the proper account along with the page reference (PR) of the journal

      ii. Record the account number of the account debited in the journal

      iii. Record the credits in the proper account along with the page reference of the journal

      iv. Record the account number of the account credited in the journal

      v. Update the balance in each ledger account affected

II. **Correcting Errors in the Journal and Ledger**

   a. Errors discovered prior to posting—draw a line in the journal and write the correct account above

   b. Errors discovered prior to posting—make a correcting journal entry

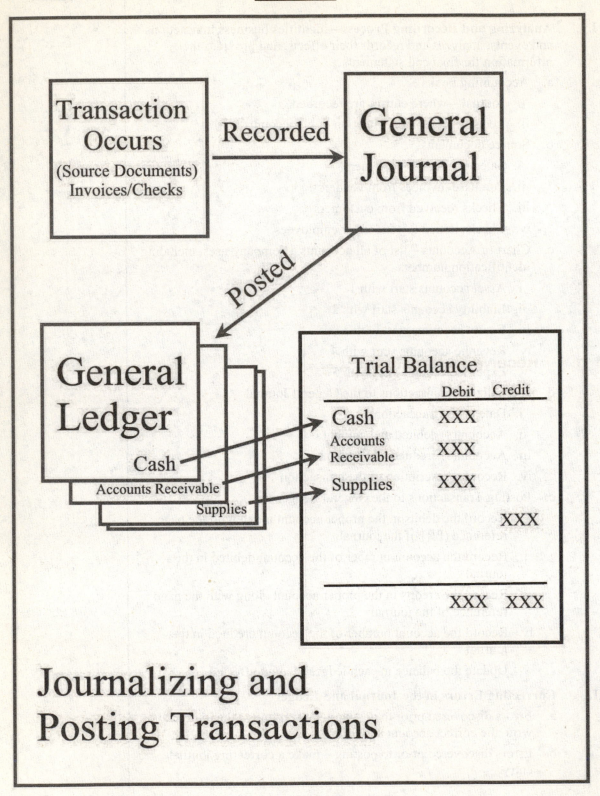

Journalizing and Posting Transactions

Matthew Leinart decided to open a business teaching people ballroom dancing. The following transactions occurred during the month of January, 2010:

a. Leinart invested $5,000 into a new checking account in the name of the business, The Dancing Quarterback.

b. Paid rent on a studio for the month of January, $500

c. Paid $600 for liability insurance for one year.

d. Bought electronic equipment and music CD's on credit in the amount of $1,200

e. Received and paid a bill for advertising, $250.

f. Collected $650 for dancing lessons for the first half of the month.

g. Received and paid the utility bill for the month of January, $200

h. Sent a bill to 'Active Seniors' for dancing lessons given but not collected, $350

i. Made a payment to creditor for equipment purchased in item c above, $200.

j. Bought supplies on account for $150.

k. Collected $1,300 for dancing lessons for the second half of the month.

l. Paid salaries to dance instructors for January, $800.

m. Leinart withdrew cash for personal use, $500.

Required:

1. Record the transactions in a journal using the following accounts; Cash (101), Accounts Receivable (105), Supplies (107), Prepaid Insurance (109), Equipment (120), Accounts Payable (201), Leinart - Capital, (301) Leinart – Drawing (310), Dancing Lesson Revenue (401), Rent Expense (502), Utilities Expense (503), Advertising Expense (504), Salaries Expense (501). (Letters have been used in lieu of dates of transactions).

2. Post the journal entries into the general ledger and balance each account in the general ledger.

3. Prepare a trial balance for The Dancing Quarterback as of January 31, 2010.

Chapter 4 – Alternate Demonstration Problem
Solution

The Dancing Quarterback
GENERAL JOURNAL
For the month ended January 31, 2010

Date	P.R.	Account Titles and Explanation	Debit	Credit
a.	101	Cash	5,000	
	301	Leinart, Capital		5,000
		to record capital contribution		
b.	502	Rent expense	500	
	101	Cash		500
		to pay the rent for January		
c.	106	Prepaid Insurance	600	
	101	Cash		600
		to record purchase of a one-year		
		liability policy		
d.	120	Equipment	1,200	
	201	Accounts payable		1,200
		to record the purchase of electronic		
		equipment on account.		
e.	504	Advertising expense	250	
	101	Cash		250
		to record payment of advertising		
		expenses		
f.	101	Cash	650	
	401	Dancing lesson revenue		650
		to record cash received for dancing		
		lessons		
g.	503	Utilities expense	200	
	101	Cash		200
		to record payment of bill for utilities		

The Dancing Quarterback
General Ledger

Cash   No. 101

DATE	PR	Debit	Credit	Balance
a	J1	5,000		5,000
b	J1		500	4,500
c	J1		600	3,900
e	J1		250	3,650
f	J1	650		4,300
g	J1		200	4,100
i	J1		200	3,900
k	J1	1,300		5,200
l	J1		800	4,400
m	J1		500	3,900

Accounts Receivable   No. 105

DATE	PR	Debit	Credit	Balance
h	J1	350		350

Supplies   No. 107

DATE	PR	Debit	Credit	Balance
j	J1	150		150

Prepaid Insurance   No. 109

DATE	PR	Debit	Credit	Balance
c	J1	600		600

Equipment   No. 120

DATE	PR	Debit	Credit	Balance
d	J1	1,200		1,200

Accounts Payable   No. 201

DATE	PR	Debit	Credit	Balance
d	J1		1,200	(1,200)
i	J1	200		(1,000)
j	J1		150	(1,150)

Leinart, Capital   No. 301

DATE	PR	Debit	Credit	Balance
a	J1		5,000	(5,000)

Leinart, Withdrawals   No. 310

DATE	PR	Debit	Credit	Balance
m	J1	500		500

Dancing Lesson Revenue   No. 401

DATE	PR	Debit	Credit	Balance
f	J1		650	(650)
h	J1		350	(1,000)
k	J1		1,300	(2,300)

Salaries Expense   No. 501

DATE	PR	Debit	Credit	Balance
l	J1		800	800

Rent Expense   No. 502

DATE	PR	Debit	Credit	Balance
b	J1	500		500

Utilities Expense   No. 503

DATE	PR	Debit	Credit	Balance
g	J1	200		250

Advertising Expense   No. 504

DATE	PR	Debit	Credit	Balance
e	J1	250		250

The Dancing Quarter Back
Trial Balance
31-Jan-10

	Debits	Credits
Cash	$ 3,900	
Accounts Receivable	350	
Supplies	150	
Prepaid Insurance	600	
Equipment	1,200	
Accounts Payable		$ 1,150
Leinart, Capital		5,000
Leinart, Withdrawal	500	
Dancing Lesson Revenue		2,300
Salary Expense	800	
Rent Expense	500	
Utilities Expense	200	
Advertising Expense	250	
	$ 8,450	$ 8,450

Problem I

The following statements are either true or false. Place a (T) in the parentheses before each true statement and an (F) before each false statement.

1. ( ) The process of recording transactions in a journal is called posting.

2. ( ) Journalizing is the process of transferring journal entry information to the ledger.

3. ( ) When an error occurs in the journal entry, the correcting process is the same regardless of when the error occurs.

4. ( ) Transactions are recorded in a journal.

5. ( ) Transactions and events are the starting points in the accounting process.

Problem II

You are given several words, phrases, or numbers to choose from in completing each of the following statements or in answering the following questions. In each case select the one that best completes the statement or answers the question and place its letter in the answer space provided.

_____ 1. A ledger is:

    a. A book of original entry in which the effects of transactions are first recorded.

    b. The collection of all accounts used by a business.

    c. A book of original entry in which any type of transaction can be recorded.

    d. A book of special journals.

    e. An account with debit and credit columns and a third column for showing the balance of the account.

_____ 2. The journal entry to record the completion of legal work for a client on credit and billing the client $1,700 for the services rendered would be:

    a. Accounts Receivable 1,700

           Unearned Legal Fees... 1,700

    b. Legal Fees Earned 1,700

           Accounts Receivable... 1,700

    c. Accounts Payable 1,700

           Legal Fees Earned 1,700

    d. Legal Fees Earned 1,700

           Sales.. 1,700

    e. Accounts Receivable 1,700

           Legal Fees Earned... 1,700

_____ 3. The journal entry to record an owner's initial investment of $1,000 cash in the business is:

    a. Owner's Name, Capital 1,000

        Cash 1,000

    b. Owner's Name Capital 1,000

        Assets 1,000

    c. Cash 1,000

        Owner's Name, Capital 1,000

    d. Land 1,000

        Owner's Name, Capital 1,000

    e. Owner's Name, Withdrawals 1,000

        Owner's Name, Capital 1,000

_____ 4. The journal entry to record a purchase of $500 cash of office supplies is:

    a. Supplies 500

        Revenue 500

    b. Supplies 500

        Accounts payable 500

    c. Cash 500

        Supplies 500

    d. Supplies 500

        Cash 500

    e. Accounts payable 500

        Supplies 500

_____ 5. To record an error in a journal entry which is discovered prior to posting you should:

    a. Draw a line through the incorrect entry and write the correct information above the line.

    b. Record a new correcting entry.

    c. Erase the incorrect entry.

    d. Do nothing.

Problem III

Following are the first 10 transactions completed by P. L. Wheeler's new business called Wheeler's Repair Shop:

a. Started the business with a cash deposit of $1,800 to a bank account in the name of the business.

b. Paid three months' rent in advance on the shop space, $675.

c. Purchased repair equipment for cash, $700.

d. Completed repair work for customers and collected cash, $1,005.50.

e. Purchased additional repair equipment on credit from Comet Company, $415.50.

f. Completed repair work on credit for Fred Baca, $175.

g. Paid Comet Company $290.50 of the amount owed from transaction (e).

h. Paid the local radio station $75 for an announcement of the shop opening.

i. Fred Baca paid for the work completed in transaction (f).

j. Withdrew $350 cash from the bank for P. L. Wheeler to pay personal expenses.

Chart of Accounts:

Cash	Accounts Payable
Accounts Receivable	P.L. Wheeler, Capital
Prepaid Rent	P.L. Wheeler, Withdrawals
Repair Equipment	Repair Services, Revenue
	Advertising Expense

Required:

Record the transactions in a general journal.

GENERAL JOURNAL

DATE	ACCOUNT TITLES AND EXPLANATION	P.R.	DEBIT	CREDIT
a.				
b.				
c.				
d.				
e.				
f.				
g.				
h.				

i.											
j.											

Problem IV

Journalize the following transactions and post to the accounts that follow.

   a. On November 5 of the current year, Sherry Dale invested $1,500 in cash, and office equipment having a market value of $950, to start a real estate agency.

   b. On November 6, the business purchased office equipment for $425 cash.

GENERAL JOURNAL

DATE	ACCOUNT TITLES AND EXPLANATION	P.R.	DEBIT	CREDIT

GENERAL LEDGER

Cash   Account No. 101

DATE	EXPLANATION	P.R.	DEBIT	CREDIT	BALANCE

	Office Equipment					Account No. 163	

DATE	EXPLANATION	P.R.	DEBIT	CREDIT	BALANCE

	Sherry Dale, Capital					Account No. 301	

DATE	EXPLANATION	P.R.	DEBIT	CREDIT	BALANCE

Problem V

Many of the important ideas and concepts discussed in Chapter 4 are reflected in the following list of key terms. Test your understanding of these terms by matching the appropriate definition with the terms. Record the number identifying the most appropriate definition in the blank space next to each term.

_____ Balance column account   _____ Ledger
_____ Chart of accounts   _____ Posting
_____ General journal   _____ Posting reference (PR) column
_____ Journal   _____ Source documents
_____ Journalizing   _____ T-account

1. An account with debit and credit columns for recording entries and another column for showing the balance of the account after each entry.

2. Another name for *business papers*; these documents are the source of information for accounting entries and can be in either paper or electronic form.

3. A record where transactions are recorded before they are posted to ledger accounts; also called *book of original entry*.

4. Process of recording transactions in a journal.

5. A column in journals where individual account numbers are entered when entries are posted to ledger accounts.

6. A list of accounts used by a company which includes an identification number for each account.

7. A record of the debits and credits of transactions; can be used to record any transaction.

8. Record containing all accounts of a business.

9. The process of transferring journal entry information to the ledger.

10. An account form used as a tool to show the effects of transactions and events on specific accounts.

Problem VI

Complete the following by filling in the blanks.

1. The _____ is known as the book of original entry, while the _____ is known as the book of final entry.

2. The _____ creates a link between a journal entry and the ledger accounts by providing a cross-reference for tracing the entry from one record to the other.

3. When an account has the opposite of a normal balance, this abnormal balance can be indicated by _____.

4. _____ _____ are the sources of accounting information which identify and describe transactions entering the accounting process.

5. A _____ ___ _____ is a list of all accounts a company uses and includes an identifying number assigned to each account.

6. If an error is discovered in a journal entry after it is posted, a _____ _____ is required.

Solutions for Chapter 4

Problem I

1. F
2. F
3. F
4. T
5. T

Problem II

1. B
2. E
3. C
4. D
5. A

Problem III

GENERAL JOURNAL

DATE	ACCOUNT TITLES AND EXPLANATION	P.R.	DEBIT		CREDIT	
a.	Cash		1 8 0 0			
	P.L. Wheeler, Capital				1 8 0 0	
b.	Prepaid Rent		6 7 5			
	Cash				6 7 5	
c.	Repair Equipment		7 0 0			
	Cash				7 0 0	
d.	Cash		1 0 0 5	50		
	Repair services revenue				1 0 0 5	50
e.	Repair Equipment		4 1 5	50		
	Accounts payable				4 1 5	50
f.	Accounts Receivable		1 7 5			
	Repair Services Revenue				1 7 5	
g.	Accounts Payable		2 9 0	50		
	Cash				2 9 0	50

College Accounting, 2nd Edition

h.	Advertising Expense					7 5						
	Cash									7 5		
i.	Cash					1 7 5						
	Accounts Receivable									1 7 5		
j.	P.L. Wheeler, Withdrawals					3 5 0						
	Cash									3 5 0		

Problem IV

GENERAL JOURNAL

DATE	ACCOUNT TITLES AND EXPLANATION	P.R.	DEBIT			CREDIT		
20— Nov. 5	Cash	101	1	5 0 0	00			
	Office Equipment	163		9 5 0	00			
	Sherry Dale, Capital	301				2	4 5 0	00
	Owner's initial investment.							
6	Office Equipment	163		4 2 5	00			
	Cash	101					4 2 5	00
	Purchased office equipment							

GENERAL LEDGER

Cash   Account No. 101

DATE	EXPLANATION	P.R.	DEBIT			CREDIT			BALANCE		
20— Nov. 5		G-1	1	5 0 0	00				1	5 0 0	00
6		G-1				4 2 5	00		1	0 7 5	00

Office Equipment   Account No. 163

DATE	EXPLANATION	P.R.	DEBIT			CREDIT			BALANCE		
20— Nov. 5		G-1		9 5 0	00					9 5 0	00
6		G-1		4 2 5	00				1	3 7 5	00

Sherry Dale, Capital   Account No. 301

DATE	EXPLANATION	P.R.	DEBIT		CREDIT			BALANCE		
20— Nov. 5		G-1			2	4 5 0	00	2	4 5 0	00

Problem V

1	Balance column account	8	Ledger
6	Chart of accounts	9	Posting
7	General journal	5	Posting reference (PR) column
3	Journal	2	Source documents
4	Journalizing	10	T-account

Problem VI

1. journal, ledger

2. Posting reference (PR) column

3. circling the amount or entering it in red

4. source documents

5. chart of accounts

6. correcting entry

CHAPTER 5
ADJUSTING ACCOUNTS AND PREPARING FINANCIAL STATEMENTS

Learning Objective 1:

Explain accrual accounting and how it improves financial statements.

Summary

Accrual accounting recognizes revenues when earned and expenses as they occur—not necessarily when cash inflows and outflows occur. This better reflects a company's financial position and performance.

Learning Objective 2:

Identify the types of accounting adjustments and their purpose.

Summary

Adjustments can be grouped according to the timing of cash receipts or payments relative to the timing of the related work performed. Adjusting entries are made for prepaid expenses, unearned revenues, accrued expenses, and accrued revenues.

Learning Objective 3:

Prepare and explain adjusting entries.

Summary

Prepaid expenses refer to items paid for in advance of receiving their benefits. Prepaid expenses are assets. Adjusting entries for prepaids involve increasing (debiting) expenses and decreasing (crediting) assets. *Accrued expenses* refer to costs incurred in a period that are both unpaid and unrecorded. Adjusting entries for recording accrued expenses involve increasing (debiting) expenses and increasing (crediting) liabilities.

Learning Objective 4:

Explain and prepare an adjusted trial balance.

Summary

An adjusted trial balance is a list of accounts and balances prepared after recording and posting adjusting entries. Financial statements are often prepared from the adjusted trial balance.

Learning Objective 5:

Prepare financial statements from an adjusted trial balance.

Summary

Revenue and expense balances are reported on the income statement. Asset, liability, and equity balances are reported on the balance sheet. We usually prepare statements in the following order: income statement, statement of owner's equity and balance sheet.

I. **Timing and Reporting**
   a. Accrual versus cash basis
      i. Accrual basis matches expenses to revenues, regardless of timing of cash receipts and payments
      ii. Cash basis recognizes revenue when cash is received and expense when cash is paid
      iii. Accrual better reflects business performance
   b. Recognizing revenues and expenses
      i. Time period assumption—business activities can be split into specific, e.g. months or years
      ii. Revenue recognition principle—record revenues when earned
      iii. Matching principle—record expenses in the same period as their related revenues

II. **Adjusting Accounts**—Framework for Adjustments
   a. Cash before Work (Deferrals)
      i. Unearned revenue
      ii. Prepaid expenses (e.g. insurance, rent)
   b. Work before Cash (Accruals)
      i. Accrued revenues
      ii. Accrued expenses (e.g. payroll)
   c. 3-Step Adjusting Process
      i. Determine current account balance
      ii. Determine what current balance should be
      iii. Record adjusting journal entry to update current account balance to what it should be
   d. Adjustments
      i. Prepaid expenses—write off expired portion
      ii. Supplies—write off used portion
      iii. Depreciation of Fixed Assets
         1. Cost – Salvage = Depreciable basis
         2. Depreciable basis/useful life (months) = Monthly Depreciation
         3. Monthly Depreciation × number of months in service = depreciation expense for the year
      iv. Salaries (Wages) payable – record all unpaid wages as of the balance sheet date

e. Adjusted Trial Balance
    i. Combine trial balance amounts with adjustments to compute adjusted balances for all accounts affected.
        1. Prepaid Insurance: Balance – adjustment = adjusted balance
        2. Supplies: Balance – adjustment = adjusted balance
        3. Depreciation
            a. Cost balance remains the same
            b. Accumulated Depreciation: Balance + adjustment = adjusted balance
        4. Wages payable: Adjusted balance = amount accrued for the period.

III.   **Preparing Financial Statements**
   a. Income Statement (Step 1)
      i. Heading—Company name, period covered (month, quarter, year)
      ii. Revenues—All revenue accounts totaled
      iii. Expenses—List expenses in order of significance
      iv. Calculate net income (loss) by subtracting expenses from revenue
   b. Statement of Owner's Equity (Step 2)
      i. Heading—Business name, period covered (month, quarter, year)
      ii. Capital at the beginning of the period
      iii. Add any capital contributions made by the owner during the period
      iv. Add net income or deduct net loss for the period
      v. Subtract any withdrawals made by the owner during the period
      vi. Capital at the end of the period
   c. Balance Sheet (Step 3)
      i. Heading—Company name, date balances presented (specific date)
      ii. Assets—list all assets and subtract contra asset accumulated depreciation. Balances should be presented in order of liquidity
      iii. Liabilities—list all liability accounts
      iv. Equity—balance is carried over from the statement of owner's equity
   d. Presentation issues
      i. All grand totals should have a double underline
      ii. All grand totals should include a dollar sign
      iii. Put a dollar sign on the first number that started the grand total

Adjusting Expired Assets

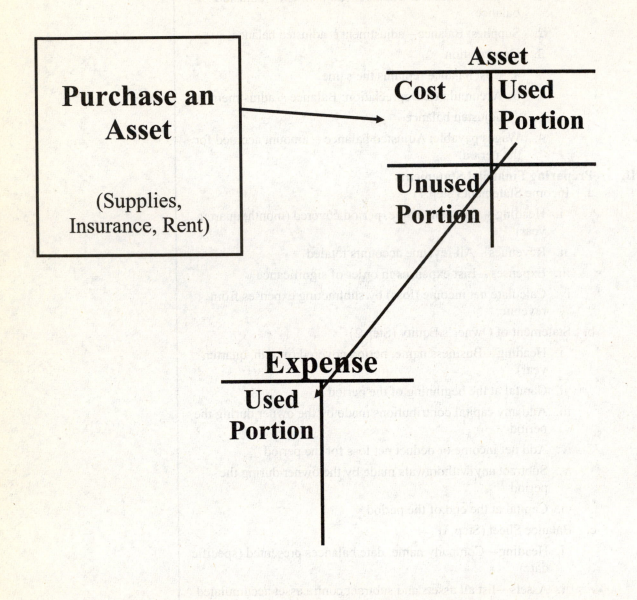

Recording Depreciation

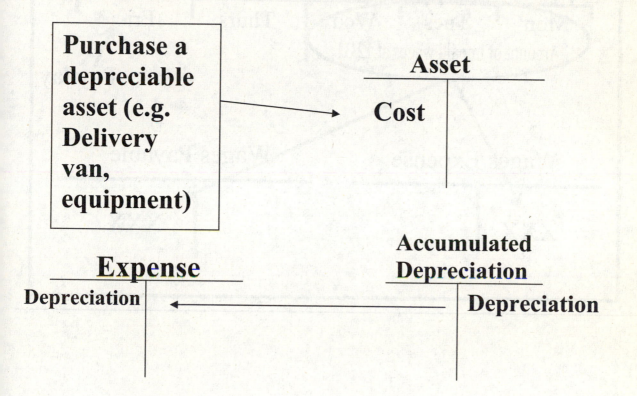

Depreciation Calculation:
 Cost – Salvage Value = Depreciable basis
 Depreciable basis/Useful life (months)
  = Monthly Depreciation Expense
 Monthly Depreciation × number of months in use
  = Depreciation Expense for the period

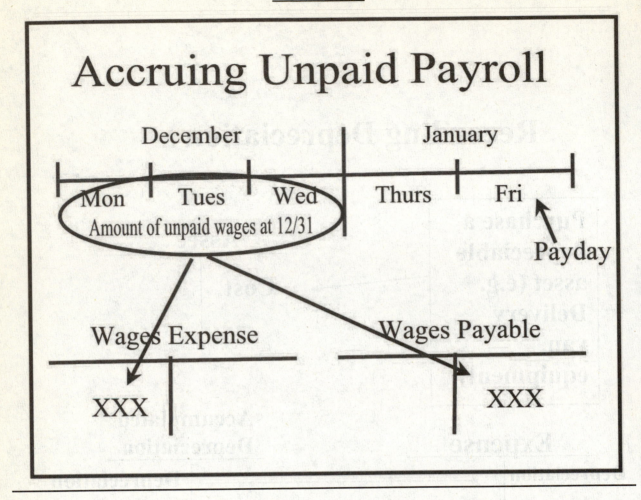

Alternate Demonstration Problem

The Dancing Quarterback reports the following unadjusted trial balance and additional information as of January 31, 2010.

The Dancing Quarter Back
Unadjusted Trial Balance
1/31/2010

	Debits	Credits
Cash	$ 3,900	
Accounts Recievable	350	
Supplies	150	
Prepaid Insurance	600	
Equipment	1,200	
Accounts Payable		$ 1,150
Leinart, Capital		5,000
Leinart, Withdrawal	500	
Dancing Lesson Revenue		2,300
Salary Expense	800	
Rent Expense	500	
Utilities Expense	200	
Advertising Expense	250	
	$ 8,450	$ 8,450

Adjusting Entry Information:

Expired insurance	350
Inventory of supplies	60
Depreciation	120
Accrued wages	200

Required:
1.   Prepare adjusting journal entries for the four adjustments necessary as of January 31, 2010.

Solution

<table>
<tr><td colspan="4">

The Dancing Quarterback
GENERAL JOURNAL
For the month ended January 31, 2010

</td></tr>
<tr><th>Date</th><th>Account</th><th>Debit</th><th>Credit</th></tr>
<tr><td>a.</td><td>Insurance Expense</td><td>350</td><td></td></tr>
<tr><td></td><td>   Prepaid Insurance</td><td></td><td>350</td></tr>
<tr><td></td><td>to write-off expired insurance</td><td></td><td></td></tr>
<tr><td></td><td></td><td></td><td></td></tr>
<tr><td>b.</td><td>Supplies Expense</td><td>90</td><td></td></tr>
<tr><td></td><td>   Supplies</td><td></td><td>90</td></tr>
<tr><td></td><td>to write-off supplies used</td><td></td><td></td></tr>
<tr><td></td><td></td><td></td><td></td></tr>
<tr><td>c.</td><td>Depreciation Expense</td><td>120</td><td></td></tr>
<tr><td></td><td>   Accumulated Depreciation</td><td></td><td>120</td></tr>
<tr><td></td><td>to record depreciaiton on equipment</td><td></td><td></td></tr>
<tr><td></td><td></td><td></td><td></td></tr>
<tr><td>d.</td><td>Salaries Expense</td><td>200</td><td></td></tr>
<tr><td></td><td>   Salaries Payable</td><td></td><td>200</td></tr>
<tr><td></td><td>to record wages unpaid at 01/31</td><td></td><td></td></tr>
<tr><td></td><td></td><td></td><td></td></tr>
</table>

Problem I

The following statements are either true or false. Place a (T) in the parentheses before each true statement and an (F) before each false statement.

1. ( )   Financial statements are prepared after adjusting entries are journalized and posted.

2. ( )   An adjusting entry is recorded to bring a revenue or expense account balance to its proper amount. This entry also updates a related asset or liability account.

3. ( )   Prepaid expenses refer to items paid for in advance of receiving their benefits.

4. ( )   Depreciation is the process of spreading the costs of plant assets over an arbitrary number of years.

5. ( )   Plant assets are long-term tangible assets used to produce and sell products and services.

6. ( )   A contra account is an account linked with a plant asset account. Its normal balance is opposite of, and it is reported as a subtraction from, that other account's balance.

Problem II

You are given several words, phrases, or numbers to choose from in completing each of the following statements or in answering the following questions. In each case select the one that best completes the statement or answers the question and place its letter in the answer space provided.

_____ 1. X Company has four employees who are each paid $40 per day for a five-day work week. The employees are paid every Friday. If the accounting period ends on Wednesday, X Company should make the following entry to accrue wages:

    a. Salaries Expense 800
         Salaries Payable   800

    b. Salaries Expense 800
         Cash   800

    c. Salaries Expense 480
         Salaries Payable...   480

    d. Salaries Expense 320
         Salaries Payable   320

    e. No entry should be made until the salaries are actually paid.

_____ 2. The Epicure Restaurant prepares monthly financial statements. On January 31 the balance in the Supplies account was $1,600. During February $2,960 of supplies were purchased and debited to Supplies. What is the adjusting entry on February 28 to account for the supplies assuming a February 28 inventory showed that $1,300 of supplies were on hand?

    a. Supplies Expense..300
         Supplies   300

    b. Supplies...300
         Supplies Expense...   300

    c. Supplies..3,260
         Cash..   3,260

    d. Supplies Expense...3,260
         Supplies   3,260

_____ 3. Each of the following could be considered a prepaid expense except:
    a. Supplies
    b. Depreciation
    c. Revenue
    d. Prepaid Insurance
    e. All of the above are prepaid expenses.

_____ 4. Examples of accrued expenses include each of the following:
    a. Salaries.
    b. Interest.
    c. Rent.
    d. Taxes.
    e. Supplies.

_____ 5. ABC Company's financial statements show the following:

Net income $195,000

Total revenues 850,000

Total expenses 655,000

ABC's profit margin is:

a. 22.9 %

b. 29.8 %

c. 435.9 %

d. 129.8 %

e. 77.1 %

_____ 6. A truck is purchased on January 1st for $17,000. It has an estimated useful life of five years and a $2,000 salvage value. The journal entry to record the adjusting entry for depreciation at the end of the year using the straight-line method is?

a. Depreciation Expense 3,000

    Accumulated Depreciation   3,000

b. Accumulated Depreciation 3,000

    Depreciation Expense   3,000

c. Depreciation Expense 3,400

    Accumulated Depreciation   3,400

d. Accumulated Depreciation 3,400

    Depreciation Expense   3,400

Problem III

Many of the important ideas and concepts discussed in Chapter 5 are reflected in the following list of key terms. Test your understanding of these terms by matching the appropriate definitions with the terms. Record the number identifying the most appropriate definition in the blank space next to each term.

_____	Accrued expenses	_____	Matching
_____	Adjusted trial balance	_____	Revenue recognition principle
_____	Adjusting entry	_____	Prepaid expenses
_____	Book value	_____	Straight-line depreciation method
_____	Contra account	_____	Time period assumption
_____	Depreciation	_____	Unadjusted trial balance

1. Costs incurred in a period that are both unpaid and unrecorded; adjusting entries for recording these items involve increasing (debiting) expenses and increasing (crediting) liabilities.

2. Prescribes expenses be reported in the same period as the revenues earned as a result of those expenses.

3. List of accounts and balances prepared after adjustments are recorded and posted to the ledger.

4. List of accounts and balances prepared before adjustments have been recorded and posted.

5. Expense created by allocating the cost of plant and equipment to the periods in which they are used; represents the expense of using the assets.

6. Journal entry at the end of an accounting period to bring an asset or liability account to its proper amount while also updating the related revenue or expense account.

7. Assumption that an organization's activities can be split into specific time periods.

8. Account linked with another account and having the opposite normal balance; reported as a subtraction from the other account's balance.

9. Method that allocates equal amounts of depreciation expense over an asset's life.

10. Items paid for in advance of receiving their benefits; classified as assets.

11. Equals the asset's original cost less its accumulated depreciation.

12. Principle that revenue be recorded in the period it is earned.

Problem IV

On October 1 of the current year, Harold Lloyd began business as a public stenographer. During the month he completed the following transactions:

October 1 Invested $3,000 in the business.

        1 Paid three months' rent in advance on the office space, $1,245.

        1 Purchased office equipment for cash, $925.50.

        2 Purchased on credit office equipment, $700, and office supplies, $75.50.

     31 Completed stenographic work during the month and collected cash, $1,725.

     31 Withdrew $725 for personal living expenses.

After the above entries were recorded in the journal and posted to the general ledger, the accounts of Harold Lloyd appeared as follows:

GENERAL LEDGER

Cash   Account No. 101

DATE	EXPLANATION	P.R.	DEBIT				CREDIT				BALANCE			
Oct. 1		G-1	3	0	0	0	00					3	0	0	0	00
1		G-1						1	2	4	5	00	1	7	5	5	00
1		G-1							9	2	5	50		8	2	9	50
31		G-2	1	7	2	5	00						2	5	5	4	50
31		G-2							7	2	5	00	1	8	2	9	50

Office Supplies   Account No. 124

DATE	EXPLANATION	P.R.	DEBIT			CREDIT			BALANCE		
Oct. 2		G-1	7	5	50				7	5	50

Prepaid Rent   Account No. 131

DATE	EXPLANATION	P.R.	DEBIT				CREDIT			BALANCE			
Oct. 1		G-1	1	2	4	5	00				1	2	4	5	00

Office Equipment   Account No. 163

DATE	EXPLANATION	P.R.	DEBIT				CREDIT			BALANCE			
Oct. 1		G-1		9	2	5	50					9	2	5	50
2		G-1		7	0	0	00				1	6	2	5	50

Accumulated Depreciation, Office Equipment   Account No. 164

DATE	EXPLANATION	P.R.	DEBIT	CREDIT	BALANCE

Accounts Payable   Account No. 201

DATE	EXPLANATION	P.R.	DEBIT			CREDIT	BALANCE		
Oct. 2		G-1	7	7	5	50		7	7	5	50

Harold Lloyd, Capital   Account No. 301

DATE	EXPLANATION	P.R.	DEBIT	CREDIT	BALANCE
Oct. 1		G-1		3 0 0 0 00	3 0 0 0 00

Harold Lloyd, Withdrawals   Account No. 302

DATE	EXPLANATION	P.R.	DEBIT	CREDIT	BALANCE
Oct. 31		G-2	7 2 5 00		7 2 5 00

Stenographic Services Revenue   Account No. 403

DATE	EXPLANATION	P.R.	DEBIT	CREDIT	BALANCE
Oct. 31		G-2		1 7 2 5 00	1 7 2 5 00

Depreciation Expense, Office Equipment   Account No. 612

DATE	EXPLANATION	P.R.	DEBIT	CREDIT	BALANCE

Rent Expense   Account No. 640

DATE	EXPLANATION	P.R.	DEBIT	CREDIT	BALANCE

Office Supplies Expense   Account No. 650

DATE	EXPLANATION	P.R.	DEBIT	CREDIT	BALANCE

On October 31, Harold Lloyd decided to adjust his accounts and prepare a balance sheet and an income statement. His adjustments were:

a. One month's rent had expired.

b. An inventory of office supplies showed $40 of unused office supplies.

c. The office equipment had depreciated $35 during October.

Required:

1. Prepare and post general journal entries to record the adjustments.

2. After posting the adjusting entries, complete the adjusted trial balance.

3. From the adjusted trial balance, complete the income statement, statement of changes in owner's equity, and balance sheet for October.

GENERAL JOURNAL

DATE	ACCOUNT TITLES AND EXPLANATION	P.R.	DEBIT	CREDIT

HAROLD LLOYD

Adjusted Trial Balance

October 31, 20—

	Account						
	Cash						
	Office supplies						
	Prepaid rent						
	Office equipment						
	Accumulated depreciation, office equipment						
	Accounts payable						
	Harold Lloyd, capital						
	Harold Lloyd, withdrawals						
	Stenographic services revenue						
	Depreciation expense, office equipment						
	Rent expense						
	Office supplies expense						
	Totals						

HAROLD LLOYD
Income Statement
For Month Ended October 31, 20—

		Revenue:							
		Stenographic services revenue							
		Operating expenses:							
		Depreciation expense, office equipment							
		Rent expense							
		Office supplies expense							
		Total operating expenses							
		Net income							

HAROLD LLOYD
Statement of Changes in Owner's Equity
For Month Ended October 31, 20—

		Harold Lloyd, Capital, October 1, 20—						
		October net income						
		Less withdrawals						
		Excess of income over withdrawals						
		Harold Lloyd, Capital, October 31, 20—						

HAROLD LLOYD
Balance Sheet
October 31, 20—

		Assets							
		Cash							
		Office supplies							
		Prepaid rent							
		Office equipment							
		Less: Accumulated depreciation							
		Total assets							
		Liabilities							
		Accounts payable							
		Owner's Equity							
		Harold Lloyd, Capital, October 31, 20—							
		Total liabilities and owner's equity							

Problem V

a. Blade Company has one employee who earns $72.50 per day. The company operates with monthly accounting periods, and the employee is paid each Friday night for a workweek that begins on Monday. Assume the calendar for October appears as shown and enter the four $362.50 weekly wage payments directly in the T-accounts below. Then enter the adjustment for the wages earned but unpaid on October 31.

OCTOBER						
S	M	T	W	T	F	S
	1	2	3	4	5	6
7	8	9	10	11	12	13
14	15	16	17	18	19	20
21	22	23	24	25	26	27
28	29	30	31			

Cash	Wages Payable	Wages Expense

b. Blade Company's October income statement should show $_____ of wages expense, and its October 31 balance sheet should show a $_____ liability for wages payable. The wages earned by its employee but unpaid on October 31 are an example of an _____ expense.

c. In the space that follows give the general journal entry to record payment of a full week's wages to the Blade Company employee on November 2.

GENERAL JOURNAL   Page 1

DATE	ACCOUNT TITLES AND EXPLANATION	P.R.	DEBIT	CREDIT

College Accounting, 2nd Edition

Solutions for Chapter 5

Problem I

1. T
2. F
3. T
4. F
5. T
6. T

Problem II

1. C
2. D
3. C
4. E
5. A
6. A

Problem III

1	Accrued expenses		2	Matching
3	Adjusted trial balance		12	Revenue recognition principle
7	Adjusting entry		10	Prepaid expenses
11	Book value		9	Straight-line depreciation method
8	Contra account		7	Time period assumption
5	Depreciation		4	Unadjusted trial balance

Problem IV

Oct. 31	Rent Expense		415.00	
	Prepaid Rent			415.00
31	Office Supplies Expense		35.50	
	Office Supplies			35.50
31	Depreciation Expense, Office Equipment		35.00	
	Accumulated Depr., Office Equipment			35.00

Cash

Date	Debit	Credit	Balance
Oct. 1	3,000.00		3,000.00
1		1,245.00	1,755.00
1		925.50	829.50
31	1,725.00		2,554.50
31		725.00	1,829.50

Office Supplies

Date	Debit	Credit	Balance
Oct. 2	75.50		75.50
31		35.50	40.00

Prepaid Rent

Date	Debit	Credit	Balance
Oct. 1	1,245.00		1,245.00
31		415.00	830.00

Office Equipment

Date	Debit	Credit	Balance
Oct. 1	925.50		925.50
2	700.00		1,625.50

Accumulated Depr., Office Equipment

Date	Debit	Credit	Balance
Oct. 31		35.00	35.00

Accounts Payable

Date	Debit	Credit	Balance
Oct. 2		775.50	775.50

Harold Lloyd, Capital

Date	Debit	Credit	Balance
Oct. 1		3,000.00	3,000.00

Harold Lloyd, Withdrawals

Date	Debit	Credit	Balance
Oct. 31	725.00		725.00

Stenographic Services Revenue

Date	Debit	Credit	Balance
Oct. 31		1,725.00	1,725.00

Depr. Expense, Office Equipment

Date	Debit	Credit	Balance
Oct. 31	35.00		35.00

Rent Expense

Date	Debit	Credit	Balance
Oct. 31	415.00		415.00

Office Supplies Expense

Date	Debit	Credit	Balance
Oct. 31	35.50		35.50

2.

HAROLD LLOYD
Adjusted Trial Balance
October 31, 20—

Cash	$1,829.50	
Office supplies	40.00	
Prepaid rent	830.00	
Office equipment	1,625.50	
Accumulated depreciation, office equipment		$ 35.00
Accounts payable		775.50
Harold Lloyd, Capital		3,000.00
Harold Lloyd, Withdrawals	725.00	
Stenographic services revenue		1,725.00
Depreciation expense, office equipment	35.00	
Rent expense	415.00	
Office supplies expense	35.50	
Totals	$5,535.50	$5,535.50

3.

HAROLD LLOYD
Income Statement
For Month Ended October 31, 20—

Revenue:		
Stenographic services revenue		$1,725.00
Operating expenses:		
Depreciation expense, office equipment	$ 35.00	
Rent expense	415.00	
Office supplies expense	35.50	
Total operating expenses		485.50
Net income		$1,239.50

HAROLD LLOYD
Statement of Changes in Owner's Equity
For Month Ended October 31, 20—

Harold Lloyd, Capital, October 1, 20—		$3,000.00
October net income	$1,239.50	
Less withdrawals	725.00	
Excess of income over withdrawals		514.50
Harold Lloyd, Capital, October 31, 20—		$3,514.50

HAROLD LLOYD
Balance Sheet
October 31, 20—
Assets

Cash		$1,829.50
Office supplies		40.00
Prepaid rent		830.00
Office equipment	$1,625.50	
Less: Accumulated depreciation	35.00	1,590.50
Total assets		$4,290.00

Liabilities

Accounts payable		$ 775.50

Owner's Equity

Harold Lloyd, Capital, October 31, 20—		3,514.50
Total liabilities and owner's equity		$4,290.00

Problem V

a.

Cash				Wages Expense		
Oct. 5	362.50			Oct. 5	362.50	
12	362.50			12	362.50	
19	362.50			19	362.50	
26	362.50			26	362.50	
				31	217.50	

Wages Payable		
	Oct. 31	217.50

b. $1,667.50; $217.50; accrued

c.
Nov 2	Wages Expense		145.00	
	Wages Payable		217.50	
	Cash			362.50

CHAPTER 6
CLOSING PROCESS AND FINANCIAL STATEMENTS

Learning Objective 1:

Prepare a work sheet and explain its usefulness.

Summary

A work sheet can be a useful tool in preparing and analyzing financial statements. It is helpful at the end of a period in preparing adjusting entries, an adjusted trial balance, and financial statements. A work sheet usually contains five pairs of columns: Unadjusted Trial Balance, Adjustments, Adjusted Trial Balance, Income Statement, and Balance Sheet & Statement of Owner's Equity.

Learning Objective 2:

Explain why temporary accounts are closed each period.

Summary

Temporary accounts are closed at the end of each accounting period for two main reasons. First, the closing process updates the capital account to include the effects of all transactions and events recorded for the period. Second, it prepares revenue, expense, and withdrawal accounts for the next reporting period by giving them zero balances.

Learning Objective 3:

Describe and prepare closing entries.

Summary

Closing entries involve four steps: (1) close credit balances in revenue (and gain) accounts to Income Summary, (2) close debit balances in expense (and loss) accounts to Income Summary, (3) close Income Summary to the capital account, and (4) close withdrawals account to owner's capital.

Learning Objective 4:

Explain and prepare a post-closing trial balance.

Summary

A post-closing trial balance is a list of permanent accounts and their balances after all closing entries are journalized and posted. Its purpose is to verify that (1) total debits equal total credits for permanent accounts and (2) all temporary accounts have zero balances.

Learning Objective 5:

Identify steps in the accounting cycle.

Summary

The accounting cycle consists of 9 steps: (1) analyze transactions, (2) journalize, (3) post, (4) prepare an unadjusted trial balance, (5) adjust accounts, (6) prepare an adjusted trial balance, (7) prepare statements, (8) close, (9) prepare a post-closing trial balance.

I. **Prepare a Worksheet**—a tool used by accountants to facilitate adjusting entries and the preparation of the financial statements.

    a. Step 1—Enter the unadjusted trial balance—the unadjusted balance for each account is entered into the appropriate debit or credit column of the worksheet.

    b. Step 2—Enter the adjustments – Enter all necessary adjustments for:

        i. Prepaid insurance expired

        ii. Supplies used

        iii. Depreciation of fixed assets

    c. Step 3—Prepare an adjusted trial balance—combine the balances in the unadjusted trial balance columns with the adjustments to compute the adjusted balances for all accounts.

    d. Step 4—Sort adjusted trial balance amounts to the financial statements

        i. Revenue and expense accounts go in the income statement columns

        ii. Assets, liabilities, equity, and withdrawals go in the balance sheet columns.

    e. Step 5—Total statement columns, compute income or loss, and balance the columns.

        i. Total the income statement columns—if revenue exceeds expenses, record the net income. If expenses exceed revenue, record the net loss.

        ii. Total the balance sheet columns. Carry over the net income or net loss to balance out the balance sheet columns.

II. **Worksheet Applications and Analysis**—

    a. Not a substitute for financial statements

    b. Helps in journalizing adjusting entries to ledger

    c. Helps in analyzing "what-if" scenarios

III. **Closing Process**—done after financial statements are prepared; starts each fiscal year with zero balances in the temporary accounts for revenue, expenses, and withdrawals.

    a. Steps in the Closing Process

        i. Step 1—Close credit balances in revenue to the income summary account

           1. Dr. Revenue accounts, Cr. Income Summary

        ii. Step 2—Close debit balances in expense accounts to the income summary account

           1. Dr. Income Summary, Cr. Expenses

   iii. Step 3—Close the Income Summary account to Owner's Equity
     1. If Net Income—Dr. Income Summary, Cr. Owner's Equity
     2. If Net Loss—Dr. Capital, Cr. Income Summary
   iv. Step 4—Closing Withdrawals to Owner's Equity
     1. Dr. Owner's Equity, Cr. Withdrawals
 b. Preparing a post-closing trial balance
   i. List of all permanent accounts (Assets, Liabilities, and Owner's Equity) and their balances in the general ledger
   ii. Exclude temporary accounts, (Revenue, Expenses and Withdrawals)

IV. Steps in the Accounting Cycle
 a. Analyze transactions
 b. Journalize transactions in the general journal
 c. Post transactions to the general ledger
 d. Prepare an unadjusted trial balance
 e. Prepare adjusting journal entries
 f. Prepare financial statements
 g. Prepare closing entries for temporary accounts
 h. Prepare a post closing trial balance

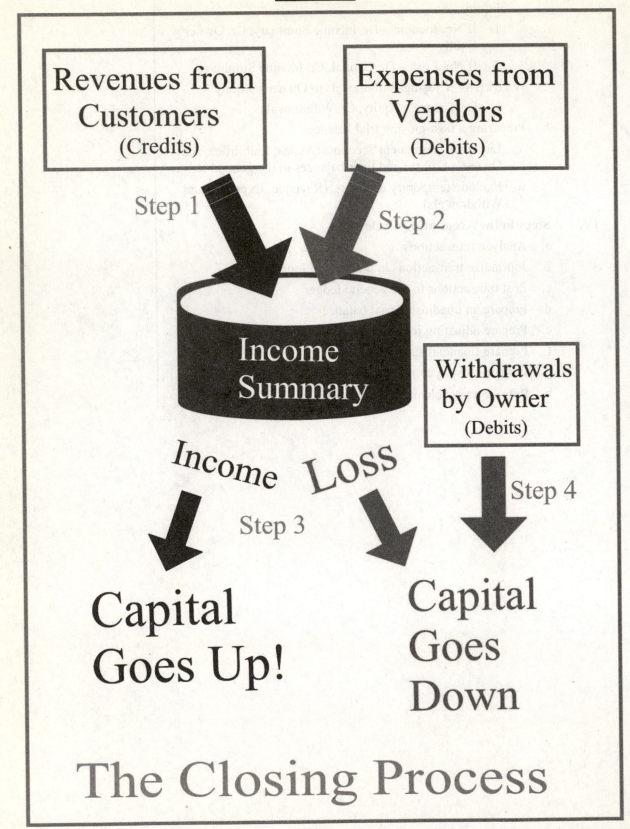

Alternate Demonstration Problem

Below is the completed worksheet for The Dancing Quarterback as of January 31, 2010.

Work Sheet
31-Jan-10

ACCOUNT TITLE	Unadjusted Trial Balance Debits	Credits	Adjustments Debits	Credits	Adjusted Trial Balance Debits	Credits	Income Statement Debits	Credits	Balance Sheet Debits	Credits
Cash	3,900				3,900				3,900	
Accounts Receivable	350				350				350	
Supplies	150			b 90	60				60	
Prepaid Insurance	600			a 350	250				250	
Equipment	1,200				1,200				1,200	
Accounts Payable		1,150				1,150				1,150
Leinart, Capital		5,000				5,000				5,000
Leinart, Withdrawal	500				500				500	
Dancing Lesson Revenue		2,300				2,300		2,300		
Salary Expense	800		d 200		1,000		1,000			
Rent Expense	500				500		500			
Utilities Expense	200				200		200			
Advertising Expense	250				250		250			
Insurance Expense			a 350		350		350			
Supplies Expense			b 90		90		90			
Depreciation Expense			c 120		120		120			
Accumulated depreciation				c 120		120				120
Salaries Payable				d 200		200				200
	8,450	8,450	760	760	8,770	8,770	2,510	2,300	6,260	6,470
Net loss								210	210	
							2,510	2,510	6,470	6,470

Required:
1. Journalize the four closing entries.
2. Prepare a post-closing trial balance.

Solution: Note: This demonstration problem shows a loss and the resulting closing entries.

The Dancing Quarterback
GENERAL JOURNAL
For the month ended January 31, 2010

Date	Account Titles and Explanation	Debit	Credit
	Closing Entries		
1	Dancing Lesson Revenue	2,300	
	Income Summary		2,300
2	Income Summary	2,510	
	Salary Expense		1,000
	Rent Expense		500
	Utilities Expense		200
	Advertising Expense		250
	Insurance Expense		350
	Supplies Expense		90
	Depreciation Expense		120
3	Leinart, Capital	210	
	Income Summary		210
4	Leinart, Capital	500	
	Leinart, Withdrawals		500

The Dancing Quarter Back
Post-Closing Trial Balance
31-Jan-10

	Debits	Credits
Cash	$ 3,900	
Accounts Receivable	350	
Supplies	60	
Prepaid Insurance	250	
Equipment	1,200	
Accumulated Depreciation		$ 120
Accounts Payable		1,150
Salaries Payable		200
Leinart, Capital		4,290
	$ 5,760	$ 5,760

Problem I

The following statements are either true or false. Place a (T) in the parentheses before each true statement and an (F) before each false statement.

1. ( ) If the Income Statement columns of a work sheet are equal after transferring from the Adjusted Trial Balance columns, then it can be concluded that there is no net income (or loss).

2. ( ) The only reason why the Statement of Owner's Equity or Balance Sheet columns of a work sheet might be out of balance would be if an error had been made in sorting revenue and expense data from the Adjusted Trial Balance columns of the work sheet.

3. ( ) After all closing entries are posted at the end of an accounting period, the Income Summary account balance is zero.

4. ( ) Throughout the current period, one could refer to the balance of the Income Summary account to determine the amount of net income or loss that was earned in the prior accounting period.

5. ( ) On a work sheet, net income would be understated if a liability was extended into the Income Statement—Credit column.

Problem II

You are given several words, phrases, or numbers to choose from in completing each of the following statements or in answering the following question. In each case select the one that best completes the statement or answers the question and place its letter in the answer space provided.

_____ 1. Equipment, Wages Expense, and The Owner, Capital would be sorted to which respective columns in completing a work sheet?

    a. Statement of Owner's Equity or Balance Sheet—Debit; Income Statement—Debit; and Statement of Owner's Equity or Balance Sheet—Debit.

    b. Statement of Owner's Equity or Balance Sheet—Debit; Income Statement—Debit; and Statement of Owner's Equity or Balance Sheet—Credit.

    c. Statement of Owner's Equity or Balance Sheet—Debit; Income Statement—Credit; and Statement of Owner's Equity or Balance Sheet—Debit.

    d. Statement of Owner's Equity or Balance Sheet—Debit; Income Statement—Credit; and Statement of Owner's Equity or Balance Sheet—Credit.

    e. Statement of Owner's Equity or Balance Sheet—Credit; Income Statement—Credit; and Statement of Owner's Equity or Balance Sheet—Credit.

_____ 2. Based on the following T-accounts and their end-of-period balances, what will be the balance of the Joe Cool, Capital account after the closing entries are posted?

Joe Cool, Capital		Joe Cool, Withdrawals		Income Summary
Dec. 31 7,000	Dec. 31 9,600			

Revenue		Rent Expense		Salaries Expense
Dec. 31 29,700	Dec. 31 3,600		Dec. 31 7,200	

Insurance Expense		Depr. Expense, Equipment		Accum. Depr. Equipment
Dec. 31 920	Dec. 31 500			Dec.31 500

a. $12,880 Debit.
b. $12,880 Credit.
c. $24,480 Credit.
d. $14,880 Credit.
e. $10,480 Debit.

_____ 3. The following items appeared on a December 31 work sheet: Based on the following information, what are the totals in the Statement of Owner's Equity or Balance Sheet columns?

	Unadjusted Trial Balance		Adjustments	
	Debit	Credit	Debit	Credit
Cash	975			
Supplies	180			70
Prepaid insurance	3,600			150
Equipment	10,320			
Accounts payable		1,140		
Unearned fees		4,500	375	
The Owner, capital		9,180		
The Owner, withdrawals	1,650			
Fees earned		5,850		375
				300
Salaries expense	2,100		315	
Rent expense	1,500			
Utilities expense	345			
	20,670	20,670		
Insurance expense			150	
Supplies expense			70	
Depreciation expense, equipment			190	
Accumulated depreciation, equipment				190
Salaries payable				315
Accounts receivable			300	
			1,400	1,400

a. $16,805.
b. $16,505.
c. $14,950.
d. $14,820.
e. Some other amount.

_____ 4. In what order are the following steps in the accounting cycle performed?

    1) Preparing an unadjusted trial balance
    2) Recording and posting closing entries
    3) Journalizing transactions
    4) Preparing a post-closing trial balance
    5) Preparing the financial statements
    6) Completing the work sheet
    7) Journalizing and posting adjusting entries
    8) Posting the entries to record transactions
    a. (1), (3), (8), (7), (6), (2), (4), (5)
    b. (3), (8), (1), (6), (5), (7), (2), (4)
    c. (1), (3), (8), (6), (7), (2), (5), (4)
    d. (3), (1), (8), (7), (6), (5), (4), (2)
    e. (3), (8), (1), (7), (6), (2), (4), (5)

_____ 5. Real accounts are:

    a. Accounts that are closed at the end of the accounting period; therefore, the revenue, expense, Income Summary, and withdrawals accounts.
    b. Accounts used to record the owner's investment in the business plus any more or less permanent changes in the owner's equity.
    c. Accounts the balance of which is subtracted from the balance of an associated account to show a more current amount then recorded in the associated account.
    d. Also called temporary accounts.
    e. Also called permanent accounts.

Problem III

Many of the important ideas and concepts discussed in Chapter 6 are reflected in the following list of key terms. Test your understanding of these terms by matching the appropriate definitions with the terms. Record the number identifying the most appropriate definition in the blank space next to each term.

_____ Accounting cycle   _____ Permanent accounts
_____ Closing entries   _____ Post-closing trial balance
_____ Closing process   _____ Temporary accounts
_____ Income Summary   _____ Working papers
                                       _____ Work sheet

1. List of permanent accounts and their balances from the ledger after the closing entries are journalized and posted.

2. Recurring steps performed each accounting period, starting with analyzing transactions and continuing through the post-closing trial balance (or reversing entries).

3. Accounts that are used to record revenues, expenses, and owner's withdrawals; they are closed at the end of the period.

4. Analyses and other informal reports prepared by accountants when organizing information for formal reports and financial statements.

5. Accounts that are used to report activities related to one or more periods; they include all balance sheet accounts whose balances are not closed.

6. Necessary steps to prepare the accounts for recording the transactions of the next period.

7. Temporary account used only in the closing process to which the balances of revenues and expenses are transferred; its balance is transferred to the owner's capital account.

8. Entries recorded at the end of each accounting period to transfer end-of-period balances in revenue, expense, and withdrawals accounts to the owner's capital.

9. Spreadsheet used to draft an unadjusted trial balance, adjusting entries, adjusted trial balance, and financial statements; an optional step in the accounting process.

Problem IV

Complete the following by filling in the blanks.

1. A work sheet is prepared after all transactions are recorded but before _____ _____.

2. Revenue accounts have credit balances; consequently, to close a revenue account and make it show a zero balance, the revenue account is _____ and the Income Summary account is _____ for the amount of the balance.

3. In extending the amounts in the Adjusted Trial Balance columns of a work sheet to the proper Income Statement or Statement of Owner's Equity and Balance Sheet columns, two decisions are:
   (a)_____and
   (b)_____.

4. Expense accounts have debit balances; therefore, expense accounts are_____ and the Income Summary account is _____ in closing the expense accounts.

5. In preparing a work sheet for a concern, its unadjusted account balances are entered in the _____ of the work sheet form, after which the _____ are entered in the second pair of columns. Next, the unadjusted trial balance amounts and the amounts in the Adjustments columns are combined to secure an _____ in the third pair of columns.

6. Only balance sheet accounts should have balances appearing on the post-closing trial balance because the balances of all temporary accounts are reduced to _____ in the closing procedure.

7. Closing entries are necessary because if at the end of an accounting period the revenue and expense accounts are to show only one period's revenues and expenses, they must begin the period with _____ balances, and closing entries cause the revenue and expense accounts to begin a new period with _____ balances.

8. Closing entries accomplish two purposes: (1) they cause all _____ accounts to begin the new accounting period with zero balances, and (2) they transfer the net effect of the past period's _____, _____, and withdrawal transactions to the owner's capital account.

Problem V

The unfinished year-end work sheet of Homer's Home Shop appears on the next page.

Required:

1. Complete the work sheet using the following adjustments information:

    a. A $725 inventory of shop supplies indicates that $1,037 of shop supplies have been used during the year.

    b. The shop equipment has depreciated $475 during the year.

    c. On December 31, wages of $388 have been earned by the one employee but are unpaid because payment is not due.

2. After completing the work sheet, prepare the year-end adjusting and closing entries.

3. Post the adjusting and closing entries to the accounts that are provided in the abbreviated general ledger.

4. After posting the adjusting and closing entries, prepare a post-closing trial balance.

WORKSHEET FOR THE YEAR ENDED DECEMBER 31, 20--

ACCOUNT	UNADJUSTED TRIAL BALANCE DR.	UNADJUSTED TRIAL BALANCE CR.	ADJUSTMENTS DR.	ADJUSTMENTS CR.	ADJUSTED TRIAL BALANCE DR.	ADJUSTED TRIAL BALANCE CR.	INCOME STATEMENT DR.	INCOME STATEMENT CR.	STMT. OF O.E. AND BALANCE SHEET DR.	STMT. OF O.E. AND BALANCE SHEET CR.
Cash	2 875 00									
Accounts receivable	2 000 00									
Shop supplies	1 762 00									
Shop equipment	5 125 00									
Accumulated Depreciation—shop equipment		725 00								
Accounts payable		575 00								
Homer Tonely, Capital		5 500 00								
Homer Tonely, withdrawals	30 000 00									
Repair services revenue		55 785 00								
Wages expense	18 250 00									
Rent expense	2 500 00									
Miscellaneous expenses	73 00									
	62 585 00	62 585 00								
Shop supplies expense										
Depreciation expense—shop equip.										
Wages payable										

2.

GENERAL JOURNAL

DATE	ACCOUNT TITLES AND EXPLANATION	P.R.	DEBIT		CREDIT	

GENERAL LEDGER

3.

Cash

Date	Debit	Credit	Balance
Dec. 31			2,875.00

Accounts Receivable

Date	Debit	Credit	Balance
Dec. 31			2,000.00

Shop Supplies

Date	Debit	Credit	Balance
Dec. 31			1,762.00

Shop Equipment

Date	Debit	Credit	Balance
Dec. 31			5,125.00

Accum. Depr., Shop Equipment

Date	Debit	Credit	Balance
Dec. 31			725.00

Accounts Payable

Date	Debit	Credit	Balance
Dec. 31			575.00

Wages Payable

Date	Debit	Credit	Balance

Homer Tonely, Capital

Date	Debit	Credit	Balance
Dec. 31			5,500.00

Homer Tonely, Withdrawals

Date	Debit	Credit	Balance
Dec. 31			30,000.00

Repair Services Revenue

Date	Debit	Credit	Balance
Dec. 31			55,785.00

Depr. Expense, Shop Equipment

Date	Debit	Credit	Balance

Wages Expense

Date	Debit	Credit	Balance
Dec. 31			18,250.00

Rent Expense

Date	Debit	Credit	Balance
Dec. 31			2,500.00

Shop Supplies Expense

Date	Debit	Credit	Balance

Miscellaneous Expenses

Date	Debit	Credit	Balance
Dec. 31			73.00

Income Summary

Date	Debit	Credit	Balance

4.

HOMER'S HOME SHOP

Post-Closing Trial Balance

December 31, 20—

Cash								
Accounts receivable								
Shop supplies								
Shop equipment								
Accumulated depreciation, shop equipment								
Accounts payable								
Wages payable								
Homer Tonely, capital								
Totals								

Solutions for Chapter 6

Problem I

1. T
2. F
3. T
4. F
5. F

Problem II

1. B
2. D
3. A
4. B
5. E

Problem III

2	Accounting cycle		5	Permanent accounts
8	Closing entries		1	Post-closing trial balance
6	Closing process		3	Temporary accounts
7	Income Summary		4	Working papers
			9	Work sheet

Problem IV

1. the adjustments are entered in the accounts

2. debited, credited

3. (a) Is the item a debit or a credit?

   (b) On which statement does it appear?

4. credited, debited

5. Unadjusted Trial Balance columns; adjustments; adjusted trial balance

6. zero

7. zero, zero

8. temporary, revenue, expense

Problem V

1.

HOMER'S HOME SHOP
Work Sheet for Year Ended December 31, 20—

	Unadjusted Trial Balance Dr.	Cr.	Adjustments Dr.	Cr.	Adjusted Trial Balance Dr.	Cr.	Income Statement Dr.	Cr.	Statement of Ch. in O.E. and Balance Sheet Dr.	Cr.
Cash	2,875				2,875				2,875	
Accounts receivable	2,000				2,000				2,000	
Shop supplies	1,762			(a)1,037	725				725	
Shop equipment	5,125				5,125				5,125	
Accum. depr., shop equipment		725		(b) 475		1,200				1,200
Accounts Payable		575				575				575
Homer Tonely, capital		5,500				5,500				5,500
Homer Tonely, withdrawals	30,000				30,000				30,000	
Repair services revenue		55,785				55,785		55,785		
Wages expense	18,250		(c) 388		18,638		18,638			
Rent expense	2,500				2,500		2,500			
Miscellaneous expenses	73				73		73			
	62,585	62,585								
Shop supplies expense			(a)1037		1,037		1,037			
Depreciation expense, shop equip.			(b) 475		475		475			
Wages payable				(c) 388		388				388
			1,900	1,900	63,448	63,448	22,723	55,785	40,725	7,663
Net income							33,062			33,062
							55,785	55,785	40,725	40,725

2.

Dec. 31	Shop Supplies Expense	1,037	
	Shop Supplies		1,037
31	Depr. Expense, Shop Equipment	475	
	Accumulated Depr., Shop Equipment		475
31	Wages Expense	388	
	Wages Payable		388
31	Repair Services Revenue	55,785	
	Income Summary		55,785
31	Income Summary	22,723	
	Rent Expense		2,500
	Wages Expense		18,638
	Miscellaneous Expenses		73
	Shop Supplies Expense		1,037
	Depr. Expense, Shop Equipment		475
31	Income Summary	33,062	
	Homer Tonely, Capital		33,062
31	Homer Tonely, Capital	30,000	
	Homer Tonely, Withdrawals		30,000

©The McGraw-Hill Companies, Inc., 2011

GENERAL LEDGER

3.

Cash

Date	Debit	Credit	Balance
Dec. 31			2,875.00

Accounts Receivable

Date	Debit	Credit	Balance
Dec. 31			2,000.00

Shop Supplies

Date	Debit	Credit	Balance
Dec. 31			1,762.00
31		1,037.00	725.00

Shop Equipment

Date	Debit	Credit	Balance
Dec. 31			5,125.00

Accum. Depr., Shop Equipment

Date	Debit	Credit	Balance
Dec. 31			725.00
31		475.00	1,200.00

Accounts Payable

Date	Debit	Credit	Balance
Dec. 31			575.00

Wages Payable

Date	Debit	Credit	Balance
Dec. 31		388.00	388.00

Homer Tonely, Capital

Date	Debit	Credit	Balance
Dec. 31			5,500.00
31		33,062.00	38,562.00
31	30,000.00		8,562.00

Homer Tonely, Withdrawals

Date	Debit	Credit	Balance
Dec. 31			30,000.00
31		30,000.00	-0-

Repair Services Revenue

Date	Debit	Credit	Balance
Dec. 31			55,785.00
31	55,785.00		-0-

Depr. Expense, Shop Equipment

Date	Debit	Credit	Balance
Dec. 31	475.00		475.00
31		475.00	-0-

Wages Expense

Date	Debit	Credit	Balance
Dec. 31			18,250.00
31	388.00		18,638.00
31		18,638.00	-0-

Rent Expense

Date	Debit	Credit	Balance
Dec. 31			2,500.00
31		2,500.00	-0-

Shop Supplies Expense

Date	Debit	Credit	Balance
Dec. 31	1,037.00		1,037.00
31		1,037.00	-0-

Miscellaneous Expenses

Date	Debit	Credit	Balance
Dec. 31			73.00
31		73.00	-0-

Income Summary

Date	Debit	Credit	Balance
Dec. 31		55,785.00	55,785.00
31	22,723.00		33,062.00
31	33,062.00		-0-

4.

HOMER'S HOME SHOP

Post-Closing Trial Balance

December 31, 20—

Cash	$ 2,875	
Accounts receivable	2,000	
Shop supplies	725	
Shop equipment	5,125	
Accumulated depreciation, shop equipment		$ 1,200
Accounts payable		575
Wages payable		388
Homer Tonely, capital		8,562
	$10,725	$10,725

CHAPTER 7
FRAUD, ETHICS, AND CONTROLS

Learning Objective 1:

Define workplace fraud and explain the four elements common to all fraud schemes.

Summary

Workplace fraud involves the use of one's job for personal gain, through deliberate misuse of the employer's assets. All workplace fraud is secret, violates the employee's job duties, provides financial benefit to the employee, and costs the employer money.

Learning Objective 2:

Describe the three major types of workplace fraud.

Summary

Asset misappropriation, corruption, and fraudulent financial statements are the three major types of workplace fraud.

Learning Objective 3:

Define internal control and identify its purpose and principles.

Summary

An internal control system consists of the policies and procedures managers use to protect assets, ensure reliable accounting, promote efficient operations, and urge adherence to company policies. It can prevent avoidable losses and help managers both plan operations and monitor company and human performance. Principles of good internal control include establishing responsibilities, maintaining adequate records, insuring assets and bonding employees, separating recordkeeping from custody of assets, dividing responsibilities for related transactions, applying technological controls, and performing regular independent reviews.

Learning Objective 4:

Explain how technology impacts an internal control system.

Summary

Technology improves managers' abilities to monitor and control business activities. It also allows for more extensive testing of records. However, technological systems often produce hard-copy evidence to review. Technology often eliminates jobs, making separation of duties more difficult, particularly in small companies.

Learning Objective 5:

Describe the limitations of internal control.

Summary

Internal control systems are limited by the human element and cost-benefit principle. Human error and/or human fraud, particularly collusion, limit the effectiveness of internal control systems. cost-benefit principle states that the costs of internal controls not exceed their benefits. In considering costs the employer consider the effects of certain controls on employee morale.

Learning Objective 6:

Explain provisions of the Sarbanes-Oxley Act that are designed to detect and curtail fraud.

Summary

The Sarbanes-Act requires each annual report to include an internal control that states managers' responsibility for maintaining adequate internal controls for financial reporting. The company must also the effectiveness of its internal controls.

Learning Objective 7:

Describe the use of documentation and verification to control cash disbursements.

Summary

A voucher system is a set of procedures and approvals designed to control cash disbursements and acceptance of obligations. The voucher system of control relies on several important documents including the voucher and its files. A key factor in this system is that only approved departments and individuals are authorized to incur certain obligations.

I. **Workplace Fraud**—Using one's job for personal financial gain by deliberate misuse of company assets. Fraud can lead to the demise of the business.

    a. Elements of Workplace Fraud Schemes

        i. Secret

        ii. Violates employee duty to employer

        iii. Provides direct or indirect benefit to employee

        iv. Costs the employer money

    b. Major Types of Workplace Fraud

        i. Asset misappropriation—theft

        ii. Corruption—bribery, kickbacks

        iii. Fraudulent financial statements—overstate or create assets/revenues, understate/hide liabilities/expenses.

    c. Detecting Fraud

        i. Tips from employees and others

        ii. Internal controls and audits

        iii. External audits

II. **Internal Control**—a system of policies and procedures adopted by a business to protect assets, ensure reliable accounting, and promote efficient operations. Adherence to company policies to ensure compliance is encouraged through both positive and negative consequences.

    a. Principles of Internal Control

        i. Establish responsibilities

            1. Should be clearly assigned

            2. Eliminate conflicting responsibilities

        ii. Maintain adequate records

            1. Preprinted checks and invoices

            2. Use a voucher system—all accounts payable transactions are coded with a unique sequential number. Purchase orders are issued, and matched to receiving documents.

            3. Clearly defined chart of accounts

            4. Timely and accurate recording of all transactions

            5. Timely and accurate financial reporting system

        iii. Insure assets and bond key employees—adequate insurance on all assets and bonding of all employees responsible for cash transactions.

        iv. Separate recordkeeping from physical custody of assets—the person responsible for physical custody of the asset should not have any responsibilities for recording transactions and/or maintaining purchasing records.

     v. Divide responsibility for related transactions—always separate the accounting function from the operational function so that two different reporting mechanisms come to the same amounts.

     vi. Apply technological controls—technology changes continue to accelerate at a mind-numbing pace. Businesses should use the most cost-beneficial technologies available and properly plan for disasters.

     vii. Perform regular and independent reviews—large Companies should use an internal audit function to review and evaluate compliance with policies and procedures.

III. Technology and Internal Control

  a. Reduced processing errors—less human error – capture necessary data one time.

  b. More Extensive Testing of Records—open architecture in software allows testing of large amount of data relatively efficiently.

  c. Limited Evidence of Processing

     i. Technology eliminates many 'hard copy' reports

     ii. Technology can track personnel transaction history

     iii. System design becomes more important that reviewing output

  d. Crucial Separation of Duties

     i. Some incompatible jobs may be consolidated by technology

     ii. Protect against unauthorized software changes

     iii. Separate users from systems designers and programmers

IV. Limitations of Internal Control

  a. Human element

     i. Humans commit fraud

     ii. Humans make errors

  b. Cost-benefit principle—cost of implementation should be less than the benefit derived.

V. Control of Cash Disbursements—when paying out funds, a Company should verify that the purchase was authorized, received and invoiced by an approved vendor.

  a. Voucher System—procedures and forms to control payments (See Appendix 7A for further discussion of elements of a voucher system)

     i. Verifying, approving and recording obligations

     ii. Issuing checks for payment of verified, approved, and recorded obligations

      b.   Elements of a Voucher System

         i.   Purchase requisition—a form used to communicate and document authorization for making purchases.

        ii.   Purchase order—a form used to communicate and document that an order has been placed to purchase goods and/or services at a specified price, quantity, terms, etc.

      iii.   Invoice—received from a vendor to document that a sale has occurred and an obligation to pay established

      iv.   Receiving Report—often a copy of the original purchase order, this documents the physical receipt of goods at the location specified.

       v.   Invoice approval/Check Authorization—a checklist to ensure all proper documents are included in the voucher package

      vi.   Voucher—a unique number assigned to a purchase transaction that establishes that a transaction has occurred and should be recorded, and authorizes the payment at an appropriate future date.

     vii.   Voucher register—each voucher is recorded into a register and posted to the general ledger.

VI.   **Sarbanes-Oxley Act (referred to as 'SOX')**

    a.   Requirements of the Act

       i.   Statement by management in annual report accepting responsibility for establishing internal controls

      ii.   Management must assess the effectiveness of internal controls

     iii.   External auditor must test internal controls

     iv.   CEO and CFO must certify the financial statements

      v.   Requires establishment of anonymous reporting of suspected activities

Alternate Demonstration Problem

The 'Jazz Derelicts' is a non-profit organization established to promote the study of Jazz Music in public schools around the country and internationally. Your father, the founding member and major contributor, has asked you to volunteer at a fundraising event and 'keep an eye out' for problems. The event just isn't producing the type of results expected. You agree to volunteer at the concert, working in the malted beverage concession stand.

Behind each beverage stand is an open cash box and multiple volunteers helping customers. It is very hot and people are very thirsty. Customers approach the stand and place their orders. For a given order, a volunteer will fill the order, take the money from the customer and make any necessary change, and put the money into the cash box.

During the event, you notice that many of the volunteers are putting customer money into their pockets. Additionally, you hear some of the volunteers soliciting additional donations from customers, and this money is also pocketed.

After the event, you talk to one of the event coordinators and determine that nobody from the organization counts the malt beverage cups before or after the event.

Required:
1. What specific internal control principles are violated at the concession stands?
2. What recommendations do you have to improve internal controls over the malt beverage concession stands for next year's event?

Solution:
1. Internal Control Principles violated:
   a. Although not specifically mentioned, the procedures were probably not well-established and communicated to the volunteers.
   b. Nobody was responsible for counting the cups used during the event.
   c. No recordkeeping function was established to record the sale of beverages.
   d. None of the volunteers were bonded.
   e. Since no recordkeeping took place, it is impossible to separate it from the physical custody.
   f. No technology used to detect fraud.
   g. No independent verification of results.

2. Recommendations:
   a. Prepare a brief set of instructions to all volunteers and review it as a group before the event starts.
   b. A supervisor should roam around and view the stands for compliance with the procedures.
   c. Sell tickets for the beverages at a different location in a secure environment.
   d. Do not collect money at the stand, ever.
   e. A ticket must be collected for all cups dispensed.
   f. Any donations should be handled by a separate booth in a secure environment.
   g. All redeemed tickets should be deposited into a locked box.
   h. Count all the cups before and after the event at each stand and calculate the number of cups sold.
   i. At the end of the event, auditors collect the boxes and count the number of tickets for each stand and record it in a journal.
   j. Compare the cup count with the ticket count and investigate any significant discrepancies.
   k. Consider banning non-compliant volunteers from future events.

Problem I

The following statements are either true or false. Place a (T) in the parentheses before each true statement and an (F) before each false statement.

1. ( ) One of the fundamental principles of internal control states that the person who has access to or is responsible for an asset should not maintain the accounting record for that asset.

2. ( ) Procedures for controlling cash disbursements are as important as those for cash receipts.

3. ( ) In order to approve an invoice for payment for the purchase of assets, the accounting department of a large company should require copies of the purchase requisition, purchase order, invoice, and receiving report.

4. ( ) All internal control policies and procedures have limitations which arise from the human element or the cost-benefit principle.

5. ( ) All workplace fraud does not cost the employer money.

6. ( ) Less human involvement in data processing allows for faster discovery in finding data entry errors.

Problem II

You are given several words, phrases, or numbers to choose from in completing each of the following statements or in answering the following questions. In each case select the one that best completes the statement or answers the question and place its letter in the answer space provided.

_____ 1. A voucher system:

    a. Permits only authorized individuals to incur obligations that will result in cash disbursements.

    b. Establishes procedures for incurring such obligations and for their verification, approval, and recording.

    c. Permits checks to be issued only in payment of properly verified, approved, and recorded obligations.

    d. Requires that every obligation be recorded at the time it is incurred and every purchase be treated as an independent transaction, complete in itself.

    e. Does all of the above.

_____ 2. A voucher is:

    a. An internal business paper (or folder) used to accumulate other papers and information needed to control cash disbursements and to ensure that the transaction is properly recorded.

    b. A business form used within a business to ask the purchasing department of the business to buy needed items.

    c. A document, prepared by a vendor, on which are listed the items sold, the sales prices, the customer's name, and the terms of sale.

    d. A form used within a business to notify the proper persons of the receipt of goods ordered and of the quantities and condition of the goods.

    e. A document on which the accounting department notes that it has performed each step in the process of checking an invoice and approving it for recording and payment.

_____ 3. Examples of workplace fraud include all of the following except that:

     a. It is due to employee mistakes due to exhaustion.

     b. It is secret.

     c. It violates the employee's duties to his employer.

     d. It is done to provide direct or indirect benefit to the employer.

     e. It costs the employer money.

_____ 4. An internal control system is designed to do the following:

     a. Urge adherence to company policies.

     b. Ensure reliable accounting.

     c. Protect assets.

     d. Promote efficient operations.

     e. All of the above.

Problem III

Many of the important ideas and concepts discussed in Chapter 7 are reflected in the following list of key terms. Test your understanding of these terms by matching the appropriate definitions with the terms. Record the number identifying the most appropriate definition in the blank space next to each term.

_____ Check register	_____ Receiving report
_____ Internal control system	_____ Vendee
_____ Invoice	_____ Vendor
_____ Invoice approval	_____ Voucher
_____ Principles of internal control	_____ Voucher register
_____ Purchase order	_____ Voucher system
_____ Purchase requisition	_____ Workplace fraud

1. Form used to report that ordered goods are received and to describe their quantity and condition.

2. Seller of goods or services.

3. Itemized record of goods prepared by the vendor that lists the customer's name, the items sold, the sales prices, and the terms of sale.

4. Internal business file that is used to accumulate documents and information to control the cash disbursements and to ensure that a transaction is properly recorded.

5. Document containing a checklist of steps necessary for approving an invoice for recording and payment; also called _check authorization_.

6. Document listing merchandise needed by a department and requesting it be purchased.

7. Another name for a cash disbursements journal which has a column for check numbers.

8. The deliberate misuse of an employer's assets for an employer's personal gain.

9. All policies and procedures used to protect assets, ensure reliable accounting, promote efficient operations, and urge adherence to company policies.

10. Set of procedures and approvals designed to control cash disbursements and acceptance of obligations.

11. Document used by the purchasing department to place an order with a seller (vendor).

12. Buyer or purchaser of goods or services.

13. Principles requiring management to establish responsibility, maintain records, insure assets, separate recordkeeping from custody of assets, divide responsibility for related transactions, apply technological controls, and perform reviews.

14. A journal used to record approved vouchers.

Problem IV

Complete the following by filling in the blanks.

1. A (n) _____ form is used by the accounting department in checking and approving an invoice for recording and payment.

2. Control of a small business is commonly gained through the direct supervision and active participation of the _____ in the affairs and activities of the business. However, as a business grows, it becomes necessary for the manager to delegate responsibilities and rely on _____ rather than personal contact in controlling the affairs and activities of the business.

3. A properly designed internal control system encourages adherence to prescribed managerial policies; and it also (a) _____
   _____ ;
   (b) _____
   _____ ; and (c) _____
   _____ .

4. A good system of internal control for cash requires a _____
   of duties so that the people responsible for handling cash and for its custody are not the same people who _____ . It also requires that all cash receipts be deposited in the bank _____ and that all payments, except petty cash payments, be made by _____ .

5. An accounting system used to control the incurrence and payment of obligations requiring the disbursement of cash is a _____ .

6. A _____ is commonly used by a selling department to notify the purchasing department of items which the selling department wishes the purchasing department to purchase.

7. The business form commonly used by the purchasing department of a large company to order merchandise is called a(n) _____ .

8. Good internal control follows certain broad principles. These principles are:

(a) Responsibilities should be clearly established, and in every situation _____ should be made responsible for each task.

(b) Adequate records should be maintained since they provide an important means of protecting _____.

(c) Assets should be _____ and employees _____.

(d) Record-keeping for assets and _____ of assets should be separated.

(e) Responsibility for related transactions should be _____ so that the work of one department or individual may act as a check on the work of others.

(f) Mechanical devices _____ where practicable.

(g) Regular and independent _____ of internal control procedures should be conducted.

Problem V

McCauley's Rug Cleaning Company uses a voucher system to control their expenditures. Determine the person/department that is responsible for providing the supporting documentation for the following documents in a standard voucher system:

Voucher Document	Document Initiated By:
Purchase requisition	
Purchase order	
Invoice	
Receiving report	
Invoice approval	
Check	

Solutions for Chapter 7

Problem I

1. T   4. T
2. T   5. F
3. T   6. F

Problem II

1. E
2. A
3. A
4. E

Problem III

7	Check register	1	Receiving report
9	Internal control system	12	Vendee
3	Invoice	2	Vendor
5	Invoice approval	4	Voucher
13	Principles of internal control	14	Voucher register
11	Purchase order	10	Voucher system
6	Purchase requisition	8	Workplace fraud

Problem IV

1. invoice approval

2. owner-manager, a system of internal control

3. (a) promotes operational efficiencies; (b) protects the business assets from waste, fraud, and theft; and (c) ensures accurate and reliable accounting data

4. separation, keep the cash records, intact each day, check

5. voucher system

6. purchase requisition

7. purchase order

8. (a) one person; (b) assets; (c) insured, bonded; (d) custody; (e) divided; (f) should be used; (g) reviews

Problem V

Voucher Document	Document Initiated By:
Purchase requisition	Requesting department
Purchase order	Purchasing department
Invoice	Supplier
Receiving report	Receiving department
Invoice approval	Accounting
Check	Cashier

CHAPTER 8
CASH AND CASH CONTROLS

Learning Objective 1:

Define cash and describe three guidelines for control of cash.

Summary

Cash includes currency, coins, amounts on deposit in bank accounts, and checks acceptable for deposit in bank accounts. Guidelines for control of cash include (1) separation of the handling of cash from its recordkeeping, (2) cash receipts should be promptly deposited in a bank, and (3) cash payments should be made by check.

Learning Objective 2:

Describe controls for cash receipts.

Summary

Control of over-the-counter cash receipts includes use of a cash register, customer review, use of receipts, a permanent transaction record locked-in the cash register, and separation of access to cash from its recordkeeping. Control of cash receipts by mail includes at least two people assigned to open mail and a listing of each sender's name, amount paid, and an explanation.

Learning Objective 3:

Describe controls for cash disbursements.

Summary

Except for very small dollar transactions, all expenditures should be made by check. A petty cash system is used to account for small dollar transactions. Employees who sign checks should not have access to accounting records.

Learning Objective 4:

Explain and record petty cash fund transactions.

Summary

Petty cash payments are for amounts for items such as postage, delivery fees, minor repairs, and supplies. A petty fund cashier safeguards the petty cash, makes payments from the petty cash fund, and keeps petty cash receipts and records. A Petty Cash account is debited only when the fund is established or increased in amount. When the fund is replenished, petty cash disbursements are recorded with debits to expense (or asset) accounts and a credit to cash.

Learning Objective 5:

Identify banking activities as controls of cash.

Summary

A bank account is a record set up by a bank, allowing a customer to endorse checks and to deposit money for safekeeping and to draw checks on it. A bank deposit ticket proves money was deposited into a bank account. A check tells the bank to pay money from a customer's (*maker*) account to a recipient (*payee*).

Learning Objective 6:

Describe a bank statement.

Summary

A bank statement shows activity in a bank account. Each bank statements lists the beginning-of-period account balance, checks and other debits decreasing the account during the period, deposits and other credits increasing the account during the period, and the end-of-period account balance.

Learning Objective 7:

Prepare and explain a bank reconciliation.

Summary

A bank reconciliation proves the accuracy of the depositor's and the bank's records. The bank statement balance is adjusted for items such as outstanding checks and unrecorded deposits made on or before the bank statement date but not reflected on the bank statement. The book balance is adjusted for items such as service charges, bank collections for the customer, and interest earned on the account.

Chapter Outline

Notes

I. **Control of Cash**

   a. Cash and Liquidity

     i. Includes currency, coin, checks, traveler's checks, money orders

     ii. Guidelines for cash control

       1. Handling of cash separate from accounting

       2. Cash receipts are promptly deposited

       3. All payments made by check

   b. Control of Cash Receipts

     i. Over the Counter Cash Receipts

       1. Locked cash register

       2. All sales recorded

       3. Permanent record internally stored

       4. Access to cash separate from the record keeping

       5. Third employee compares tape to deposit

       6. Cash short/over recorded for discrepancies

     ii. Cash Receipts by Mail

       1. Mail opened and checks are recorded

       2. Checks sent to cashier with a copy of the record, for deposit to the bank.

       3. Copy of record sent to accounting and recorded in GL

       4. Bank account is reconciled to the GL by a different person

   c. Control of Cash Disbursements—all cash payments are made by check except for small incidental items.

     i. Petty Cash System

       1. Small amount of cash is entrusted to an employee

       2. Petty cash voucher (receipt) prepared as payments are made

       3. Vouchers submitted at month end for reimbursement

       4. Record journal entry, assuring that total debits = total credits. Any difference is recorded in Cash Over and Short account

II. **Banking Activities as Controls**—Banks are independent third parties with strong controls that can be relied upon for accuracy.

   a. Basic Bank Services

     i. Bank account set up by a bank for a customer

     ii. Signature card to verify the owner's signature

     iii. Deposit ticket for recording cash receipts

     iv. Checks for making payments to vendors and employees

     v. Electronic Funds Transfer for 'paperless' transactions

    b. Bank Statement—shows all activity for a month
- i. Beginning Balance
- ii. Deposits Made
- iii. Checks written (cleared)
- iv. Collections made directly
- v. Service Charges
- vi. Ending balance

    c. Bank Reconciliation—one of the strongest controls available for detecting and correcting errors that can occur in the accounting process. Performed by comparing the activity on the bank statement with the activity recorded on the GL to identify:
- i. Transactions recorded on the GL not on the Bank Statement
  1. Outstanding Checks
  2. Deposits in Transit
- ii. Transactions recorded by the Bank, not on the GL
  1. Collections
  2. Service charges
  3. NSF charges
- iii. Calculate adjusted bank and book balances
  1. Bank balance + Deposits in Transit – Outstanding checks =Adjusted balance
  2. Book balance + Collections + Interest Earned – Service charges/NSF charges = Adjusted balance
  3. Adjusted balances should match
- iv. Adjustments to the General Ledger
  1. All items on the 'book' side of the bank reconciliation should be adjusted in the GL.

Bank Reconciliation

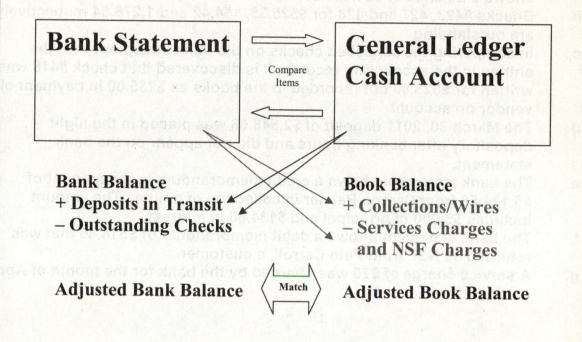

Bank Statement	→ Compare Items	**General Ledger Cash Account**

Bank Balance
+ Deposits in Transit
− Outstanding Checks

Book Balance
+ Collections/Wires
− Services Charges
and NSF Charges

Adjusted Bank Balance ⟺ Match **Adjusted Book Balance**

➤ Items on the bank statement, not in GL
➤ Items recorded on GL, not on bank statement

Alternate Demonstration Problem

Prepare a bank reconciliation for Katie's Koffee Kup Kafe, for the month ended April 30, 2011. The following information is available to reconcile the book balance of cash with its bank statement balance as of April 30, 2011.

a. After all posting is complete on April 30, 2011, the company's book balance of Cash has a $20,907.50 debit balance, but its bank statement shows a balance of $24,822.25.

b. Checks #423, 427 and 428 for $525.35, 154.42 and 1,278.54 respectively are outstanding

c. In comparing the cancelled checks on the bank statement with the entries in the accounting records, it is discovered that check #418 was written for $325.00 but recorded in the books as $235.00 in payment of a vendor on account.

d. The March 30, 2011 deposit of $2,548.68 was placed in the night depository after banking hours and did not appear on the bank statement.

e. The bank statement shows a credit memorandum in the amount of $5,134.58 from Carson Palmer in collection of a note. The amount includes $5,000 of principal and $134.58 in interest.

f. The bank statement shows a debit memorandum of $514.46 that was returned as NSF from Pete Carroll, a customer.

g. A service charge of $25 was charged by the bank for the month of April.

Katie's Koffee Kup Kafe Bank Reconciliation For the month ended April 30, 2011				
Bank statement balance	$ 24,822.25	Book balance	$	20,907.50
Add:		Add:		
Deposit in transit	2,548.68	Collection of Note		
		Principal		5,000.00
		Interest		134.58
Deduct:		Deduct:		
Outstanding checks		Service charge		(25.00)
#423	(525.35)	NSF check		(514.46)
#427	(154.42)	Error on check #418		(90.00)
#428	(1,278.54)			
Adjusted bank balance	$ 25,412.62	Adjusted book balance	$	25,412.62

Katie's Koffee Kup Kafe
General Journal
For the month ended April 30, 2011

Date	Account	Debit	Credit
30-Apr	Cash	5,134.58	
	Notes Receivable		5,000.00
	Interest income		134.58
	to record collection of note from		
	Carson Palmer		
30-Apr	Miscellaneous Expense	25.00	
	Cash		25.00
	to record service charge for the month		
30-Apr	Accounts Receivable	514.46	
	Cash		514.46
	to record NSF check from Pete Carroll		
30-Apr	Accounts Payable	90.00	
	Cash		90.00
	to correct error on check #418		

Problem I

The following statements are either true or false. Place a (T) in the parentheses before each true statement and an (F) before each false statement.

1. ( ) After the petty cash fund is established, the Petty Cash account is not debited or credited again unless the size of the fund is changed.

2. ( ) If 20 canceled checks are listed on the current month's bank statement, then no less than 20 checks could have been issued during the current month.

3. ( ) Cash includes currency and coins only.

4. ( ) Control of cash receipts that arrive by mail includes that two people should be present when opening the mail.

5. ( ) Outstanding checks are added to the bank balance when performing a bank reconciliation.

Problem II

You are given several words, phrases, or numbers to choose from in completing each of the following statements or in answering the following questions. In each case select the one that best completes the statement or answers the question and place its letter in the answer space provided.

_____ 1. Liquidity is:

    a. The portion of a corporation's equity that represents investments in the corporation by its stockholders.

    b. Cash or other assets that are reasonably expected to be realized in cash or be sold or consumed within one year or one operating cycle of the business.

    c. A characteristic of an asset indicating how easily the asset can be converted into cash or used to buy services or satisfy obligations.

    d. Obligations that are due to be paid or liquidated within one year or one operating cycle of the business.

    e. Economic benefits or resources without physical substance, the value of which stems from the privileges or rights that accrue to their owner.

_____ 2. Each of the following items would cause Brand X Sales Company's book balance of cash to differ from its bank statement balance.

    A. A service charge made by the bank.

    B. A check listed as outstanding on the previous month's reconciliation and that is still outstanding.

    C. A customer's check returned by the bank marked "NSF."

    D. A deposit which was mailed to the bank on the last day of November and is unrecorded on the November bank statement.

    E. A check paid by the bank at its correct $422 amount but recorded in error in the General Journal at $442.

    F. An unrecorded credit memorandum indicating the bank had collected a note receivable for Brand X Sales Company and deposited the proceeds in the company's account.

    G. A check written during November and not yet paid and returned by the bank.

Which of the above items require entries on the books of Brand X Sales Company?

    a. A., B., C., and E.

    b. A., C., E., and F.

    c. A., B., D., and F.

    d. A., B., D., E., and G.

    e. C., D., E., and F.

_____ 3. A cash register receipt showed $825. A count of cash in the register showed $821. The entry to record cash sales would include:

    a. Debit to Sales for $825.

    b. Debit to Cash for $821.

    c. Debit to Sales for $821.

    d. Credit to Cash for $821.

    e. Credit to Cash for $825.

_____ 4. A bank reconciliation is completed and The Video Store is notified of a customer's NSF check for $300. The journal entry to record the NSF check that is returned as uncollectible would include:

    a. Miscellaneous Expense 300

          Accounts Receivable   300

    b. Accounts Receivable 300

          Cash   300

    c. Accounts Payable 3,260

          Cash   3,260

    d. Cash...3,260

          Accounts Receivable   3,260

Problem III

Many of the important ideas and concepts discussed in Chapter 8 are reflected in the following list of key terms. Test your understanding of these terms by matching the appropriate definitions with the terms. Record the number identifying the most appropriate definition in the blank space next to each term.

_____	Bank reconciliation	_____	Deposit ticket
_____	Bank statement	_____	Electronic funds transfer (EFT)
_____	Canceled checks	_____	Liquid asset
_____	Cash	_____	Liquidity
_____	Cash Over and Short	_____	Outstanding checks
_____	Check	_____	Petty cash
_____	Days' sales uncollected	_____	Signature card
_____	Deposit in transit		

1. Company's ability to pay for its short-term obligations.

2. Checks written and recorded by the depositor but not yet paid by the bank at the bank statement date.

3. Asset such as cash that is easily converted into other types of assets or used to pay for goods, services or liabilities.

4. Checks that the bank has paid and deducted from the customer's account during the period.

5. An income statement account used to record cash overages and cash shortages arising from missing petty cash receipts or from errors in making change.

6. Report that explains the difference between the balance of a checking account in the depositor's records and the balance reported on the bank statement.

7. Small amount of cash in a fund to pay minor expenses.

8. Includes the signatures of each person authorized to sign checks on the account.

9. Use of electronic communication to transfer cash from one party to another.

10. Lists items such as currency, coins, and checks deposited and their corresponding dollar amounts.

11. Document signed by the depositor instructing the bank to pay a specified amount to a designated recipient.

12. Includes currency, coins, and amounts on deposit in bank checking or savings accounts.

13. Bank report on the depositor's beginning and ending cash balances, and a listing of its changes, for a period.

14. Deposits recorded by the company but not yet by its bank.

Problem IV

Complete the following by filling in the blanks.

1. If a cashier errs while making change and gives a customer too much money back, the resulting cash shortage is recorded with a debit to an account called _____.

2. If the size of the petty cash fund remains unchanged, the Petty Cash account _____ (is, is not) debited in the entry to replenish the petty cash fund.

3. A bank reconciliation is prepared to account for the difference between the _____ and the _____.

4. After preparing a bank reconciliation, journal entries _____(should, should not) be made to record those items listed as outstanding checks.

5. Days' sales uncollected is used in evaluating the _____ of a company.

6. A _____ _____ lists currency, coins and checks deposited along with their dollar amounts.

7. A _____ _____ is a report which explains any differences between the checking account balance according to the depositor's records and the balance reported on the bank statement.

Problem V

On November 5 of the current year Cullen Company drew Check No. 23 for $50 to establish a petty cash fund.

1. Give the general journal entry to record the establishment of the fund.

DATE	ACCOUNT TITLES AND EXPLANATION	P.R.	DEBIT		CREDIT	

After making a payment from petty cash on November 25, the petty cashier noted that there was only $2.50 cash remaining in the fund. The cashier prepared the following list of expenditures from the fund and requested that the fund be replenished.

Nov. 9	Express freight on merchandise purchased	$ 9.75
12	Miscellaneous expense to clean office	10.00
15	Office supplies	3.50
18	Delivery of merchandise to customer	8.00
23	Miscellaneous expense for collect telegram	3.25
25	Express freight on merchandise purchased	13.00

Check No. 97 in the amount of $47.50 was drawn to replenish the fund.

©The McGraw-Hill Companies, Inc., 2011

2. In the General Journal below give the entry to record the check replenishing the petty cash fund.

DATE	ACCOUNT TITLES AND EXPLANATION	P.R.	DEBIT	CREDIT

Problem VI

Information about the following eight items is available to prepare Verde Company's December 31 bank reconciliation.

Two checks (1) No. 453 and (2) No. 457 were outstanding on November 30. Check No. 457 was returned with the December bank statement but Check No. 453 was not. (3) Check No. 478, written on December 26, was not returned with the canceled checks; and (4) Check No. 480 for $96 was incorrectly entered in the Cash Disbursements Journal and posted as though it were for $69. (5) A deposit placed in the bank's night depository after banking hours on November 30 appeared on the December bank statement, but (6) one placed there after hours on December 31 did not. (7) Enclosed with the December bank statement was a debit memorandum for a bank service charge and (8) a check received from a customer and deposited on December 27 but returned by the bank marked "Not Sufficient Funds."

1. If an item in the above list should not appear on the December 31 bank reconciliation, ignore it. However, if an item should appear, enter its number in a set of parentheses to show where it should be added or subtracted in preparing the reconciliation.

2.

VERDE COMPANY
Bank Reconciliation
December 31, 20—

Book balance of cash............... $X,XXX   Bank statement balance.................. $X,XXX
  Add: Add:
    ( )   ( )
    ( )   ( )
    ( )   ( )
  Deduct: Deduct:
    ( )   ( )
    ( )   ( )
    ( )   ( )
Reconciled balance.................. $X,XXX   Reconciled balance......................... $X,XXX

3. Certain of the above items require entries on Verde Company's books. Place the numbers of these items within the following parentheses:
( ), ( ), ( ), ( ), ( ), ( )

Problem VII

The bank statement dated September 30, 2011, for the Smith Company showed a balance of $2,876.35 which differs from the $1,879.50 book balance of cash on that date. In attempting to reconcile the difference, the accountant noted the following facts:

1. The bank recorded a service fee of $15 that was not recorded on the books of Smith Company.

2. A deposit of $500 was made on the last day of the month but was not recorded by the bank.

3. A check for $176 had been recorded on the Smith Company books as $167. The bank paid the correct amount.

4. A check was written during September but has not been processed by the bank. The amount was $422.85.

5. A check for $1,000 is still outstanding from August.

6. A check for $100 deposited by Smith Company was returned marked "Not Sufficient Funds."

7. A credit memorandum stated that the bank collected a note receivable of $200 for Smith Company and charged Smith a $2 collection fee. Smith Company had not previously recorded the collection.

Prepare, in good form, a bank reconciliation which shows the correct cash balance on September 30, 2011.

Solutions for Chapter 8

Problem I

1. T   4. T
2. F   5. F
3. F

Problem II

1. C
2. B
3. B
4. B

Problem III

6	Bank reconciliation	10	Deposit ticket
13	Bank statement	9	Electronic funds transfer (EFT)
4	Canceled checks	3	Liquid asset
12	Cash	1	Liquidity
5	Cash Over and Short	2	Outstanding checks
11	Check	7	Petty cash
14	Deposit in transit	8	Signature card

Problem IV

1. Cash Over and Short

2. is not

3. book balance of cash, bank statement balance

4. should not

5. liquidity

6. deposit ticket

7. bank reconciliation

Problem V

1. Nov. 5 Petty Cash 50.00
           Cash 50.00
           Established a petty cash fund.

2. Nov. 25 Transportation-In 22.75
           Miscellaneous Expenses 13.25
           Office Supplies.. 3.50
           Delivery Expense 8.00
           Cash 47.50
           Reimbursed the petty cash fund.

Problem VI

1. Book balance of cash................ $X,XXX   Bank statement balance .... $X,XXX
    Add: Add:
      (   )   (6)
    Deduct: Deduct:
      (4)   (1)
      (7)   (3)
      (8)   (   )
2. (4), (7), (8)

Problem VII

SMITH COMPANY
Bank Reconciliation
September 30, 2011

Book balance of cash	$1,879.50	Bank statement balance	$2,876.35
Add:		Add:	
Proceeds of note less			
Collection fee	198.00	Deposit on 9/30/07	500.00
	2,077.50		3,376.35
Deduct:		Deduct:	
NSF check $100.00		Outstanding checks:	
Service fee 15.00		August $1,000.00	
Recording error 9.00	124.00	September 422.85	1,422.85
Reconciled balance	$1,953.50	Reconciled balance	$1,953.50

Learning Objective 1:

Describe the laws that affect employee payroll.

Summary

Law requires employers to withhold amounts from employee pay for Social Security taxes, Medicare taxes, and for federal and state income taxes.

Learning Objective 2:

Compute employee gross pay.

Summary

Gross pay is the amount of compensation the employee earned during the period before deductions for items like taxes. It is commonly computed as the employee's hourly wage rate multiplied by the number of hours the employee worked during the pay period.

Learning Objective 3:

Compute employee deductions for taxes and net pay.

Summary

Employees pay 6.2% of their gross pay (up to $106,800) for Social Security taxes and 1.45% of their income for Medicare taxes. Based on the number of withholding allowances the employee chooses, the employer computes federal and state income tax withholdings from tax tables.

Learning Objective 4:

Record employee payroll information in a payroll register.

Summary

A payroll register is often used to keep a record of pay period dates, hours worked, gross pay, deductions, and net pay of each employee for each pay period. The payroll register provides information the accountant can use to make journal entries and prepare tax documents.

Learning Objective 5:

Journalize payroll transactions in a general journal.

Summary

The accountant debits Wage Expense for the total gross pay and credits tax liability accounts for amounts owed, and Accrued Wages Payable for employees' net pay. Paying the payroll results in a debit to Accrued Wages Payable and a credit to Cash.

Learning Objective 6:

Prepare an earnings record for each employee.

Summary

Employee earnings records summarize each employee's earnings, deductions, net pay, and total earnings during each calendar year. This information is used in computing taxes and in preparing tax documents required by law.

Learning Objective 7:

Explain how an employer can control payroll.

Summary

The employer can control payroll by hiring trustworthy employees, maintaining confidential records in locked files, and by separating important payroll duties.

College Accounting, 2nd Edition

I.   **Legal Aspects of Employee Payroll**—There is a legal
        relationship that is created between Employees and Employers.
        Employees are bound to follow the direction of supervisors and
        employers must pay them, collect taxes and report the information
        to the state and federal governments.

    a. Fair Labor Standards Act

        i.   Minimum wage established

        ii. 40 hour work week

        iii. 150% overtime rate

    b. Federal and State Income Tax Withholding

        i.   Employee files a W-4 withholding certificate

        ii. Withholding allowances for each child or dependent

        iii. Employees can elect 'exempt'.

    c. Federal Insurance Contributions Act (FICA)

        i.   Social security—6.2% (subject to maximum wage base)

        ii. Medicare—1.45%

        iii. Amount matched by employer

        iv. Self-employment tax for sole proprietors

II.   **Computing Employee Gross Pay**

    a. Employee completes time sheet

    b. Multiply hours worked times rate (150% for hours over 40)

III.   **Computing Withholdings from Employee Gross Pay**

    a. Federal Income Tax Withholding

        i.   Amount from tax table

        ii. Tables for weekly, bi-weekly, semi-monthly, monthly

        iii. Based on W-4 withholding allowances and filing status.

        iv. Can use rate schedules as alternative

    b. State Income Tax Withholding

        i.   Tables similar to Federal

    c. FICA Withholding

        i.   Social security—6.2% (subject to maximum wage base)

        ii. Medicare—1.45%

    d. Voluntary Deductions

        i.   Retirement plans

        ii. Health plans

        iii. Charitable gifts

e. Computing Net Pay
   i. Gross Wages – Federal Tax
   ii. – State Tax
   iii. – FICA
   iv. – Voluntary deductions
   v. = Net Pay

IV. **Payroll Register**
  a. Permanent record of prayroll transactions each pay period
  b. Source for journal entry to record payroll
   i. Dr. Wages/Salaries expense
   ii. Cr. Various liability accounts (Wages payable for net pay)
  c. Tracks wages subject to employer taxes
   i. FICA
   ii. Federal unemployment
   iii. State unemployment

V. **Paying Employees**
  a. Open a special payroll bank account
  b. Transfer funds to special account
   i. Dr. Cash – Payroll
   ii. Cr. Cash
  c. To distribute checks to employees
   i. Dr. Wages payable
   ii. Cr. Cash – Payroll

VI. **Employee Earnings Records**
  a. Legal requirement to track individual employee
   i. Earnings
   ii. Deductions
  b. Source for W-2 reporting annually

VII. **Control over Payroll**
  a. Fiduciary responsibility to report information
  b. Big penalties for failure to pay withheld taxes
  c. IRS will close business in arrears for payroll taxes
  d. Payroll fraud
   i. Ghost employees
   ii. Over reported hours
   iii. Overstated sales commissions
   iv. Very expensive for employers

e. Payroll Control
   i. Careful hiring practices
   ii. Review all timesheets
   iii. Payroll data secured
   iv. All payroll changes supported by proper documents
   v. Separation of inconsistent duties
      1. Independent distribution of checks
      2. Independent reconciliation of bank account

The Payroll Process

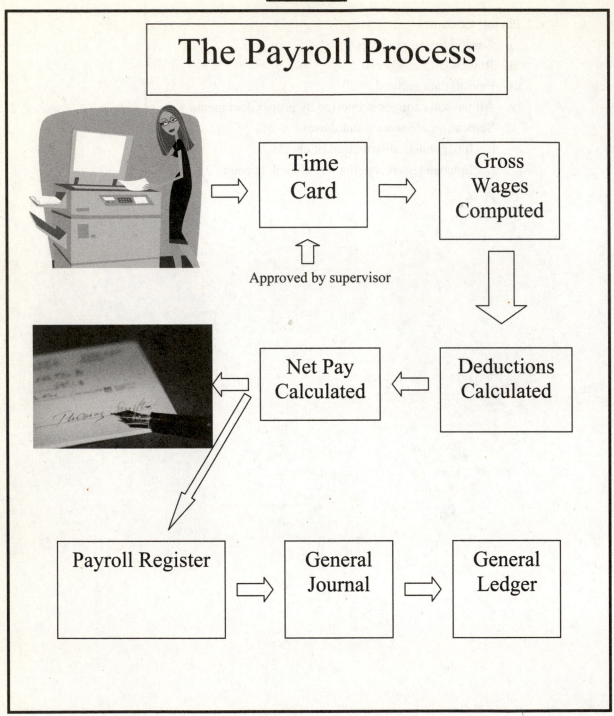

Time Card

Gross Wages Computed

Approved by supervisor

Net Pay Calculated

Deductions Calculated

Payroll Register

General Journal

General Ledger

Alternate Demonstration Problem

Floyd's Beauty Shop reports the information below related to its employees for the week ending April 7, 2011. The Company pays its employees one and one-half times their normal hourly wage for all hours worked beyond 40 hours.

Employee	Hours Worked	Hourly Wage	Withholding Allowances
Floyd Woodcock	42	12.67	2
Ralph Kafooty	48	11.25	2
Evelyn Woodhead	41	14.35	1

Required:
1. Compute each employee's gross pay for the week
2. Compute the amount Floyd's Beauty Shop must withhold from its employees' pay for the week ending April 7, 2011, for:
   a. Federal income taxes (use wage bracket withholding tables in Exhibit 9.4)
   b. State income taxes (assume Floyd's withholds 8% of the amount of federal income taxes withheld)
   c. Social Security taxes (6.2%)
   d. Medicare taxes (1.45%)
3. Compute net pay for the week for each employee
4. Prepare the journal entry to record the payroll for the week.
5. Prepare the journal entry to pay the payroll assuming Floyds uses a special payroll account.

Solution

Employee	Regular Hours	Overtime Hours	Regular Rate	Overtime Rate	Total Wages
Floyd Woodcock	40	2	12.67	19.01	544.82
Ralph Kafooty	40	8	11.25	16.88	585.04
Evelyn Woodhead	40	1	14.35	21.53	595.53
Total Gross Wages					1725.39

Employee	Federal Income Tax	State Income Tax	Social Security	Medicare Tax	Total Deductions
Floyd Woodcock	37.00	3.84	33.78	7.90	82.52
Ralph Kafooty	43.00	4.32	36.27	8.48	92.07
Evelyn Woodhead	55.00	5.20	36.92	8.64	105.76
Total Gross Wages	135.00	13.36	106.97	25.02	280.35

Employee	Gross Wages	Total Deductions	Net Pay
Floyd Woodcock	544.82	82.52	462.30
Ralph Kafooty	585.04	92.07	492.97
Evelyn Woodhead	595.53	105.76	489.77
Total Gross Wages	1,725.39	280.35	1,445.04

<table>
<tr><th colspan="5">Floyd's Beauty Shop
General Journal</th></tr>
<tr><th></th><th>Date</th><th>Account</th><th>Debit</th><th>Credit</th></tr>
<tr><td></td><td></td><td></td><td></td><td></td></tr>
<tr><td>4</td><td>7-Apr</td><td>Wages expense</td><td>1725.39</td><td></td></tr>
<tr><td></td><td></td><td>Federal Tax Payable</td><td></td><td>135.00</td></tr>
<tr><td></td><td></td><td>State Tax Payable</td><td></td><td>13.36</td></tr>
<tr><td></td><td></td><td>Social Security Tax Payable</td><td></td><td>106.97</td></tr>
<tr><td></td><td></td><td>Medicare Tax Payable</td><td></td><td>25.02</td></tr>
<tr><td></td><td></td><td>Wages Payable</td><td></td><td>1,445.04</td></tr>
<tr><td></td><td></td><td>to record the payroll of April 7</td><td></td><td></td></tr>
<tr><td></td><td></td><td></td><td></td><td></td></tr>
<tr><td>5</td><td>7-Apr</td><td>Cash-Payroll</td><td>1445.04</td><td></td></tr>
<tr><td></td><td></td><td>Cash</td><td></td><td>1,445.04</td></tr>
<tr><td></td><td></td><td>to transfer funds to the payroll account</td><td></td><td></td></tr>
<tr><td></td><td></td><td></td><td></td><td></td></tr>
<tr><td></td><td>7-Apr</td><td>Wages Payable</td><td>1445.04</td><td></td></tr>
<tr><td></td><td></td><td>Cash-Payroll</td><td></td><td>1,445.04</td></tr>
</table>

Problem I

The following statements are either true or false. Place a (T) in the parentheses before each true statement and an (F) before each false statement.

1. ( ) Employee benefit costs represent expenses to the employer in addition to the direct costs of salaries and wages.

2. ( ) Since federal income taxes withheld from an employee's wages are expenses of the employee, not the employer, they should not be treated as liabilities of the employer.

3. ( ) As the number of withholding allowances claimed increases, the amount of income tax to be withheld increases.

4. ( ) A special payroll bank account is used to replenish the regular bank account after all the employees are paid.

5. ( ) A penalty of 100% can be levied on any unpaid employee withholding taxes.

6. ( ) An accounts payable register is used to prepare the journal entry to record the payroll in the general ledger.

7. ( ) Net pay is gross pay plus all deductions.

8. ( ) The employer uses Circular E from the IRS to compute federal taxes withheld from employees wages.

9. ( ) The Fair Labor Standards Act sets a minimum at $7.75 currently.

10. ( ) An individual who is a sole proprietor must pay only the employee's portion of FICA taxes.

Problem II

You are given several words, phrases, or numbers to choose from in completing each of the following statements or in answering the following questions. In each case select the one that best completes the statement or answers the question and place its letter in the answer space provided.

For the next three questions, use the following information as to earnings and deductions taken from a company's payroll records for the pay period ended November 15:

Employee's Name	Earnings to End of Previous Week	Gross Pay This Week	Federal Income Taxes	Medical Insurance Deducted
Rita Hawn	$25,700	$ 800	$155.00	$ 35.50
Dolores Hopkins	930	800	134.00	35.50
Robert Allen	106,700	1,000	193.00	42.00
Calvin Ingram	18,400	740	128.00	42.00
		$3,340	$610.00	$155.00

_____ 1. Employees' FICA taxes are withheld at an assumed rate of 6.2% on the first $106,800 earned for Social Security and 1.45% of all wages earned for Medicare. The journal entry to accrue the payroll should include a:

a. Debit to Accrued Payroll Payable for $3,340.

b. Debit to FICA Taxes Payable—Medicare for $48.43.

c. Debit to Payroll Taxes Expense for $765.

d. Credit to FICA Taxes Payable—Social Security for $151.28.

e. Credit to Accrued Payroll Payable for $2,575.

_____ 2. The amount of the net pay is:

   a. $3340.00

   b. $2575.00

   c. $2375.29

   d. $4205.00

   e. $4304.71

_____ 3. The journal entry to record Wages Expense should include a:

   a. Debit to Wages Expense for $3,340.

   b. Credit to Wages Expense for $3,340.

   c. Debit to Wages Expense for $2375.29.

   d. Credit to Wages Expense for $2375.29.

   e. None of the above are correct.

Problem III

Many of the important ideas and concepts that are discussed in Chapter 9 are reflected in the following list of key terms. Test your understanding of these terms by matching the appropriate definitions with the terms. Record the number identifying the most appropriate definition in the blank space next to each term.

_____ Circular E
_____ Employee
_____ Employee benefits
_____ Employee earnings records
_____ Employee's Withholding Allowance
         Certificate (Form W-4)
_____ FICA taxes
_____ Gross pay
_____ Independent contractor
_____ Individual employee earnings records

_____ Net pay
_____ Payroll bank account
_____ Payroll deductions
_____ Payroll register

_____ Sales-per-employee ratio
_____ Self-employment tax
_____ Wage bracket withholding table
_____ Withholding allowance

1. Withholding allowance certificate, filed with the employer, identifying the number of withholding allowances claimed.

2. Table of the amounts of income tax withheld from employee's wages.

3. Taxes assessed on both employers and employees under the Federal Insurance Contributions Act (FICA); these taxes fund Social Security and Medicare programs.

4. Additional compensation paid to or on behalf of employees, such as premiums for medical, dental, life, and disability insurance and contributions to pension plans, and vacation pay.

5. Total compensation earned by an employee.

6. Amounts withheld from an employee's gross pay; also called _withholdings_.

7. Gross pay less all deductions; also called _take home pay_.

8. Record of an employee's gross pay, deductions, net pay, and year-to-date information.

9. Bank account used solely for paying employees, each pay period an amount equal to the total employees' net pay is deposited in it and the employees' payroll checks are drawn on that account.

10. Record for a pay period that shows the pay period dates, regular and overtime worked, gross pay, net pay, and deductions.

11. IRS federal income tax withholding tables.

12. Someone whose work is under the direction of an employer.

13. Someone who does a job for an employer, but decides how to do the work.

14. Records that summarize each employee's earnings, deductions, and net pay during each calendar year.

15. Social Security and Medicare taxes for person who operate their own businesses.

16. Determines the amount of federal income taxes to withhold from an employee's pay.

Problem IV

Complete the following by filling in the blanks.

1. The _____ pay minus the total payroll _____ equals the amount of the net pay.

2. The two components of FICA taxes are _____ and _____.

3. The amount to be withheld from an employee's wages for federal income taxes is determined by
   (a)_____ and
   (b)_____.

4. According to the wage bracket withholding table of Exhibit 11A.6 in your text, $ _____ should be withheld from the wages of an employee for federal income taxes if the employee has two exemptions and earned $680 in a week.

5. The _____ contains all the data needed to prepare the general journal entry to record payroll.

6. An employee's time worked, gross earnings, deductions, and net pay for a full year are summarized in a _____.

7. A person who operates their own business as a sole proprietor or independent contractor pays
   _____ _____ _____.

8. An _____ is someone whose work is under the direction of the employer.

9. An _____ _____ performs a job for an employer, but decides how to do the work.

10. _____ _____ are amounts withheld from an employee's gross pay.

Problem V

The following information as to earnings and deductions for the pay period ended November 15 was taken from a company's payroll records:

Employee's Name	Earnings to End of Previous Week	Gross Pay This Week	Federal Income Taxes	Medical Insurance Deducted
Rita Hawn..	$25,700	$ 800	$155.00	$ 35.50
Dolores Hopkins.............................	930	800	134.00	35.50
Robert Allen	106,700	1,000	193.00	42.00
Calvin Ingram................................	18,400	740	128.00	42.00
		$3,340	$610.00	$155.00

Required:

Calculate the employees' FICA taxes withheld assuming a rate of 6.2% on the first $94,200 earned for Social Security and 1.45% of all wages earned for Medicare, and prepare a journal entry to accrue the payroll under the assumption that all of the employees work in the office.

DATE	ACCOUNT TITLES AND EXPLANATION	P.R.	DEBIT	CREDIT

Problem VI

The Payroll Register of Whiteman Sales for the <u>first week</u> of the year follows. The deductions and net pay of the first three employees have been calculated and entered.

1. Complete the payroll information opposite the name of the last employee, Fred Clarke. Use an assumed 8% FICA tax rate (Medicare and Social Security rates have been combined and rounded for ease of calculation in this problem). In addition to FICA taxes, Mr. Clarke should have $111 of federal income taxes, $20 of medical insurance, and no union dues withheld from his wages, which are chargeable to office salaries. The overtime premium rate is 50%.

PAYROLL REGISTER

EMPLOYEE'S NAME	CLOCK CARD NUMBER	DAILY TIME							TOTAL HOURS	O.T. HOURS	REG. PAY RATE		REGULAR PAY		O.T. PREMIUM PAY		GROSS PAY		
		M	T	W	T	F	S	S											
Delbert Landau	12	8	8	8	7	4	0	0	35		11	00	385	00			385	00	1
Maria Garza	9	8	8	8	5	4	0	0	35		12	00	396	00			396	00	2
Ralph Webster	15	8	8	7	8	4	0	0	35		13	00	455	00			455	00	3
Fred Clarke	4	8	8	8	8	8	4	0	44	4	14	00							4
																			5

Week ending January 8, 2011

	DEDUCTIONS								PAYMENT				DISTRIBUTION					
	FICA TAXES		FEDERAL INCOME TAXES		MEDICAL INSURANCE		UNION DUES		TOTAL DEDUC-TIONS		NET PAY		CHECK NUMBER	SALES SALARIES		OFFICE SALARIES	DELIVERY WAGES	
1	30	80	65	00	20	00	10	00	125	80	259	20					385	00
2	31	68	63	00	20	00	10	00	124	68	271	32		396	00			
3	36	40	68	00	20	00	10	00	134	40	320	60		455	00			
4																		
5																		

2. Complete the Payroll Register by totaling its columns, and give the general journal entry to record its information.

DATE	ACCOUNT TITLES AND EXPLANATION	P.R.	DEBIT	CREDIT

Whiteman Sales uses a special payroll bank account in paying its employees. Each payday, after the general journal entry recording the information of its Payroll Register is posted, a single check for the total of the employees' net pay is drawn and deposited in the payroll bank account. This transfers funds equal to the payroll total from the regular bank account to the payroll bank account. Then special payroll checks are written on the payroll bank account and given to the employees. For the January 8 payroll, four payroll checks beginning with payroll Check No. 102 were drawn and delivered to the employees. Record this information in the Payroll Register.

3. Make the entry to record the transfer of cash to the payroll bank account for the January 8 payroll.

DATE	ACCOUNT TITLES AND EXPLANATION	P.R.	DEBIT	CREDIT

Solutions for Chapter 9

Problem I

1. T
2. F
3. F
4. F
5. T
6. F
7. F
8. T
9. F
10. F

Problem II

1. D
2. C
3. A

Problem III

11	Circular E	14	Individual employee earnings records
12	Employee	7	Net pay
4	Employee benefits	9	Payroll bank account
8	Employee earnings records	6	Payroll deductions
1	Employee's Withholding Allowance Certificate (Form W-4)	10	Payroll register
3	FICA taxes	15	Self-employment tax
5	Gross pay	2	Wage bracket withholding table
13	Independent contractor	16	Withholding allowance

Problem IV

1. gross, deductions
2. Social Security taxes, Medicare taxes
3. (a) the amount of his or her wages,
   (b) the number of his or her withholding allowances
4. $68
5. Payroll Register
6. Employee's Individual Earnings Record
7. self-employment tax
8. employee
9. independent contractor
10. Payroll deductions

Problem V

Nov. 15   Office Salaries Expense..   3,340.00
        FICA Taxes Payable..   199.71
        Employees' Federal Income Taxes Payable.......................   610.00
        Employees' Hospital Insurance Payable............................   155.00
        Accrued Payroll Payable 2,375.29

($800 + $800 + $100 + $740) x .062 = $151.28 Soc. Sec Tax
$3,340 *0.0145 = $48.43 Medicare
$151.28 + $48.43 = $199.71

Problem VI

1.

PAYROLL REGISTER

EMPLOYEE'S NAME	CLOCK CARD NUMBER	M	T	W	T	F	S	S	TOTAL HOURS	O.T. HOURS	REG. PAY RATE		REGULAR PAY		O.T. PREMIUM PAY		GROSS PAY		
Delbert Landau	12	8	8	8	7	4	0	0	35		11	00	385	00			385	00	1
Maria Garza	9	8	8	8	5	4	0	0	35		12	00	396	00			396	00	2
Ralph Webster	15	8	8	7	8	4	0	0	35		13	00	455	00			455	00	3
Fred Clarke	4	8	8	8	8	8	4	0	44	4	14	00	560	00	84	00	644	00	4
													1,796	00	84	00	1,880	00	5

Week ending January 8, 2011

	DEDUCTIONS									PAYMENT				DISTRIBUTION					
	FICA TAXES		FEDERAL INCOME TAXES		HOSPITAL INSURANCE		UNION DUES		TOTAL DEDUC-TIONS		NET PAY		CHECK NUMBER	SALES SALARIES		OFFICE SALARIES		DELIVERY WAGES	
1	150	40	65	00	20	00	10	00	245	40	139	60	102					385	00
2	31	68	63	00	20	00	10	00	124	68	271	32	103	396	00				
3	36	40	68	00	20	00	10	00	134	40	320	60	104	455	00				
4	51	52	111	00	20	00			182	52	461	48	105			644	00		
5	270	00	307	00	80	00	30	00	687	00	1193	00		851	00	644	00	385	00

2.   Jan. 8   Sales Salaries Expense 851.00
               Office Salaries Expense 644.00
               Delivery Wages Expense 385.00
                  FICA Taxes Payable..   270.00
                  Employees' Federal Income Taxes Payable 307.00
                  Employees' Medical Insurance Payable 80.00
                  Employees' Union Dues Payable......................................   30.00
                  Accrued Payroll Payable 1,193.00

3.   Jan. 8   Accrued Payroll Payable 1,193.00
               Cash...   1,193.00

CHAPTER 10
EMPLOYER PAYROLL TAX REPORTING

Learning Objective 1:

Describe laws that impact employer's payroll obligations.

Summary

Law requires employers to match their employees' Social Security and Medicare taxes. Employers must also pay federal and state unemployment taxes and workers' compensation insurance premiums.

Learning Objective 2:

Compute employer's FICA taxes and record them in a general journal.

Summary

The employer pays 6.2% of each employee's annual gross pay (up to $106,800) for Social Security taxes and 1.45% of their annual gross pay for Medicare taxes. The accountant debits Payroll Tax Expense and credits Employer FICA—Social Security Tax Payable and Employer—FICA Medicare Tax Payable.

Learning Objective 3:

Journalize employer's deposit of federal income taxes and FICA taxes withheld and prepare a deposit coupon.

Summary

The employer must periodically deposit amounts withheld from employee pay in a federal depository. This is done by either electronic funds transfer or by completing a Form 8109. The accountant debits Employer FICA—Social Security Tax Payable and Employer FICA—Medicare Tax Payable and credits Cash.

Learning Objective 4:

Prepare Form 941, Employer's Quarterly Federal Tax Return.

Summary

The accountant files this federal tax form within one month after each quarter ends. It reports on the employer's Federal Unemployment Taxes for the quarter.

Learning Objective 5:

Prepare Form W-2, Employee's Wage and Tax Statement, and Form W-3, Transmittal of Wage and Tax Statements.

Summary

After each calendar year-end the employer sends each employee a Form W-2, which summarizes the employee's wages and deductions for the year just ended. The employer transmits copies of these W-2's to the Social Security Administration and includes a Form W-3 that summarizes all the individual W-2's.

Learning Objective 6:

Compute employer's state and federal unemployment taxes and record them in a general journal.

Summary

The employer pays unemployment taxes of up to 6.2% of employee gross pay. Employers with stable employment histories and low turnover typically pay lower SUTA rates. Employers also receive credits for SUTA taxes and often pay FUTA taxes of only 0.8% of their employee's annual gross pay. The accountant debits Payroll Tax Expense and credits Federal Unemployment Taxes Payable and State Unemployment Taxes Payable.

Learning Objective 7:

Prepare unemployment tax returns.

Summary

The employer files a quarterly state unemployment tax return. Federal unemployment taxes are reported annually on Form 940, the Employer's Federal Unemployment Tax Return.

Learning Objective 8:

Compute and record workers' compensation insurance premiums for employers.

Summary

Most states require the employer to provide benefits or pay insurance premiums for employees injured while on the job. Premium amounts are based on total estimated salary amounts and how hazardous the job is.

I.   **Laws Impacting Employer's Payroll Tax**
   - a.   Employer Identification Number (EIN)
     - i.   Unique number for all businesses
     - ii.   Functions like a Social Security number for employers
     - iii.   Use form SS-4 to apply
   - b.   Employer FICA Tax
     - i.   Social Security—6.2% (Subject to maximum wage base)
     - ii.   Medicare Tax—1.45%
     - iii.   Matched amount paid by employee
   - c.   Federal and State Unemployment Tax Acts
     - i.   Federal—FUTA—0.8% of first $7,000 wages for each employee
     - ii.   State—SUTA—Rates vary based on merit rating
   - d.   Workers' Compensation Insurance
     - i.   Provides benefits for workers injured on the job
     - ii.   Premium is based on job description and wages

II.   **Employer's Payroll Taxes**
   - a.   Computing Employer's FICA Tax
     - i.   Same amount as employee withholding
     - ii.   Dr. Payroll Tax Expense
     - iii.   Cr. FICA Tax Payable
   - b.   Payroll Tax Deposits
     - i.   If annual taxes < $50,000, monthly depositor
     - ii.   If annual taxes > $50,000, semi-weekly depositor
     - iii.   Make deposits using a Federal depository on form 8109
     - iv.   Severe penalties for non-payment of payroll taxes
       1. 100% penalty
       2. Closure of the business
     - v.   Payroll register is source for deposit information

III.   **Employer's Payroll Tax Reporting**
   - a.   Employer's Quarterly Federal Tax Return
     - i.   Form 941—Due by the end of the month following the end of quarter
     - ii.   Reconciles to the deposits made

    b. Employer's Annual Withholding Reporting

      i. Form W-2

        1. Sent to all employees at the end of the year

        2. Due by January 31st

        3. Copy filed with State and Federal government

      ii. Form W-3

        1. Transmittal form for W-2's

        2. Shows total of all employee wages and taxes for the year

        3. Due by February 28th (or 29th in leap year)

IV. Federal (FUTA) and State (SUTA) Unemployment Taxes

    a. Basic rules

      i. Apply only to first $7,000 of wages

      ii. Rates based on Company experience—lower claims, lower rates

      iii. State unemployment reduces Federal unemployment rate

    b. Computing Employer's Unemployment Taxes

      i. Payroll records must track wage base information for all employees

      ii. Amount = wages subject to FUTA x rate

      iii. Journal Entry to record unemployment tax

        1. Dr. Payroll Tax Expense

        2. Cr. FUTA (or SUTA) Tax Payable

    c. Reporting Employer's Unemployment Taxes

      i. Form 940 is due by January 31st

      ii. State Unemployment forms due each quarter by the end of the following month

      iii. Journal Entry to record payment

        1. Dr. FUTA (or SUTA) Tax Payable

        2. Cr. Cash

V. Workers' Compensation Insurance

    a. Computing Estimated Workers' Compensation Insurance Premium

      i. Estimate total payroll for the year by job classification

      ii. Multiply each job classification wages x rate

      iii. Journal Entry

        1. Dr. Workers' Compensation Insurance Expense

        2. Cr. Cash

b. Computing Actual Workers' Compensation Insurance Premium

   i.   Actual wages for the year by job classification

   ii. Multiply each job classification wages x rate

   iii. Record additional premium (or refund)

Employer Taxes

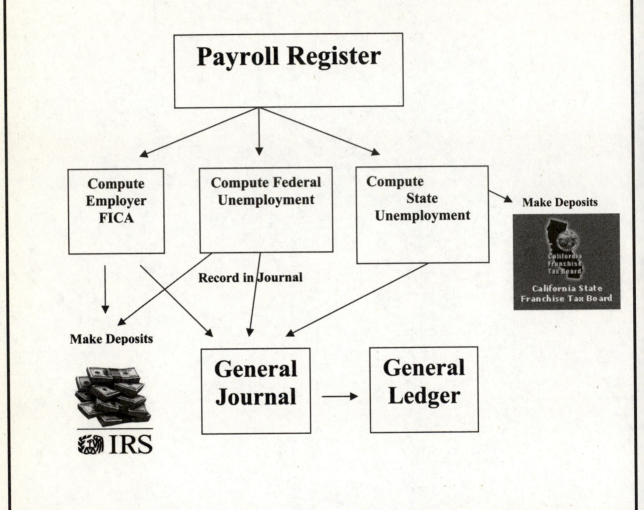

Alternate Demonstration Problem

This demonstration problem uses the same information presented in Chapter 9 to continue with calculating and recording employer payroll taxes.

Below is the payroll information for Floyd's Beauty Shop for the week ended April 7.

Employee	Regular Hours	Overtime Hours	Regular Rate	Overtime Rate	Total Wages
Floyd Woodcock	40	2	12.67	19.01	544.82
Ralph Kafooty	40	8	11.25	16.88	585.04
Evelyn Woodhead	40	1	14.35	21.53	595.53
Total Gross Wages					1725.39

Employee	Federal Income Tax	State Income Tax	Social Security	Medicare Tax	Total Deductions
Floyd Woodcock	37.00	3.84	33.78	7.90	82.52
Ralph Kafooty	43.00	4.32	36.27	8.48	92.07
Evelyn Woodhead	55.00	5.20	36.92	8.64	105.76
Total Gross Wages	135.00	13.36	106.97	25.02	280.35

Employee	Gross Wages	Total Deductions	Net Pay
Floyd Woodcock	544.82	82.52	462.30
Ralph Kafooty	585.04	92.07	492.97
Evelyn Woodhead	595.53	105.76	489.77
Total Gross Wages	1,725.39	280.35	1,445.04

Required:
1. Compute the following employer payroll taxes for the week ended April 7
   a. FICA – Social Security – 6.2% on all wages
   b. FICA – Medicare – 1.45% on all wages
   c. FUTA – 0.8% on wages of $1,267.22
   d. SUTA – 3.2% on wages of $1,267.22
2. Prepare a journal entry to record the employer taxes on April 7.
3. Prepare a journal entry to record the payment of the taxes on April 10.

Solution:

FICA-Social Security	1,725.39	6.20%	106.97
FICA-Medicare	1,725.39	1.45%	25.02
FUTA	1,267.22	0.80%	10.14
SUTA	1,267.22	3.20%	40.55
			182.68

<table>
<tr><th colspan="5">Floyd's Beauty Shop
General Journal</th></tr>
<tr><th>Date</th><th>Account</th><th>Debit</th><th>Credit</th></tr>
<tr><td></td><td></td><td></td><td></td></tr>
<tr><td>2   7-Apr</td><td>Payroll tax expense</td><td>182.68</td><td></td></tr>
<tr><td></td><td>Social Security Tax Payable</td><td></td><td>106.97</td></tr>
<tr><td></td><td>Medicare Tax Payable</td><td></td><td>25.02</td></tr>
<tr><td></td><td>FUTA Tax Payable</td><td></td><td>10.14</td></tr>
<tr><td></td><td>SUTA Tax Payable</td><td></td><td>40.55</td></tr>
<tr><td></td><td>to record employer taxes for week</td><td></td><td></td></tr>
<tr><td></td><td></td><td></td><td></td></tr>
<tr><td>3   7-Apr</td><td>Social Security Tax Payable</td><td>106.97</td><td></td></tr>
<tr><td></td><td>Medicare Tax Payable</td><td>25.02</td><td></td></tr>
<tr><td></td><td>FUTA Tax Payable</td><td>10.14</td><td></td></tr>
<tr><td></td><td>SUTA Tax Payable</td><td>40.55</td><td></td></tr>
<tr><td></td><td>Cash</td><td></td><td>182.68</td></tr>
<tr><td></td><td></td><td></td><td></td></tr>
</table>

Problem I

The following statements are either true or false. Place a (T) in the parentheses before each true statement and an (F) before each false statement.

1. ( ) Federal unemployment taxes are withheld from employees' wages at the rate of 1.45% on the first $87,000 earned.

2. ( ) Social Security taxes are levied equally on the employee and the employer.

3. ( ) Each time a payroll is recorded, a separate journal entry usually is made to record the employer's FICA and state and federal unemployment taxes.

4. ( ) Since Jon Company has very little employee turnover, the company has received a very favorable merit rating. As a result, Jon Company should expect to pay substantially smaller amounts of FICA taxes than normal.

5. ( ) Employer's FICA taxes are reported annually on a Form 940.

6. ( ) EIN stands for Employee Identification Number.

7. ( ) The general journal entry to record employer FICA tax includes a debit to Payroll Tax Expense.

8. ( ) Federal Unemployment Taxes can be reduced by a credit of as much as 4.5%.

9. ( ) Form 8109 is the Federal Tax Deposit Coupon.

10. ( ) Form 941 is the Employer's Quarterly Federal Tax Return.

Problem II

You are given several words, phrases, or numbers to choose from in completing each of the following statements or in answering the following questions. In each case select the one that best completes the statement or answers the question and place its letter in the answer space provided.

For the next three questions, use the following information as to earnings and deductions taken from a company's payroll records for the pay period ended November 15:

Employee's Name	Earnings to End of Previous Week	Gross Pay This Week	Federal Income Taxes	Medical Insurance Deducted
Rita Hawn..........................	$25,700	$ 800	$155.00	$ 35.50
Dolores Hopkins..........................	930	800	134.00	35.50
Robert Allen	106,700	1,000	193.00	42.00
Calvin Ingram..........................	18,400	740	128.00	42.00
		$3,340	$610.00	$155.00

_____ 1. Assume a state unemployment tax rate of 5.4% on the first $7,000 paid each employee and a federal unemployment tax rate of 0.8% on the first $7,000 paid each employee. The journal entry to record the employer's payroll taxes resulting from the payroll should include a debit to Payroll Taxes Expense for:

a. $249.31

b. $277.91

c. $293.23

d. $349.03

e. The entry does not include a debit to Payroll Taxes Expense.

_____ 2. Employees' FICA taxes are withheld at an assumed rate of 6.2% on the first $106,800 earned for Social Security and 1.45% of all wages earned for Medicare. The journal entry to record the employer's payroll taxes resulting from the payroll should include a credit to Employer FICA-Social Security Taxes Payable:

a. $414.16
b. $208.07
c. $207.08
d. $48.43
e. $255.51.

_____ 3. Employees' FICA taxes are withheld at an assumed rate of 6.2% on the first $87,000 earned for Social Security and 1.45% of all wages earned for Medicare. The journal entry to record the employer's payroll taxes resulting from the payroll should include a credit to Employer FICA-Medicare Taxes Payable:

a. $24.22
b. $207.08
c. $96.86
d. $48.43
e. $255.51.

Problem III

Many of the important ideas and concepts that are discussed in Chapter 10 are reflected in the following list of key terms. Test your understanding of these terms by matching the appropriate definitions with the terms. Record the number identifying the most appropriate definition in the blank space next to each term.

_____ Authorized depository
_____ Employer identification number (EIN)
_____ Employer Quarterly Unemployment Tax Report
_____ Federal depository bank
_____ Federal Reserve Bank
_____ FUTA taxes
_____ Form 940
_____ Form 940-EZ
_____ Form 941

_____ Form 8109
_____ Form 8109-B
_____ Form SS-4
_____ Form W-2
_____ Form W-3
_____ Look-back rule
_____ Merit rating
_____ SUTA taxes
_____ Workers' compensation insurance

1. Yearly report by an employer to each employee showing the employee's wages subject to FICA and federal income taxes along with the amounts of taxes withheld.

2. IRS form used to report an employer's federal unemployment taxes (FUTA) on an annual filing basis.

3. Rating assigned to an employer by a state based on the employer's past record regarding unemployment.

4. Payroll taxes on employers assessed by the federal government to support the federal unemployment insurance program.

5. State payroll taxes on employers to support unemployment programs.

6. IRS form filed to report FICA taxes owed and remitted.

7. Bank authorized to accept deposits of amounts payable to the federal government.

8. A bank that can accept payroll deposits from its own checking account customers.

9. A number issued by the federal government that uniquely identifies a business.

10. A report filed with the state that shows an employer's unemployment taxes owed.

11. A bank that can accept payroll deposits from any business.

12. The Employer's Annual Federal Unemployment Tax Return.

13. A preprinted Federal Tax Deposit Coupon.

14. A Federal Tax Deposit Coupon used by new businesses or when the business does not have a supply of preprinted Forms 8109.

15. An Internal Revenue Service form filed by a business in order to receive an employer identification number.

16. The Transmittal of Wage and Tax Statements form.

17. A rule used to classify business as monthly or semiweekly depositors.

18. An insurance program that provides benefits to workers who are injured on the job.

Problem IV

Complete the following by filling in the blanks.

1. Good employer merit ratings give employers a reduction in their state unemployment tax rates as a reward for_____.

2. Employers pay FICA taxes _____ to those withheld from employees.

3. According to law, a _____ showing wages earned and taxes withheld must be given by the employer to each employee within one month after the year-end.

4. According to the Federal Insurance Contributions Act, an employer must file an Employer's Quarterly Federal Tax Return (Form _____) within one month after the end of each _____.

5. An _____ _____ _____ is a unique number which identifies each business.

6. Most employers are required to provide _____ _____ _____ for their employees in case they are injured on the job.

7. A _____-_____ _____ is used to classify businesses as monthly or semiweekly depositors.

8. Form _____ is an IRS form used to report an employer's federal unemployment taxes on an annual filing basis.

Problem V

The following information as to earnings and deductions for the pay period ended November 15 was taken from a company's payroll records:

Employee's Name	Earnings to End of - Previous Week	Gross Pay This Week	Federal Income Taxes	Medical Insurance Deducted
Rita Hawn...	$25,700	$ 800	$155.00	$ 35.50
Dolores Hopkins...............................	930	800	134.00	35.50
Robert Allen	106,700	1,000	193.00	42.00
Calvin Ingram...................................	18,400	740	128.00	42.00
		$3,340	$610.00	$155.00

Required:

Prepare a journal entry to record the employer's payroll taxes resulting from the payroll. Assume a state unemployment tax rate of 5.4% on the first $7,000 paid each employee and a federal unemployment tax rate of 0.8% on the first $7,000 paid each employee.

DATE	ACCOUNT TITLES AND EXPLANATION	P.R.	DEBIT	CREDIT

Problem VI

The Payroll Register of Whiteman Sales for the <u>first week</u> of the year follows. The deductions and net pay for all employees have been calculated and entered in the table below:

Week ending January 8, 2011

	DEDUCTIONS								PAYMENT				DISTRIBUTION					
	FICA TAXES		FEDERAL INCOME TAXES		HOSPITAL INSURANCE		UNION DUES		TOTAL DEDUC-TIONS		NET PAY		CHECK NUMBER	SALES SALARIES		OFFICE SALARIES		DELIVERY WAGES	
1	150	40	65	00	20	00	10	00	245	40	139	60	102					385	00
2	31	68	63	00	20	00	10	00	124	68	271	32	103	396	00				
3	36	40	68	00	20	00	10	00	134	40	320	60	104	455	00				
4	51	52	111	00	20	00			182	52	461	48	105			644	00		
5	270	00	307	00	80	00	30	00	687	00	1193	00		851	00	644	00	385	00

Make the general journal entry to record the payroll taxes levied on Whiteman Sales as a result of the payroll entered in its January 8 Payroll Register. The company has a merit rating that reduces its state employment tax rate to 1% of the first $7,000 paid each employee. (Assume the federal unemployment tax rate is 0.8%.)

DATE	ACCOUNT TITLES AND EXPLANATION	P.R.	DEBIT		CREDIT	

Solutions for Chapter 10

Problem I

1. F
2. T
3. T
4. F
5. F
6. F
7. T
8. F
9. T
10. T

Problem II

1. A
2. C
3. D

Problem III

8	Authorized depository	13	Form 8109
9	Employer identification number (EIN)	14	Form 8109-B
10	Employer Quarterly Unemployment Tax Report	15	Form SS-4
7	Federal depository bank	1	Form W-2
11	Federal Reserve Bank	16	Form W-3
4	FUTA taxes	17	Look-back rule
2	Form 940	3	Merit rating
12	Form 940-EZ	5	SUTA taxes
6	Form 941	18	Workers' compensation insurance

Problem IV

1. providing stable employment for employees
2. Equal
3. Form W-2 (Wage and Tax Statement)
4. 941, calendar quarter
5. Employer identification number
6. workers' compensation insurance
7. look-back rule
8. 940

Problem V

15	Payroll Taxes Expense	249.31	
	FICA Taxes Payable		199.71
	State Unemployment Taxes Payable		43.20
	Federal Unemployment Taxes Payable		6.40

*$800+$800+$100+$740 = $2,440 *0.062 = $151.28 Social Security*
*$3,340 *0.0145 = $48.43 Medicare*
$151.28 + $48.43 = $199.71 FICA Taxes Payable
$800 × 0.054 = $43.20; $800 × 0.008 = $6.40

Problem VI

Jan. 8	Payroll Taxes Expense	184.24	
	FICA Taxes Payable		270.00
	State Unemployment Taxes Payable		18.80
	Federal Unemployment Taxes Payable		15.04

CHAPTER 11
MERCHANDISE SALES AND ACCOUNTS RECEIVABLE

Learning Objective 1:

Analyze and record transactions for merchandise sales.

Summary

A merchandiser records sales at the invoice price of the sale. The sale may be for cash or on credit.

Learning Objective 2:

Describe how to compute and record sales discounts.

Summary

When cash discounts from the sales price are offered and customers pay within the discount period, the seller debits Sales Discounts, a contra account to Sales.

Learning Objective 3:

Explain how to record sales returns and allowances.

Summary

Refunds or credits given to customers for unsatisfactory merchandise are recorded as debits to Sales Returns and Allowances, a contra account to Sales.

Learning Objective 4:

Describe the use of special journals and subsidiary ledgers.

Summary

Special journals are used for recording transactions of similar type, each meant to cover one kind of transaction. Four of the most common special journals are the sales journal, cash receipts journal, purchases journal, and cash disbursements journal. Special journals are efficient and cost-effective tools in the journalizing and posting process.

Learning Objective 5:

Journalize and post transactions using a sales journal.

Summary

The sales journal is an efficient means to record sales of inventory on credit. The sales journal will typically debit Accounts Receivable and credit Sales and Sales Tax Payable (if applicable).

Learning Objective 6:

Prepare and prove the accuracy of the accounts receivable subsidiary ledger.

Summary

Account balances in the general ledger and the accounts receivable subsidiary ledger are tested for accuracy after posting is complete. This procedure is twofold: (1) prepare a trial balance of the general ledger to confirm that debits equal credits and (2) prepare a schedule of accounts receivable to confirm that the controlling account's balance equals the subsidiary ledger's balance.

Learning Objective 7:

Journalize and post transactions using a cash receipts journal.

Summary

A cash receipts journal is typically used to record cash receipts from credit customers, cash from cash sales, and cash received from other sources.

I. **Merchandising Sales**—merchandise represents products that a Company buys that will be resold. Merchandisers can be either wholesalers (selling to other resellers) or retailers (selling to consumers directly)

   a. Credit Sales—Sales on account that will be paid based on credit terms.

     i. Dr. Accounts Receivable

     ii. Cr. Sales

   b. Cash Sales—Sales in a retail environment where customers pay for merchandise with currency, checks or credit cards.

     i. Dr. Cash

     ii. Cr. Sales

   c. Credit Terms—Established at the time of sales

     i. n/30—Net 30 days—Payment is due within 30 days

     ii. 2/10, n/30—2% discount if paid within 10 days, otherwise the balance is due within 30 days.

     iii. Other—n/10 EOM, 2/10, n/60

   d. Cash Receipts

     i. Journal to record cash received from customer without a discount

       1. Dr. Cash

       2. Cr. Accounts Receivable

     ii. Journal entry to record cash received from customer with a discount

       1. Dr. Cash

       2. Dr. Sales Discounts

       3. Cr. Accounts Receivable (gross amount of the invoice)

   e. Sales Returns and Allowances

     i. Sales Returns—when the goods are physically returned to the seller

     ii. Sales Allowances—when a price adjustment is made for non-conforming or substandard merchandise

     iii. Journal Entry to record return or allowance

       1. Dr. Sales Returns and Allowances

       2. Cr. Accounts Receivable

   f. Recording and Posting Merchandise Sales

     i. Recording sales with sales tax included

       1. Dr. Accounts Receivable

       2. Cr. Sales Tax Payable

       3. Cr. Sales

ii. Recording payment of sales taxes
1. Dr. Sales Tax Payable
2. Cr. Cash

II. **Special Journals and Subsidiary Ledgers**
a. Sales Journal
i. Record all credit sales in columnar form
ii. Post totals to the General Ledger directly
iii. Post detail transactions to the AR subsidiary Ledger
b. Accounts Receivable Subsidiary Ledger
i. Separate page for each customer
ii. All transactions posted to Accounts Receivable in the GL must be also posted in the subsidiary ledger
c. Proving the Ledgers
i. Compute ending balances for each customer monthly.
ii. Prepare a schedule of accounts receivable listing all customer balances at the end of the month.
iii. Compare the balance in accounts receivable on the general ledger with total from schedule of accounts receivable
iv. Investigate and correct all discrepancies.

III. **Cash Receipts Journal**
a. Journalizing and posting when cash is received from credit customers—Debit to cash and sales discounts; credit to accounts receivable
b. Journalizing and posting cash sales—Debit to cash; credit to sales
c. Journalizing and posting cash from other sources—Debit to cash; credit to other accounts

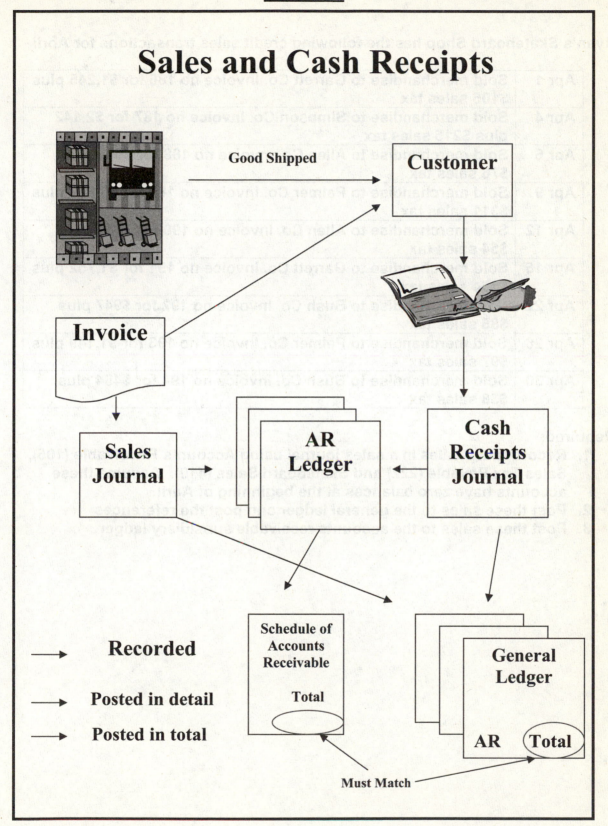

Sales and Cash Receipts

Good Shipped

Customer

Invoice

Sales Journal

AR Ledger

Cash Receipts Journal

→ **Recorded**

→ **Posted in detail**

→ **Posted in total**

Schedule of Accounts Receivable

Total

General Ledger

AR   Total

Must Match

Alternate Demonstration Problem

Ryan's Skateboard Shop has the following credit sales transactions for April

Apr 1	Sold merchandise to Garrett Co. Invoice no 186 for $1,245 plus $105 sales tax
Apr 4	Sold merchandise to Simpson Co. Invoice no 187 for $2,142 plus $215 sales tax
Apr 6	Sold merchandise to Allen Co. Invoice no 188 for $865 plus $76 sales tax
Apr 9	Sold merchandise to Palmer Co. Invoice no 189 for $3,867 plus $311 sales tax
Apr 12	Sold merchandise to Allen Co. Invoice no 190 for $643 plus $54 sales tax
Apr 15	Sold merchandise to Garrett Co. Invoice no 191 for $1,752 plus $154 sales tax
Apr 22	Sold merchandise to Bush Co. Invoice no 192 for $947 plus $85 sales tax
Apr 26	Sold merchandise to Palmer Co. Invoice no 193 for $1,149 plus $97 sales tax
Apr 30	Sold merchandise to Bush Co. Invoice no 194 for $484 plus $38 sales tax

Required:

1. Record these sales in a sales journal using Accounts Receivable (105), Sales Tax Payable (222) and Skateboard Sales (410). Assume these accounts have zero balances at the beginning of April.
2. Post these sales to the general ledger and post the references
3. Post these sales to the accounts receivable subsidiary ledger.

Solution:

Ryan's Skateboard Shop
Sales Journal
For the month ended April 30, 2011

Date	Customer	Invoice Number	PR	Accounts Receivable (Dr.)	Sales Tax Payable (Cr.)	Skateboard Sales (Cr.)
4/1	Garrett	186	a	1245	105	1350
4/4	Simpson	187	b	2142	215	2357
4/6	Allen	188	c	865	76	941
4/9	Palmer	189	d	3867	311	4178
4/12	Allen	190	e	643	54	697
4/15	Garrett	191	f	1752	154	1906
4/22	Bush	192	g	947	85	1032
4/26	Palmer	193	h	1149	97	1246
4/30	Bush	194	i	484	38	552
				13094	1135	14229
				-105	-222	-140

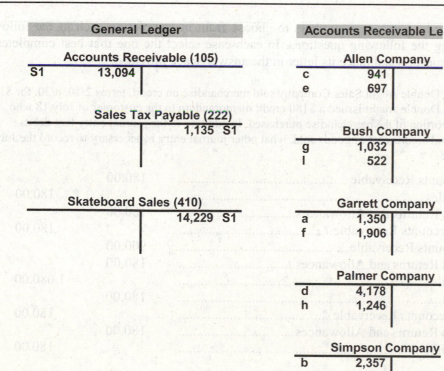

General Ledger

Accounts Receivable (105)

| S1 | 13,094 | |

Sales Tax Payable (222)

| | | 1,135 | S1 |

Skateboard Sales (410)

| | | 14,229 | S1 |

Accounts Receivable Le

Allen Company

| c | 941 |
| e | 697 |

Bush Company

| g | 1,032 |
| l | 522 |

Garrett Company

| a | 1,350 |
| f | 1,906 |

Palmer Company

| d | 4,178 |
| h | 1,246 |

Simpson Company

| b | 2,357 |

Problem I

The following statements are either true or false. Place a (T) in the parentheses before each true statement and an (F) before each false statement.

1. ( ) Sales returns and allowances or discounts are not included in the calculation of net sales.

2. ( ) A credit memorandum may originate with either party to a transaction, but the sender of a credit memorandum will credit the account of the receiver.

3. ( ) At month-end, the total sales recorded in the Sales Journal is debited to Accounts Receivable and credited to Sales.

4. ( ) Sales is a General Ledger account.

5. ( ) Transactions recorded in a journal do not necessarily result in equal debits and credits to General Ledger accounts.

6. ( ) If a general journal entry is used to record a charge sale, the credit of the entry must be posted twice.

7. ( ) A subsidiary ledger contains detailed information on a specific account in the general ledger.

8. ( ) A columnar journal has only one column.

Problem II

You are given several words, phrases or numbers to choose from in completing each of the following statements or in answering the following questions. In each case select the one that best completes the statement or answers the question and place its letter in the answer space provided.

_____ 1. On July 18, Double Aught Sales Company sold merchandise on credit, terms 2/10, n/30, for $1,080. On July 21, Double Aught issued a $180 credit memorandum to the customer of July 18 who returned a portion of the merchandise purchased. In addition to the journal entry that debits inventory and credits cost of goods sold, what other journal entry is necessary to record the July 21 transaction?

a.	Accounts Receivable	180.00	
	Sales		180.00
b.	Sales Returns and Allowances..............................	180.00	
	Accounts Receivable..		180.00
c.	Accounts Receivable	900.00	
	Sales Returns and Allowances..............................	180.00	
	Sales		1,080.00
d.	Sales..	180.00	
	Accounts Receivable..		180.00
e.	Sales Returns and Allowances..............................	180.00	
	Sales		180.00

_____ 2. The following information is available from the balance sheet of Foster Company:

Cash	$22,300
Short-term investments	10,500
Accounts receivable	47,360
Merchandise inventory	52,100
Accounts payable	66,800
J. Foster, capital	57,300

Foster's acid-test ratio is:

a. 0.5
b. 1.2
c. 2.0
d. 1.4
e. 2.3

_____ 3. A company that uses special journals and a General Journal borrowed $1,500 from the bank in exchange for a note payable to the bank. In which journal would the transaction be recorded?

a. Sales Journal
b. Purchases Journal
c. Cash Receipts Journal
d. Cash Disbursements Journal
e. General Journal

_____ 4. A book of original entry that is designed and used for recording only a specified type of transaction is a:

a. Check Register
b. Subsidiary Ledger
c. General Ledger
d. Special Journal
e. Schedule of Accounts Payable

_____ 5. A company that uses special journals and a General sold $1,500 of merchandise on credit. In which journal would the transaction be recorded?

a. Sales Journal
b. Purchases Journal
c. Cash Receipts Journal
d. Cash Disbursements Journal
e. General Journal

Problem III

Many of the important ideas and concepts discussed in Chapter 11 are reflected in the following list of key terms. Test your understanding of these terms by matching the appropriate definitions with the terms. Record the number identifying the most appropriate definition in the blank space next to each term.

_____ Accounts receivable ledger   _____ Merchandise

_____ Cash discount   _____ Merchandiser

_____ Columnar journal   _____ Retailer

_____ Controlling account   _____ Sales discount

_____ Credit memorandum   _____ Sales journal

_____ Credit period   _____ Schedule of accounts receivable

_____ Credit terms   _____ Special journal

_____ Discount period   _____ Subsidiary ledger

_____ EOM   _____ Wholesaler

_____ General Journal

1. Term used by a seller to describe a cash discount granted to customers for paying within the discount period.

2. Abbreviation for *end of month;* used to describe credit terms for some transactions.

3. Description of the amounts and timing of payments that a buyer agrees to make in the future.

4. Time period that can pass before a customer's payment is due.

5. All-purpose journal for recording the debits and credits of transactions and events.

6. Notification that the sender has credited the recipient's account in the sender's records.

7. Time period in which a cash discount is available and the buyer can make a reduced payment.

8. Reduction in the price of merchandise that is granted by a seller to a buyer when payment is made within the discount period.

9. Products that a company owns to sell to their customers.

10. Entity that earns net income by buying and selling merchandise.

11. An intermediary that buys products from manufacturers or other wholesalers and sells them to retailers or other wholesalers.

12. Intermediary that buys products from manufacturers or wholesalers and sells them to customers.

13. List of balances of all the accounts in the accounts receivable ledger that are summed to show the total amount of accounts receivable outstanding.

14. General ledger account, the balance of which (after posting) equals the sum of the balances of the accounts in a related subsidiary ledger.

15. Any journal used for recording and posting transactions of a similar type.

16. A subsidiary ledger listing individual credit customer accounts.

17. List of individual accounts with a common characteristic; linked to a controlling account in the general ledger.

18. Journal with more than one column.

19. Journal used to record sales of merchandise on credit.

    College Accounting, 2ⁿᵈ Edition

Problem IV

On December 31, 2011, Valentine Variety Store's merchandise activities during the 2011 year disclosed the following:

Invoice cost of merchandise purchases	$48,500
Purchase discounts received	900
Purchase returns and allowances received	400
Cost of transportation-in	2,500

Required: Using the data above, complete the Cost of Net Purchases for Valentine Variety Store for December 31, 2011. Use the form provided below.

VALENTINE VARIETY STORE

Purchases									
Less: Purchases returns									
and allowances $_____									
Purchase discounts _____									
Add: Transportation-in									
Net Purchases									

Problem V

1. A reduction in a payable that is granted if it is paid within the discount period is a _____ discount.

2. When a company records sales returns with general journal entries, the credit of an entry recording such a return is posted to two different accounts. This does not cause the trial balance to be out of balance because_____
   _____.

3. Cash sales _____ (are, are not) normally recorded in the Sales Journal.

4. The posting principle upon which a subsidiary ledger and its controlling account operate requires that the controlling account be debited for an amount or amounts equal to the sum of _____ _____ to the subsidiary ledger and that the controlling account be credited for an amount or amounts equal to the sum of _____ to the subsidiary ledger.

5. When a subsidiary Accounts Receivable Ledger is maintained, the equality of the debits and credits posted to the General Ledger is proved by preparing _____. At the same time the balances of the customer accounts in the Accounts Receivable Ledger are proved by preparing_____.

Problem VI

Below are four transactions completed by McGuff Company on September 30 of the current year. Following the transactions are the company's journals with prior September transactions recorded therein.

Requirement One: Record the four transactions in the company's journals.

Sept. 30 Received an $808.50 check from Ted Clark in full payment of the September 20, $825 sale, less the $16.50 discount.

30 Received a $550 check from a tenant in payment of his September rent.

30 Sold merchandise costing $840 to Inez Smythe for $1,675 on credit, Invoice No. 655.

30 Cash sales for the last half of the month totaled $9,450.50. This merchandise cost $ 4,275.

GENERAL JOURNAL

DATE	ACCOUNT TITLES AND EXPLANATION	P.R.	DEBIT	CREDIT

SALES JOURNAL

DATE	ACCOUNT DEBITED	INVOICE NUMBER	P.R.	Accts Receivable Dr Sales Cr.	Cost of Goods Sold Dr. Inventory Cr.
20— SEPT. 3	N.R. Boswell	651	√	1 8 7 5 00	9 5 0 00
15	Inez Smythe	652	√	1 5 0 0 00	8 0 0 00
20	Ted Clark	653	√	8 2 5 00	4 2 0 00
24	N.R. Boswell	654	√	2 2 5 0 00	1 2 5 00

CASH RECEIPTS JOURNAL

DATE	ACCOUNT CREDITED	P.R.	CASH DEBIT	SALES DISCOUNT DEBIT	ACCOUNTS RECEIVABLE CREDIT	SALES CREDIT	OTHER ACCOUNTS CREDIT	Cost of Goods Sold Dr. Inventory Cr.
20— Sept. 1	Rent Earned	406	5 5 0 00				5 5 0 00	
13	N.R. Boswell	√	1 8 3 7 50	3 7 50	1 8 7 5 00			
15	Sales	√	9 0 0 0 00			9 0 0 0 00		4 6 0 0 00

Requirement Two: The individual postings from the journals of McGuff Company through September 29 have been made. Complete the individual postings from the journals.

Requirement Three: Foot and crossfoot the journals and make the month-end postings.

Requirement Four: Test the subsidiary ledgers by preparing schedule of accounts receivable.

N.R. Boswell

2200 Falstaff Street

DATE	EXPLANATION	P.R.	DEBIT			CREDIT			BALANCE		
20 Sept. 3		S-8	1	875	00				1	875	00
13		R-9				1	875	00			
24		S-8	2	250	00				2	250	00

Ted Clark

10765 Catonsville Avenue

DATE	EXPLANATION	P.R.	DEBIT			CREDIT			BALANCE		
20 Sept. 20		S-8		825	00					825	00

Inez Smythe

785 Violette Circle

DATE	EXPLANATION	P.R.	DEBIT			CREDIT			BALANCE		
20 Sept. 15		S-8	1	500	00				1	500	00

GENERAL LEDGER

Cash   Account No. 101

DATE	EXPLANATION	P.R.	DEBIT			CREDIT			BALANCE		

Accounts Receivable   Account No. 106

DATE	EXPLANATION	P.R.	DEBIT			CREDIT			BALANCE		

Inventory   Account No. 107

DATE	EXPLANATION	P.R.	DEBIT	CREDIT	BALANCE

Rent Earned   Account No. 406

DATE	EXPLANATION	P.R.	DEBIT	CREDIT	BALANCE
20 Sept. 1		R-9		5 5 0 00	5 5 0 00

Sales   Account No. 413

DATE	EXPLANATION	P.R.	DEBIT	CREDIT	BALANCE

Sales Discounts   Account No. 415

DATE	EXPLANATION	P.R.	DEBIT	CREDIT	BALANCE

Cost of Goods Sold   Account No. 613

DATE	EXPLANATION	P.R.	DEBIT	CREDIT	BALANCE

MCGUFF COMPANY

Schedule of Accounts Receivable

September 30, 20

Study Guide, Chapter 11

Solutions for Chapter 11

Problem I

1. F 5. F
2. T 6. F
3. T 7. T
4. T 8. F

Problem II

1. B
2. B
3. C
4. D
5. A

Problem III

16	Accounts receivable ledger	9	Merchandise
8	Cash discount	10	Merchandiser
18	Columnar journal	12	Retailer
14	Controlling account	1	Sales discount
6	Credit memorandum	19	Sales journal
4	Credit period	13	Schedule of accounts receivable
3	Credit terms	15	Special journal
7	Discount period	17	Subsidiary ledger
2	EOM	11	Wholesaler
5	General journal		

Problem IV

VALENTINE VARIETY STORE

Purchases..			$48,500
Less: Purchases returns and allowances.......................	$400		
Purchase discounts	900	1,300	$47,200
Add: Transportation-in			2,500
Net purchases			$49,700

Problem V

1. cash

2. only the balance of one of the accounts, Accounts Receivable account, appears on the trial balance.

3. are not

4. the debits posted, the credits posted

5. a trial balance, a schedule of accounts receivable

Problem VI

SALES JOURNAL

DATE	ACCOUNT DEBITED	INVOICE NUMBER	P.R.	Accts Receivable Dr Sales Cr.					Cost of Goods Sold Dr. Inventory Cr.				
20 SEPT. 3	N.R. Boswell	651	√		1	8	7	5	00		9	5	0	00
15	Inez Smythe	652	√		1	5	0	0	00		8	0	0	00
20	Ted Clark	653	√			8	2	5	00		4	2	0	00
24	N.R. Boswell	654	√		2	2	5	0	00		1	2	5	00
30	Inez Smythe	655	√		1	6	7	5	00		8	4	0	00
30	Totals.				8	1	2	5	00	3	1	3	5	00
						(106/413)					(501/107)			

CASH RECEIPTS JOURNAL

DATE	ACCOUNT CREDITED	P.R.	CASH DEBIT	SALES DISCOUNT DEBIT	ACCOUNTS RECEIVABLE CREDIT	SALES CREDIT	OTHER ACCOUNTS CREDIT	Cost of Goods Sold Debit Inventory Cr.
20— Sept. 1	Rent Earned	406	5 5 0 00				5 5 0 00	
13	N.R. Boswell	✓	1 8 3 7 50	3 7 50	1 8 7 5 00			
15	Sales	✓	9 0 0 00			9 0 0 00		
30	Ted Clark	✓	8 0 8 50	1 6 50	8 2 5 00			4 6 0 0 00
30	Rent Earned	406	5 5 0 00				5 5 0 00	
30	Sales	✓	9 4 5 0 50			9 4 5 0 50		4 2 7 5 00
30	Totals		22 1 9 6 50	5 4 00	2 7 0 0 00	18 4 5 0 50	1 1 0 0 00	8 8 7 5 00
			(101)	(415)	(106)	(413)	(✓)	(501/107)

GENERAL LEDGER

Cash — No. 101

Date	Debit	Credit	Balance
Sept. 30	22,196.50		22,196.50

Accounts Receivable — No. 106

Date	Debit	Credit	Balance
Sept. 30	8,125.00		8,125.00
30		2,700.00	5,425.00

Inventory — No. 107

Date	Debit	Credit	Balance
Bal for.			14,390.00
Sept 30		3,135.00	11,255.00
30		8,875.00	2,380.00

Rent Earned — No. 406

Date	Debit	Credit	Balance
Sept. 1		550.00	550.00
30		550.00	1,100.00

Sales — No. 413

Date	Debit	Credit	Balance
Sept. 30		8,125.00	8,125.00
30		18,450.50	26,575.50

Sales Discounts — No. 415

Date	Debit	Credit	Balance
Sept. 30	54.00		54.00

Cost of Goods Sold — No. 501

Date	Debit	Credit	Balance
Sept. 30	3,135.00		3,135.00
30	8,875.00		12,010.00

ACCOUNTS RECEIVABLE LEDGER

N.R. Boswell

Date	Debit	Credit	Balance
Sept. 3	1,875.00		1,875.00
13		1,875.00	-0-
24	2,250.00		2,250.00

Ted Clark

Date	Debit	Credit	Balance
Sept. 20	825.00		825.00
30		825.00	-0-

Inez Smythe

Date	Debit	Credit	Balance
Sept. 15	1,500.00		1,500.00
30	1,675.00	5,625.00	3,175.00

MCGUFF COMPANY
Schedule of Accounts Receivable
September 30, 20--

N.R. Boswell	$2,250.00
Inez Smythe	3,175.00
Total accounts receivable	$5,425.00

CHAPTER 12
MERCHANDISE PURCHASES AND ACCOUNTS PAYABLE

Learning Objective 1:

Analyze and record transactions for merchandise purchases.

Summary

A merchandiser records sales at list price less any trade discounts. The merchandiser records applicable purchase discounts for cash payment within the discount period as well as applicable purchase returns and freight charges.

Learning Objective 2:

Journalize and post transactions using a purchases journal.

Summary

The purchases journal is an efficient means to record the purchase of inventory on credit. The purchases journal will typically debit merchandise inventory (and transportation-in if applicable) and credit accounts payable.

Learning Objective 3:

Prepare and prove the accuracy of an accounts payable subsidiary ledger.

Summary

Account balances in the general ledger and the accounts payable subsidiary ledger are tested for accuracy after posting is complete. This procedure is twofold: (1) prepare a trial balance of the general ledger to confirm that debits equal credits and (2) prepare a schedule to confirm that the controlling account's balance equals the subsidiary ledger's balance.

Learning Objective 4:

Journalize and post transactions using a cash disbursements journal.

Summary

This journal, also called a cash payments journal, is used to record cash payments for purchases, expenses, and other items.

Chapter Outline

I.   **Accounting for Merchandise Purchases**
    a. Purchasing procedures
        i.   Purchase requisition—authorizes the purchase of goods
        ii. Purchase order—communicates intention to buy goods to the vender chosen
        iii. Receiving report—evidences the physical receipt of the goods when they arrive
        iv. Invoice—evidences the transaction including all necessary details about the purchase
    b. Accounting for Purchases and Freight Charges
        i.   Record transactions into a Purchases account
        ii. Purchases is an expense account included in COGS
        iii. Charge freight to Freight In (Transportation In) which is an expense account.
    c. Trade Discounts
        i.   List price is published in the merchandise catalog.
        ii. Trade discounts given based on volume and relationship.
        iii. List × discount = purchase price
    d. Purchase discounts
        i.   Based on terms of the purchase
            1. 2/10 n/30 – 2% discount in 10 days, otherwise due in 30
            2. n/30 – Due in 30 days
            3. COD – Cash on Delivery
        ii. Credit period from invoice date to due date.
        iii. Discount period from invoice date to discount date.
        iv. Discounts taken are recorded to Purchase Discounts as a credit
        v.   Purchase Discounts is a Contra-Expense account
    e. Purchase Returns and Allowances
        i.   Returns are physically sent back to the vendor
        ii. Allowances are adjustments in price due to non-conformance or sub-standard goods
        iii. Company issues a debit memorandum for purchase returns
        iv. Purchase Returns and Allowances is a Contra-Expense account
    f. Transportation Costs and Ownership Transfer
        i.   Designation of Title Transfer—FOB (Free on Board)
            1. Shipping Point—Sellers location
                a. Title transfers when goods leave seller
                b. Buyer responsible for freight and insurance cost

2. Destination Point—Buyers location
   a. Title transfers when goods received by buyer
   b. Seller responsible for freight and insurance cost

II. **Purchases Journal and Accounts Payable Subsidiary Ledger**
   a. Purchases Journal
      i. Record all credit purchase transactions each month
      ii. Record all necessary details about the transaction
         1. Date
         2. Vendor
         3. Purchase amount
         4. Freight amount
         5. Shipping terms—FOB
         6. Total amount due
      iii. Total amounts at the end of the month and post to the GL
   b. Posting to the Accounts Payable Subsidiary Ledger
      i. Separate page for each vendor/supplier
      ii. Post each purchase transaction to the individual vendor accounts
      iii. Any transactions that affect Accounts Payable must be posted to the subsidiary ledger
         1. Invoices
         2. Debit Memorandums
         3. Payments
   c. Proving the Accounts Payable Ledger
      i. Balance each vendor account and prepare a schedule of accounts payable
      ii. Total from schedule must agree with balance in AP in the GL

III. **Cash Disbursements Journal**
   a. Credit to Cash; Debit to Accounts Payable, Purchase Discounts and other accounts.
   b. For control over cash disbursements, all payments (except for those of small amounts) are made by check.

Purchases and Cash Payments

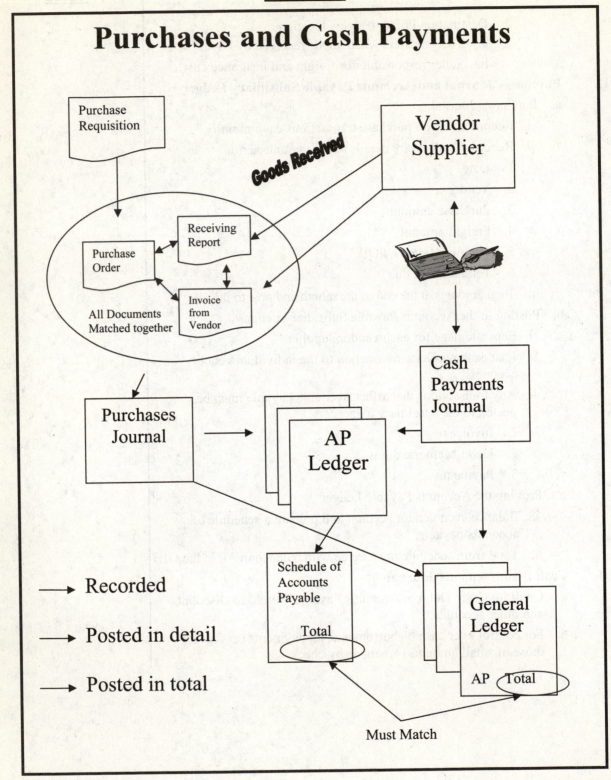

Purchase Requisition

Vendor Supplier

Goods Received

Receiving Report

Purchase Order

Invoice from Vendor

All Documents Matched together

Cash Payments Journal

Purchases Journal

AP Ledger

→ Recorded

→ Posted in detail

→ Posted in total

Schedule of Accounts Payable

Total

General Ledger

AP   Total

Must Match

Alternate Demonstration Problem

Ryan's Skateboard Shop has the following credit purchase transactions for April

Apr 2	Purchased merchandise from Parker Co., $1,450, Terms 2/10, N30, FOB Destination Point
Apr 5	Purchased merchandise from Coletrane Co., $2,650, N30, FOB Shipping Point, Freight $240
Apr 8	Purchased merchandise from Getz Co., $850, Terms 2/10, N30, FOB Shipping Point, Freight $86
Apr 9	Purchased merchandise from Rollins Co., $2,650, N30, FOB Shipping Point, Freight $270
Apr 14	Purchased merchandise from Getz Co., $1,810, Terms 2/10, N30, FOB Shipping Point, Freight $150
Apr 17	Purchased merchandise from Coletrane Co., $1,840, N30, FOB Shipping Point, Freight $210
Apr 23	Purchased merchandise from Parker Co., $2,825, Terms 2/10, N30, FOB Destination Point
Apr 25	Purchased merchandise from Young Co., $850, Terms 2/10, N30, FOB Shipping Point, Freight $65
Apr 29	Purchased merchandise from Rollins Co., $3,450, N30, FOB Shipping Point, Freight $325

Required:
1. Record these purchases in a purchase journal using Accounts Payable (205), Freight In (525) and Purchases (510). Assume these accounts have zero balances at the beginning of April.
2. Post these purchases to the general ledger and post the references.
3. Post these purchases to the accounts payable subsidiary ledger.

Solution:

Ryan's Skateboard Shop
Purchase Journal
For the month ended April 30, 2011

Date	Customer	Terms	PR	Purchases (Dr.)	Freight In (Dr.)	Accounts Payable (Cr.)
4/2	Parker	2/10,N30	a	1,450	-	1,540
4/5	Coletrane	N30	b	2,650	240	2,890
4/8	Getz	2/10,N30	c	850	86	936
4/9	Rollins	N30	d	2,650	270	2,920
4/14	Getz	2/10,N30	e	1,810	150	1,960
4/17	Coletrane	N30	f	1,840	210	2,050
4/23	Parker	2/10,N30	g	2,825	-	2,825
4/25	Young	2/10,N30	h	850	65	915
4/29	Rollins	N30	i	3,450	325	3,775
				18,375	1,346	19,721
				(510)	(525)	(205)

General Ledger

Accounts Payable (205)

		19,721	P1

Purchases (510)

P1	18,375	

Freight In (525)

P1	1,346	

Accounts Payable Ledger

Coletrane Company

	2,890	b
	2,050	f

Getz Company

	936	c
	1,960	e

Parker Company

	1,450	a
	2,825	g

Rollins Company

	2,920	d
	3,775	I

Young Company

	915	h

Problem I

The following statements are either true or false. Place a (T) in the parentheses before each true statement and an (F) before each false statement.

1. ( ) Cash discounts on merchandise purchased are debited to the inventory account.

2. ( ) Transportation costs on merchandise purchased are debited to the inventory account.

3. ( ) A debit memorandum may originate with either party to a transaction, but the memorandum gets its name from the action of the selling party.

4. ( ) Recording the purchase of merchandise on account requires a debit to the inventory account and a credit to accounts payable.

5. ( ) A Purchases Journal is used to record all purchases.

6. ( ) Transactions recorded in a journal do not necessarily result in equal debits and credits to General Ledger accounts.

7. ( ) A Cash Disbursements Journal is used to record all receipts of cash.

8. ( ) FOB stands for freight on board.

Problem II

You are given several words, phrases or numbers to choose from in completing each of the following statements or in answering the following questions. In each case select the one that best completes the statement or answers the question and place its letter in the answer space provided.

_____ 1. A company that uses special journals and a General Journal paid a creditor for office supplies purchased on account. In which journal would the transaction be recorded?

      a. Sales Journal

      b. Purchases Journal

      c. Cash Receipts Journal

      d. Cash Disbursements Journal

      e. General Journal

_____ 2. A book of original entry that is designed and used for recording only a specified type of transaction is a:

      a. Check Register

      b. Subsidiary Ledger

      c. General Ledger

      d. Special Journal

      e. Schedule of Accounts Payable

_____ 3. Net income for a merchandise is computed as?

      a. Net sales plus cost of goods sold minus expenses

      b. Net sales minus cost of goods sold minus expenses

      c. Gross sales minus cost of goods sold minus expenses

      d. Net sales minus cost of goods sold plus expenses

      e. Gross sales minus cost of goods sold plus expenses

_____ 4. Cost of goods sold is computed as?

    a. Beginning inventory plus net purchases plus ending inventory

    b. Beginning inventory plus gross purchases plus ending inventory

    c. Ending inventory plus beginning inventory plus net purchases

    d. Beginning inventory plus net purchases minus ending inventory

    e. Ending inventory plus beginning inventory minus gross purchases

_____ 5. A company that uses special journals and a General Journal purchased merchandise on credit. In which journal would the transaction be recorded?

    a. Purchases Journal

    b. Sales Journal

    c. Cash Receipts Journal

    d. Cash Disbursements Journal

    e. General Journal

Problem III

Many of the important ideas and concepts discussed in Chapter 12 are reflected in the following list of key terms. Test your understanding of these terms by matching the appropriate definitions with the terms. Record the number identifying the most appropriate definition in the blank space next to each term.

_____ Accounts payable ledger	_____ Purchase discount
_____ Cash disbursements journal	_____ Purchase order
_____ Credit period	_____ Purchase requisition
_____ Credit terms	_____ Purchases journal
_____ Debit memorandum	_____ Receiving report
_____ Discount period	_____ Schedule of accounts payable
_____ FOB	_____ Trade discount
_____ Inventory	_____ Transportation-in
_____ Invoice	_____ Vendor
_____ List price	
_____ Merchandise inventory	
_____ Merchandiser	
_____ Net purchases	

1. Reduction below a list or catalog price that can vary for wholesalers, retailers, and customers.

2. Notification that the sender has debited the recipient's account in the sender's records.

3. Merchandise a company owns and expects to sell in its normal operations.

4. Catalog price of an item before any trade discount is deducted.

5. Products that a company owns to sell to their customers; also called merchandise.

6. Term used by a purchaser to describe a cash discount granted to the purchaser for paying within the discount period.

7. Time period in which a cash discount is available and the buyer can make a reduced payment.

8. Abbreviation for *free on board;* the point at which ownership of goods passes to the buyer; FOB *shipping point* (or *factory*) means the buyer pays shipping costs and accepts ownership of the goods at the seller's place of business; FOB *destination* means the seller pays shipping costs and accepts ownership of the goods until at the buyer's place of business;

9. Special journal normally used to record all payments of cash.

10. Entity that earns net income by buying and selling merchandise.

11. List of the balances of all accounts in the accounts payable ledger that are summed to show the total amount of accounts payable outstanding.

12. A journal that is used to record all purchases on credit.

13. Time period that can pass before a customer's payment is due.

14. Net cost of merchandise purchased.

15. Seller of goods or services

16. Description of the amounts and timing of payments that a buyer (debtor) agrees to make in the future.

17. Document used by the purchasing department to place an order with a seller (vendor).

18. Freight costs paid by the buyer.

19. Document listing merchandise needed by a department and requesting it be purchased.

20. Form used to report that ordered goods are received and to describe their quantity and condition.

21. Itemized record of goods prepared by the vendor that lists the customer's name, items sold, sales prices, and terms of sale.

Problem VI

1. Trade discounts _____ (are, are not) credited to the Inventory account.

2. A store received a credit memorandum from a wholesaler for unsatisfactory merchandise that the store sent back for credit. The store should record the memorandum with a _____ (debit, credit) to its Inventory account and a _____ (debit, credit) to its Accounts Payable account.

3. When special journals are used, credit purchases of store supplies or office supplies should be recorded in the _____.

4. The posting principle upon which a subsidiary ledger and its controlling account operate requires that the controlling account be debited for an amount or amounts equal to the sum of _____ _____ to the subsidiary ledger and that the controlling account be credited for an amount or amounts equal to the sum of _____ to the subsidiary ledger.

5. Cash purchases of store supplies or office supplies should be recorded in a(n) _____ _____.

Problem VII

Below are five transactions completed by McGuff Company on September 30 of the current year. Following the transactions are the company's journals with prior September transactions recorded therein.

Requirement One: Record the five transactions in the company's journals.

Sept. 30   Received merchandise and an invoice dated September 28, terms 2/10, n/60 from Johnson Company, $4,000.

     30   Purchased store equipment on account from Olson Company, invoice dated September 30, terms n/10, EOM, $950.

     30   Issued Check No. 525 to Kerry Meadows in payment of her $650 salary.

     30   Issued Check No. 526 for $1,715 to Olson Company in full payment of its September 20 invoice, less–a $35 discount.

     30   Received a credit memorandum from Olson Company for unsatisfactory merchandise received on September 24 and returned for credit, $625.

GENERAL JOURNAL

DATE	ACCOUNT TITLES AND EXPLANATION	P.R.	DEBIT	CREDIT

PURCHASES JOURNAL

DATE	ACCOUNT	DATE OF INVOICE	TERMS	P.R.	ACCOUNTS PAYABLE CREDIT			INVENTORY DEBIT			OTHER ACCOUNTS DEBIT	
20--- Sept. 8	Johnson Company	9/6	2/10, n/60	√	3	7 5 0	00	3	7 5 0	00		
22	Olson Company	9/20	2/10, n/60	√	1	7 5 0	00	1	7 5 0	00		
24	Olson Company	9/22	2/10. n/60	√	5	6 2 5	00	5	6 2 5	00		

CASH DISBURSEMENTS JOURNAL

DATE	CH. NO.	PAYEE	ACCOUNT DEBITED	P.R.	CASH CREDIT	INVENTORY CREDIT	OTHER ACCOUNTS DEBIT	ACCOUNTS PAYABLE DEBIT
20--								
Sept. 15	523	Kerry Meadows	Salaries Expense	622	6 5 0 00		6 5 0 00	
16	524	Johnson Company	Johnson Company	√	3 6 7 5 00	7 5 00		3 7 5 0 00

Requirement Two: The individual postings from the journals of McGuff Company through September 29 have been made. Complete the individual postings from the journals.

Requirement Three: Foot and crossfoot the journals and make the month-end postings.

Requirement Four: Test the subsidiary ledgers by preparing schedule of accounts payable.

ACCOUNTS PAYABLE LEDGER

Johnson Company
118 E. Seventh Street

DATE	EXPLANATION	P.R.	DEBIT	CREDIT	BALANCE
20--- Sept. 8		P-8		3 7 5 0 00	3 7 5 0 00
16		D-7	3 7 5 0 00		- 0 -

Olson Company
788 Hazelwood Avenue

DATE	EXPLANATION	P.R.	DEBIT	CREDIT	BALANCE
20--- Sept. 22		P-8		1 7 5 0 00	1 7 5 0 00
24		p-8		5 6 2 5 00	7 3 7 5 00

GENERAL LEDGER

Cash   Account No. 101

DATE	EXPLANATION	P.R.	DEBIT	CREDIT	BALANCE

Inventory   Account No.107

DATE	EXPLANATION	P.R.	DEBIT	CREDIT	BALANCE

Store Equipment   Account No. 165

DATE	EXPLANATION	P.R.	DEBIT	CREDIT	BALANCE

College Accounting, 2nd Edition

Accounts Payable — Account No.201

DATE	EXPLANATION	P.R.	DEBIT	CREDIT	BALANCE

Salaries Expense — Account No.622

DATE	EXPLANATION	P.R.	DEBIT	CREDIT	BALANCE
20--- Sept. 15		D-7	6 5 0 00		6 5 0 00

MCGUFF COMPANY

Schedule of Accounts Payable

September 30, 20--

Solutions for Chapter 12

Problem I

1.	F	5.	F
2.	T	6.	F
3.	F	7.	F
4.	T	8.	F

Problem II

1.	D
2.	D
3.	B
4.	D
5.	A

Problem III

11	Accounts payable ledger	6	Purchase discount
9	Cash disbursements journal	17	Purchase order
13	Credit period	19	Purchase requisition
16	Credit terms	12	Purchases journal
2	Debit memorandum	20	Receiving report
7	Discount period	11	Schedule of accounts payable
8	FOB	1	Trade discount
3 or 5	Inventory	18	Transportation-in
21	Invoice	15	Vendor
4	List price		
3 or 5	Merchandise inventory		
10	Merchandiser		
14	Net purchases		

Problem VI

1. are not

2. credit, debit

3. Purchases Journal

4. the debits posted, the credits posted

5. Cash Disbursements Journal

Problem VII

DATE	GENERAL JOURNAL		DEBIT	CREDIT
Sept 30	Accounts Payable-Olson Company	201/√	625.00	
	Inventory	107		625.00

PURCHASES JOURNAL

DATE	ACCOUNT	DATE OF INVOICE	TERMS	P.R.	ACCOUNTS PAYABLE CREDIT	INVENTORY DEBIT	OTHER ACCOUNTS DEBIT
20—							
Sept. 8	Johnson Company	9/6	2/10, n/60	√	3 750 00	3 750 00	
22	Olson Company	9/20	2/10, n/60	√	1 750 00	1 750 00	
24	Olson Company	9/22	2/10. n/60	√	5 625 00	5 625 00	
30	Johnson Company	9/28	2/10, n/60	√	4 000 00	4 000 00	
30	Str Equip/Olsn Co.	9/30	n/10 EOM	165√	950 00		950 00
30	Totals				16 075 00	15 125 00	950 00
					(201)	(107)	(√)

CASH DISBURSEMENTS JOURNAL

DATE	CH. NO.	PAYEE	ACCOUNT DEBITED	P.R.	CASH CREDIT	INVENTORY CREDIT	OTHER ACCOUNTS DEBIT	ACCOUNTS PAYABLE DEBIT
20—								
Sept. 15	523	Kerry Meadows	Salaries Expense	622	650 00		650 00	
16	524	Johnson Company		√	3 675 00	75 00		3 750 00
30	525	Kerry Meadows	Salaries Expense	622	650 00		650 00	
30	526	Olson Company		√	1 715 00	35 00		1 750 00
30	Totals				6 690 00	110 00	1 300 00	5 500 00
					(101)	(107)	(√)	(201)

GENERAL LEDGER

Cash   No. 101

Date	Debit	Credit	Balance
Bal For.			22,196.50
30		6,690.00	15,506.50

Accounts Payable   No. 201

Date	Debit	Credit	Balance
Sept 30		16,075.00	16,075.00
30	5,500.00		10,575.00
30	625.00		9,950.00

Inventory   No. 107

Date	Debit	Credit	Balance
Sept. 30	15,125.00		15,125.00
30		625.00	14,500.00
30		110.00	14,390.00

Salaries Expense   No. 622

Date	Debit	Credit	Balance
Sept. 15	650.00		650.00
30	650.00		1,300.00

Store Equipment   No. 165

Date	Debit	Credit	Balance
Sept. 30	950.00		950.00

ACCOUNTS PAYABLE LEDGER

Johnson Company

Date	Debit	Credit	Balance
Sept. 8		3,750.00	3,750.00
16	3,750.00		-0-
30		4,000.00	4,000.00

Olson Company

Date	Debit	Credit	Balance
Sept. 22		1,750.00	1,750.00
24		5,625.00	7,375.00
30		950.00	8,325.00
30	1,750.00		6,575.00
30	625.00		5,950.00

MCGUFF COMPANY
Schedule of Accounts Payable
September 30, 20--

Johnson Company	$4,000.00
Olson Company	5,950.00
Total accounts payable	$9,950.00

CHAPTER 13

MERCHANDISER'S ADJUSTMENTS AND TRIAL BALANCE

Learning Objective 1:

Use a trial balance for a merchandiser.

Summary

The merchandiser's trial balance includes accounts for merchandise inventory, sales, and purchases. Under a periodic inventory system the unadjusted merchandise inventory balance is its balance as of the beginning of the period.

Learning Objective 2:

Prepare the adjusting entries for inventory.

Summary

Two entries are needed to adjust inventory. First, debit Income Summary and credit Merchandise Inventory for the beginning balance of merchandise inventory from the unadjusted trial balance. Second, debit Merchandise Inventory and credit Income Summary for the ending balances of inventory, determined by a physical count.

Learning Objective 3:

Prepare adjusting entries for prepaid and accrued expenses.

Summary

Prepaid assets, like prepaid insurance or supplies, are used during a period. An adjusting entry records the amount used as expense and reduces the related asset to the amount that remains for future use. Depreciation is a special case of prepaid expenses. Accrued expenses are costs, like employee salaries, that occur before the end of an accounting period but that won't be paid until the next period. An adjusting entry records these expenses and creates a liability for the amount owed.

Learning Objective 4:

Compute net sales and net purchases.

Summary

Net sales is computed as sales minus sales returns and allowances minus sales discounts. Net purchases is computed as purchases plus transportation-in minus purchase returns and allowances minus purchase discounts. Balances for each of these accounts come from the ending unadjusted trial balance.

Learning Objective 5:

Compute cost of goods sold.

Summary

The inventory equation is used to compute cost of goods sold. Beginning inventory plus net purchases minus ending inventory equals cost of goods sold. Ending inventory is determined from a physical count of the inventory that remains unsold at the end of the period.

Learning Objective 6:

Compute gross profit.

Summary

Gross profit is computed as net sales minus cost of goods sold. It is an important measure of performance for a merchandiser.

Learning Objective 7:

Prepare the adjusting entry for accrued revenue.

Summary

Accrued revenue is revenue earned for work performed before the end of a period, but amounts won't be collected until the next period. An adjusting entry is recorded with a debit to Accounts Receivable and a credit to Sales (or Revenue).

Learning Objective 8:

Prepare the adjusting entry for unearned revenue.

Summary

When a business receives cash before it performs work, it has a liability to perform that future work. When the work is performed, Unearned Revenue (a liability) is reduced with a debit and Revenue is increased with a credit.

Learning Objective 9:

Describe the alternatives in accounting for prepayments.

Summary

Debiting all prepaid expenses to expense accounts when they are purchased is acceptable. When this is done, adjusting entries must transfer any unexpired amounts from expense accounts to asset accounts. Crediting all unearned revenues to revenue accounts when cash is received is also acceptable. In this case, the adjusting entries must transfer any unearned amounts from revenue accounts to unearned revenue accounts.

I.   **Merchandiser's Trial Balance**

    a.   Using a Trial Balance

        i.   Merchandise inventory are products the merchandiser plans to sell

        ii. Under period inventory system, balance of Merchandise Inventory account does not change during the year

        iii. Include separate accounts for sales, purchases, and related accounts

    b.   Adjusting Entries for Merchandise Inventory

        i.   Dr. Income Summary, Cr. Merchandise Inventory—to transfer beginning balance to Income Summary

        ii. Dr. Merchandise Inventory, Cr. Income Summary—to record ending balance

II.   **Expense Adjustments**

    a.   Prepaids—cash paid before work performed

        i.   Prepaid Insurance—as time passes the policy expires

            1.   Dr. Insurance Expense

            2.   Cr. Prepaid Insurance

        ii. Supplies—some are used during the period

            1.   Count balance of unused supplies

            2.   Expense = Beginning supplies balance plus supplies purchased minus ending supplies balance

            3.   Dr. Supplies Expense, Cr. Supplies

        iii. Depreciation Expense

            1.   Expense = (Cost – salvage value)/useful life

            2.   Dr. Depr. Expense, Cr. Accumulated Depreciation

III. **Partial Work Sheet—**

    a.   Adjusted Trial Balance—Can be used to prepare financial statements and compute key amounts for a merchandiser

    b.   Computing Net Sales and Net Purchases

        i.   Net sales = Sales – sales discounts – sales returns and allowances

        ii. Net purchases = Purchases – purchase discounts – purchase returns and allowances + cost of transportation-in

        iii. Cost of goods sold = Beginning inventory + net purchases – ending inventory

        iv. Gross profit = Net sales – cost of goods sold

IV. **Revenue Adjustments**

   a. Accrued Revenues—earned during the period but both unrecorded and not yet received in cash

      i. Dr. Accounts Receivable, Cr. Sales Revenue

         1. Based on amount of work performed

   b. Unearned Revenues—for cash received before work is performed

      i. Dr. Cash, Cr. Unearned Sales Revenue

         1. For amount of cash received

         2. A liability until work is performed

      ii. Dr. Unearned Sales Revenue, Cr. Sales Revenue

         1. For amount of work performed

V. **Links to Financial Statements—effects on financial statements if adjustments are not made.**

   a. Prepaid expenses

      i. Assets/Equity overstated

      ii. Expenses understated

   b. Unearned revenues

      i. Liabilities overstated

      ii. Equity/Revenue understated

   c. Accrued Expenses

      i. Liability/Expenses understated

      ii. Equity overstated

   d. Accrued Revenues

      i. Assets/Revenue/Equity understated

Components of Gross Profit

Sales

- Sales Returns and Allowances

- Sales Discounts
_____

Net Sales

Purchases

- Purchases Returns and Allowances
- Purchases Discounts
+ Freight In
+ Beginning Inventory
- Ending Inventory
_____

Cost of Goods Sold

Net Sales
- Cost of Goods Sold
_____

Gross Profit

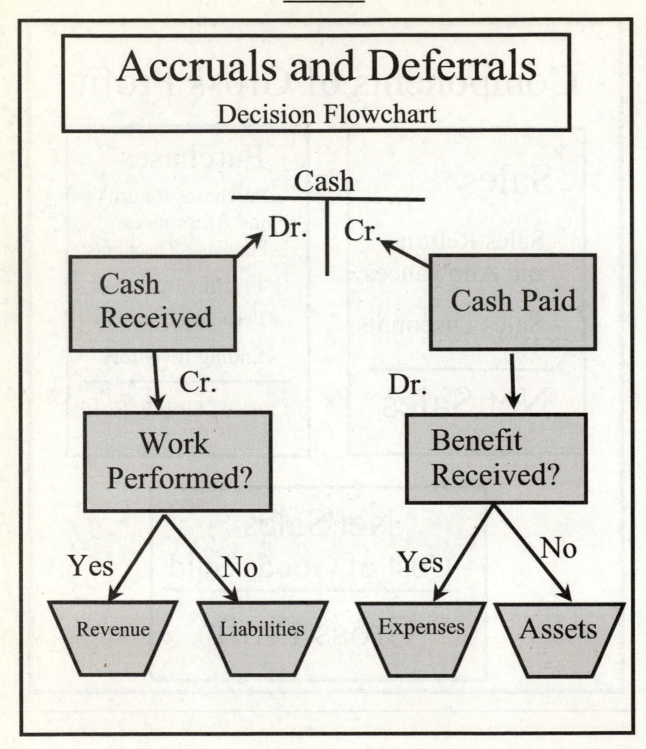

Accruals and Deferrals
Decision Flowchart

Cash

Dr. | Cr.

Cash Received → Dr.

Cash Paid → Cr.

Cr. → Work Performed?

Dr. → Benefit Received?

Work Performed?
- Yes → Revenue
- No → Liabilities

Benefit Received?
- Yes → Expenses
- No → Assets

Alternate Demonstration Problem

The following information relates to Jason's Surf Shop on December 31, 2010. The company, which uses the calendar year as its annual reporting period, initially records prepaid and unearned items in balance sheet accounts (assets and liabilities, respectively)

a. The company's weekly payroll is $4,225, paid each Friday for a five-day work week. Assume December 31, 2010 falls on a Wednesday, but the employees will not be paid their wages until Friday, January 2, 2011.
b. Nine months earlier, on April 1, 2010, the company purchased a truck that cost $14,000. Its useful life is predicted to be five years, at which time the truck is estimated to be worth $2,000 in salvage value.
c. On October 1, 2010, the company agreed to work on a group of surfboards for the local surf team. The company is paid $4,800 in advance for the repair of 24 surfboards. The amount received was debited to Cash and credited to Unearned Surf Repair Revenue. As of 12/31/10, 18 of the surfboards had been repaired.
d. On July 1, 2010, the company purchased a 12-month insurance policy for $1,200. The transaction was recorded with a debit to Prepaid Insurance and credit to Cash.
e. On December 31, 2010, the company had completed $800 worth of surfboard repairs that were waiting for customers to pick them up. They had not been billed yet.

Required:

1. Prepare any necessary adjusting entries on December 31, 2010, in relation to transactions and events a through e.
2. Prepare T-accounts for the accounts affected by adjusting entries and post the adjusting entries. Determine the adjusted balances for the Unearned Revenue and Prepaid Insurance accounts.
3. Complete the following table and determine the amounts and effects of your adjusting entries on the year 2010 income statement and December 31, 2010 balance sheet.

Entry	Amount in the entry	Effect on Net Income	Effect on Assets	Effect on Liabilities	Effect on Equity
a					
b					
c					
d					
e					

Solution:

		Jason's Surf Shop		
		General Journal		
Date		Account	Debit	Credit
12/31	a	Wages Expense	2,535	
		Wages Payable		2,535
		to accrue wages for last week		
		in December (4,225/5 * 3 days)		
12/31	b	Depreciation Expense	1,800	
		Accumulated Depreciation - Truck		1,800
		to record depreciation on the Truck		
		(14,000- 2,000)/60 months * 9 mo.)		
12/31	c	Unearned Surfboard Repair Revenue	3,600	
		Surfboard Repair Revenue		3,600
		to adjust unearned revenue for		
		surfboards repaired at 12/31		
		(4,800/24 boards * 18 completed)		
12/31	d	Insurance Expense	600	
		Prepaid Insurance		600
		to write-off expired insurance		
		($1,200/12 months * 6 months)		
12/31	e	Accounts Receivable	800	
		Surfboard Repair Revenue		800
		to accrue revenue for completed		
		repairs		

General Ledger

Wages Expense			Prepaid Insurance		
a	2,535		*	1,200	600	d
			#	600		

Depreciation Expense - Truck	
b	1,800

	Unearned Revenue		
c	3,600	4,800	*
		1,200	#

Insurance Expense	
d	600

Accounts Receivable	
e	800

Surfboard Repair Revenue		
	3,600	c
	800	e
	4,400	#

Wages Payable		
	2,535	a

Accumulated Depreciation - Truck		
	1,800	b

* Unadjusted balance
\# Adjusted balance

Entry	Amount in the entry	Effect on Net Income	Effect on Assets	Effect on Liabilities	Effect on Equity
a	2,535	(2,535)	-	2,535	(2,535)
b	1,800	(1,800)	(1,800)	-	(1,800)
c	3,600	3,600	-	(3,600)	3,600
d	600	(600)	(600)	-	(600)
e	800	800	800	-	800

Problem I

The following statements are either true or false. Place a (T) in the parentheses before each true statement and an (F) before each false statement.

1. ( ) The effect of a debit to an unearned revenue account and a corresponding credit to a revenue account is to transfer the earned portion of the fee from the liability account to the revenue account.

2. ( ) Under the periodic inventory system, the balance in Merchandise Inventory in an unadjusted trial balance is its balance as of the beginning of the accounting period.

3. ( ) Cost of transportation-in is subtracted in computing net purchases.

4. ( ) Merchandise available for sale equals beginning inventory plus the cost of net purchases.

5. ( ) If a business records receipts of unearned revenues with debits to cash and credits to revenue accounts, no adjusting entries are required at the end of the period.

Problem II

You are given several words, phrases, or numbers to choose from in completing each of the following statements or in answering the following questions. In each case select the one that best completes the statement or answers the question and place its letter in the answer space provided.

_____ 1.   Net income for a merchandiser is computed as?

   a. Net sales plus cost of goods sold minus expenses
   b. Net sales minus cost of goods sold minus expenses
   c. Gross sales minus cost of goods sold minus expenses
   d. Net sales minus cost of goods sold plus expenses
   e. Gross sales minus cost of goods sold plus expenses

_____ 2.   Cost of goods sold is computed as?

   a. Beginning inventory plus net purchases plus ending inventory
   b. Beginning inventory plus gross purchases plus ending inventory
   c. Ending inventory plus beginning inventory plus net purchases
   d. Beginning inventory plus net purchases minus ending inventory
   e. Ending inventory plus beginning inventory minus gross purchases

_____ 3.   Lori Teach owns a sole proprietorship. During April, Lori's business received $250 cash in advance for future services. The following entry should be made when the money is received:

   a. Cash 250
         Accounts Receivable   250
   b. Accounts Receivable 250
         Unearned Revenue   250
   c. Cash 250
         Unearned Revenue   250
   d. Unearned Revenue 250
         Services Revenue   250
   e. No entry should be made until services are actually rendered.

_____ 4. On December 1, B & B Security Service collected three months' fees of $6,000 in advance of providing services and credited Unearned Security Service Fees. They provided the monthly service from that date forward. The December 31st adjustment will require that Unearned Service Fees be

    a. Credited for $ 2,000.

    b. Debited for $ 6,000.

    c. Credited for $ 6,000.

    d. Debited for $ 4,000.

    e. Debited for $ 2,000.

_____ 5. The Epicure Restaurant prepares monthly financial statements. On January 31 the balance in the Supplies account was $1,600. During February $2,960 of supplies were purchased and debited to Supplies. What is the adjusting entry on February 28 to account for the supplies assuming a February 28 inventory showed that $1,300 of supplies were on hand?

    a. Supplies Expense 300

        Supplies 300

    b. Supplies...300

        Supplies Expense.. 300

    c. Supplies...3,260

        Cash 3,260

    d. Supplies Expense 3,260

        Supplies 3,260

_____ 6. (Appendix 13A) Hanover Company prepares monthly financial statements and follows the procedure of crediting revenue accounts when it records cash receipts of unearned revenues. During April, the business received $4,800 for services to be rendered during April and May. On April 30, $2,000 of the amounts received had been earned. What is the adjusting journal entry on April 30 for service fees?

    a. Service Fees Earned 2,000

        Unearned Service Fees 2,000

    b. Unearned Service Fees 2,800

        Service Fees Earned 2,800

    c. Cash 2,000

        Service Fees Earned 2,000

    d. Unearned Service Fees 2,000

        Service Fees Earned 2,000

    e. Service Fees Earned 2,800

        Unearned Service Fees 2,800

_____ 7. (Appendix 13A) Xanadu Company prepares monthly financial statements. On August 31, the balance in the Office Supplies account was $300. During September, $500 of supplies were purchased and debited to Office Supplies Expense. What is the adjusting journal entry on September 30 to account for the supplies assuming a September inventory of supplies showed that $250 were on hand?

a. Office Supplies 350

      Office Supplies Expense 350

b. Office Supplies Expense 250

      Office Supplies 250

c. Office Supplies Expense 50

      Office Supplies 50

d. Office Supplies Expense 350

      Office Supplies 350

e. Office Supplies 250

      Office Supplies Expense 250

Problem III

Many of the important ideas and concepts discussed in Chapter 13 are reflected in the following list of key terms. Test your understanding of these terms by matching the appropriate definitions with the terms. Record the number identifying the most appropriate definition in the blank space next to each term.

_____ Accrued revenues   _____ Net purchases
_____ Cost of goods sold   _____ Net sales
_____ Gross profit   _____ Unearned revenues
_____ Merchandise inventory

1. Net sales minus cost of goods sold.

2. Liability created when customers pay in advance for products or services; earned when products or services are later delivered.

3. Net cost of merchandise purchased.

4. Computed as sales minus sales discounts and minus sales returns minus and allowances.

5. Revenues earned in a period that are both unrecorded and not yet received in cash.

6. Goods that a company owns and expects to sell to customers.

7. Cost of inventory sold to customers during a period.

Problem IV

Prepare the adjusting journal entries for Accent Kitchens who provides kitchen remodeling services. Accent Kitchens had the following transactions at the end of the year which require attention:

   a. Provided $3,500 of services to customers which have not yet been billed to these customers.
   b. Accrued salaries at 12/31 are $500
   c. Received $1,500 deposit for services to be provided in January.

Required: Prepare the general journal entries to record the adjustments.

GENERAL JOURNAL

DATE	ACCOUNT TITLES AND EXPLANATION	P.R.	DEBIT	CREDIT
12/31				
12/31				
12/31				

Problem V

Riverview Properties operates an apartment building. On December 31, at the end of an annual accounting period, its Rent Earned account had a $335,500 credit balance, and the Unearned Rent account had a $3,600 credit balance. The following information was available for the year-end adjustments: (a) the credit balance in the Unearned Rent account resulted from a tenant paying his rent for six months in advance beginning on November 1; (b) also, a tenant in temporary financial difficulties had not paid his rent for the month of December. The amount due was $475.

Required: Enter the necessary adjustments directly in the T-accounts below.

Rent Receivable	Unearned Rent	Rent Earned
	Nov. 1 3,600	Balance 335,500

After the foregoing adjustments are entered in the accounts, the company's Rent Earned account has a $_____ balance which should appear on its income statement as revenue earned during the year. Its Unearned Rent account has a $_____ balance, and this should appear on the company's balance sheet as a _____. Likewise, the company's Rent Receivable account has a $_____ balance, and this should appear on its balance sheet as a _____.

Solutions for Chapter 13

Problem I

1. T
2. T
3. F
4. T
5. F

Problem II

1. B
2. D
3. C
4. E
5. D
6. E
7. C

Problem III

5	Accrued revenues	3	Net purchases
7	Cost of goods sold	4	Net sales
1	Gross profit	2	Unearned revenues
6	Merchandise inventory		

Problem IV

GENERAL JOURNAL

DATE	ACCOUNT TITLES AND EXPLANATION	P.R.	DEBIT	CREDIT
12/31	Accounts Receivable		3 5 0 0	
	Consulting Services			3 5 0 0
12/31	Salaries Expense		5 0 0	
	Salaries Payable			5 0 0
12/31	Cash		1 5 0 0	
	Unearned Services			1 5 0 0

Problem V

Rent Receivable		
Dec. 31	475	

Unearned Rent			
Dec. 31	1,200	Nov. 1	3,600

Rent Earned		
	Bal.	335,500
	Dec. 31	1,200
	31	475

Rent Earned, $337,175
Unearned Rent, $2,400, liability
Rent Receivable, $475, asset

Learning Objective 1:

Prepare a work sheet for a merchandising business.

Summary

A work sheet can be useful in organizing data, preparing financial statements, and preparing closing entries. The work sheet includes columns for the unadjusted trial balance, the adjusting entries, and the adjusted trial balances. Balances in the adjusted trial balance columns are then extended into either income statement or balance sheet columns.

Learning Objective 2:

Define and prepare multiple-step and single-step income statements.

Summary

Multiple-step income statements include greater detail for sales and expenses than do single-step income statements. They also show details of net sales and report expenses in categories reflecting different activities.

Learning Objective 3:

Prepare a statement of owner's equity.

Summary

The statement of owner's equity is used to summarize changes in the owner's capital account during the year. The beginning balance of owner's capital is updated for the net income or loss for the period, additional owner investments during the period, and any owner withdrawals during the period. The ending balance of owner's capital is included on the end of period balance sheet.

Learning Objective 4:

Explain and prepare a classified balance sheet.

Summary

Classified balance sheets report assets and liabilities in two categories: current and noncurrent. Current assets often include cash, accounts receivable, and merchandise inventory. Noncurrent assets often include long-term investments, plant assets, and intangible assets. Current liabilities often include accounts payable and wages payable. Noncurrent liabilities often include notes payable, bonds payable, and leases.

Learning Objective 5:

Prepare journal entries to close temporary accounts.

Summary

Closing entries involve four steps: (1) close temporary accounts having credit balances to Income Summary, (2) close temporary accounts having debit balances to Income Summary, (3) close Income Summary to the owner's capital account, (4) close the owner withdrawals account to the owner's capital account.

Learning Objective 6:

Prepare a post-closing trial balance.

Summary

After journalizing and posting the closing entries, a trial balance is prepared using the ending balances in the permanent accounts. This post-closing trial balance proves the equality of debits and credits in the general ledger.

Learning Objective 7:

Prepare reversing entries and explain their purpose.

Summary

Reversing entries are an optional step. They are applied to accrued expenses and revenues. The purpose of reversing entries is to simplify subsequent journal entries. Financial statements are unaffected by the choice to use or not use reversing entries.

I.   Preparing the Work Sheet

    a.   Similar to that for service business, but also includes sales and purchases accounts

    b.   Steps in preparing the work sheet

        i.   Enter unadjusted trial balance

        ii.   Enter adjustment in the adjustments columns

        iii.   Prepare adjusted trial balance

        iv.   Sort adjusted trial balance amounts to financial statement columns

           1.   Assets, Liabilities and Equity listed in balance sheet columns

           2.   Revenues and Expenses listed in income statement columns

        v.   Total financial statement columns and balance worksheet with Net Income or Net Loss on both the income statement and balance sheet columns

II.   Financial Statement Formats

    a.   Multiple-step Income Statement—show detailed computations of net sales and other expenses, and report subtotals

        i.   Three main sections

           1.   Gross profit

           2.   Income from operations—gross profit less operating expenses

           3.   Net income

        ii.   Some companies further classify operating expenses into two sections

           1.   Selling expenses—include expenses of promoting sales, making sales, and delivering goods

           2.   General and administrative expenses – not directly to sales, but support overall operations

        iii.   Nonoperating activities include items unrelated to company's main operations

           1.   Other revenue and gains—e.g. interest revenue, gains from asset disposals

           2.   Other expenses and losses—e.g. interest expense, losses from asset disposals

    b.   Single-Step Income Statement

        i. Revenues

        ii. Expenses

    c. Statement of Owner's Equity

       i. Summarize changes in owner's equity due to

         1. Net income or loss for the year

         2. Owner investments during the year

         3. Owner withdrawals during the year

    d. Classified Balance Sheet

    e. Classification structure

       i. Assets and liabilities split between current and noncurrent

       ii. Current items are expected to be converted to cash or liquidated within one year or the operating cycle, which ever is longer.

       iii. Operating cycle is time from spending cash for goods and services to receiving cash for goods and services.

    f. Classification Categories

       i. Current Assets—Cash, Accounts Receivable, Inventory, Prepaids, Supplies

       ii. Non-current Assets—Property and Equipment, Intangibles, Long-term investments

       iii. Current Liabilities—Accounts Payable, Notes Payable, current portion of Long-term debt, Salaries payable, Accrued liabilities

       iv. Noncurrent Liabilities—Long-term debt

       v. Equity—Capital

III. **Completing the Accounting Cycle**

    a. Closing entries

       i. Close temporary accounts with credit balances to Income Summary

       ii. Close temporary accounts with debit balances to Income Summary

       iii. Close Income Summary to Owner's Capital

       iv. Close Withdrawals to Owner's Capital

    b. Post-closing trial balance

       i. List of permanent accounts and their balances after the closing process

Income Statement Formats

Multiple-step
-Gross profit
-Operating expenses
-Nonoperating items
-Net income

Single-step
- Revenues
- Expenses
- Net income

Classified Balance Sheet

Assets	Liabilities & Equity
Current assets	Current liabilities
Noncurrent assets	Noncurrent liabilities
Long-term investments	Long-term debt
Plant assets	Equity
Intangible assets	

Alternate Demonstration Problem

Presented below is the adjusted trial balance for Ryan's Skateboard Shop as of December 31, 2010. The beginning merchandise inventory balance on January 1, 2010 was $24,617.

Ryan's Skateboard Shop Adjusted Trial Balance 31-Dec-10		
	Debits	Credits
Cash	$ 4,585	
Accounts receivable	12,846	
Merchandise inventory	24,617	
Office supplies	1,250	
Store supplies	842	
Store equipment	13,854	
Accumulated depreciation-Store Eq.		$ 4,866
Accounts payable		2,645
Notes payable		5,000
R. Spuddy, Capital		29,435
R. Spuddy, Withdrawals	1,200	
Income summary	1,867	
Sales		108,252
Sales discounts	3,545	
Sales returns and allowances	2,645	
Purchases	66,848	
Purchases discounts		1,364
Purchases returns and allowances		4,652
Transportation-in	1,684	
Sales Salaries expense	14,864	
Depreciation expense-store equipment	1,646	
Office supplies expense	465	
Interest expense	3,456	
Totals	$ 156,214	$ 156,214

Required:
1. Prepare a multiple-step income statement.
2. Prepare closing journal entries.

Solution:

Income Statement		
For the year ended December 31, 2010		
Revenue:		
Sales	108,252	
Sales discounts	(3,545)	
Sales returns and allowances	(2,645)	
Net Sales		$ 102,062
Cost of goods sold:		
Beginning Inventory	26,464	
Purchases	66,848	
Less: Purchases discounts	(1,364)	
Less: Purchases returns and allowances	(4,652)	
Transportation-in	1,684	
Net purchases	62,516	
Goods available for sale	89,000	
Less: Ending inventory	24,617	
Cost of goods sold		64,383
Gross profit		37,670
Sales salaries expense	14,864	
Depreciation expense-store equipment	1,646	
Office supplies expense	465	
Operating expenses		16,975
Operating income		20,704
Interest expense		(3,456)
Net income		$ 17,248

Ryan's Skateboard Shop					
General Journal					
Date		Account		Debit	Credit
		Closing Entries			
12/31	Sales			108,252	
		Sales returns and allowances			3,545
		Sales discounts			2,645
		Income summary			102,062
12/31	Income summary			62,516	
	Purchases returns and allowances			1,364	
	Purchases discounts			4,652	
		Purchases			66,848
		Transportation-in			1,684
12/31	Income summary			20,431	
		Sales salaries expense			14,864
		Depreciation expense-store equipment			1,646
		Office supplies expense			465
		Interest expense			3,456
12/31	Income summary			17,248	
		R. Spuddy, Capital			17,248
12/31	R. Spuddy, Capital			1,200	
		R. Spuddy, Withdrawals			1,200

Problem I

The following statements are either true or false. Place a (T) in the parentheses before each true statement and an (F) before each false statement.

1. ( ) On an adjusted trial balance, the balance in Income Summary is the difference between the beginning balance of Merchandise Inventory and the ending balance of Merchandise Inventory.
2. ( ) Income Summary is closed to the owner's withdrawals account.
3. ( ) Expenses are closed at the end of the period by debiting the expense accounts.
4. ( ) Revenue is closed at the end of the period by crediting the Income Summary account.
5. ( ) A multi-step income statement shows detailed computations of net sales and expenses and reports subtotals for different classes of items.

Problem II

You are given several words, phrases, or numbers to choose from in completing each of the following statements or in answering the following question. In each case select the one that best completes the statement or answers the question and place its letter in the answer space provided.

_____ 1. Based on the following information, calculate the missing amounts.

Sales..	$28,800	Cost of goods sold...............	?
Beginning inventory	?	Gross profit	$10,800
Purchases....................................	18,000	Expenses	?
Ending inventory	12,600	Net income..........................	3,600

    a. Beginning inventory, $16,200; Cost of goods sold, $12,600; Expenses, $1,800.
    b. Beginning inventory, $23,400; Cost of goods sold, $10,800; Expenses, $7,200.
    c. Beginning inventory, $9,000; Cost of goods sold, $14,400; Expenses, $3,600.
    d. Beginning inventory, $12,600; Cost of goods sold, $18,000; Expenses, $7,200.
    e. Beginning inventory, $19,800; Cost of goods sold, $25,200; Expenses, $14,400.

_____ 2. The following information is taken from a single proprietorship's income statement. Calculate ending inventory for the business.

Sales..	$165,250	Purchase returns.................	$ 390
Sales returns.............................	980	Purchase discounts.............	1,630
Sales discounts.........................	1,960	Transportation-in................	700
Beginning inventory	16,880	Gross profit	58,210
Purchases.................................	108,380	Net income..........................	17,360

    a. $19,840.
    b. 22,080.
    c. $21,160.
    d. 44,250.
    e. Some other amount.

_____ 3.   The four steps necessary to record and post the closing entries of the period include all of the following except:

    a. Close revenue accounts to Income Summary.
    b. Close expense accounts to Income Summary.
    c. Close expense accounts to revenue.
    d. Close Income Summary to the owner's capital account.
    e. Close the withdrawals account to the owner's capital account.

_____ 4.   Each of the following are part of the multi-step income statement except:

    a. Gross profit.
    b. Income summary.
    c. General and administrative expenses.
    d. Net income.
    e. Cost of goods sold.

Problem III

Many of the important ideas and concepts discussed in Chapter 14 are reflected in the following list of key terms. Test your understanding of these terms by matching the appropriate definitions with the terms. Record the number identifying the most appropriate definition in the blank space next to each term.

_____ Classified balance sheet	_____ Multiple-step income statement
_____ Current assets	_____ Operating cycle
_____ Current liabilities	_____ Periodic inventory system
_____ General and administrative expenses	_____ Reversing entries
_____ Intangible assets	_____ Selling expenses
_____ Long-term investments	_____ Single-step income statement
_____ Long-term liabilities	_____ Unclassified balance sheet

1. Assets such as notes receivable or investments in stocks and bonds that are held for more than the longer of one year or the operating cycle.

2. Balance sheet that presents the assets and liabilities in relevant subgroups.

3. Optional entries recorded at the beginning of a new period that prepare the accounts for new journal entries as if adjusting entries hadn't occurred.

4. Balance sheet that broadly groups the assets, liabilities and owner's equity.

5. Long-term assets (resources) used to produce or sell products or services; these assets lack physical form and their benefits are uncertain.

6. Cash or other assets that are expected to be sold, collected, or used within the longer of one year or the company's operating cycle.

7. Obligations due to be paid or settled within the longer of one year or the operating cycle.

8. Obligations that are not due to be paid within the longer of one year or the operating cycle.

9. Normal time between paying cash for merchandise and receiving cash from customers.

10. Method that records the cost of inventory purchased but does not continuously track the quantity available or sold to customers; records are updated at the end of each period to reflect the physical count and costs of goods available.

©The McGraw-Hill Companies, Inc., 2011

11. Income statement format that includes cost of goods sold as an operating expense and shows only one subtotal for total expenses.

12. Expenses of promoting sales such as displaying and advertising merchandise, making sales, and delivering goods to customers.

13. Expenses that support the operating activities of a business.

14. Income statement format that shows subtotals between sales and net income and details of net sales.

Problem IV

Complete the following by filling in the blanks.

1. Revenue accounts have credit balances; consequently, to close a revenue account and make it show a zero balance, the revenue account is _____ and the Income Summary account is _____ for the amount of the balance.

2. In extending the amounts in the Adjusted Trial Balance columns of a work sheet to the proper Income Statement or Statement of Owner's Equity and Balance Sheet columns, two decisions are:
(a)_____and
(b)_____.

3. Expense accounts have debit balances; therefore, expense accounts are_____ and the Income Summary account is _____ in closing the expense accounts.

4. In preparing a work sheet for a business, unadjusted account balances are entered in the _____ of the work sheet form, after which the _____ are entered in the second pair of columns. Next, the unadjusted trial balance amounts and the amounts in the Adjustments columns are combined to secure an _____ in the third pair of columns.

5. Only balance sheet accounts should have balances appearing on the post-closing trial balance because the balances of all temporary accounts are reduced to _____ in the closing procedure.

Problem V

The following amounts appeared on Valentine Variety Store's adjusted trial balance as of December 31, 2010, the end of its fiscal year:

Valentine Variety Store Adjusted Trial Balance 31-Dec-10		
	Debits	Credits
Cash	$ 4,000	
Merchandise inventory	15,000	
Other assets	8,000	
Liabilities		$ 4,000
V. Valentine, Capital		22,300
V. Valentine, Withdrawals	10,000	
Income summary		2,000
Sales		80,000
Sales returns and allowances	600	
Purchases	48,500	
Purchases discounts		900
Purchases returns and allowances		400
Transportation-in	2,500	
General and administrative expenses	8,000	
Selling expenses	13,000	
Totals	$ 109,600	$ 109,600

Required: Using the adjusted trial balance above, prepare a multiple-step income statement for Valentine Variety Store for December 31, 2010. Use the form provided below.

VALENTINE VARIETY STORE

Income Statement

For the Year Ended December 31, 2010

	Revenue:											
	Sales											
	Less: Sales returns and allowances											
	Net sales											
	Cost of goods sold:											
	Merchandise inventory, December 31, 2009											
	Purchases											
	Less: Purchases returns											
	and allowances $_____											
	Purchase discounts _____											
	Net purchases											
	Add: Transportation-in											
	Cost of goods purchased											
	Goods available for sale											
	Merchandise inventory, December 31, 2010											
	Cost of goods sold											
	Gross profit from sales											
	Operating expenses:											
	General and administrative expenses											
	Selling expenses											
	Total operating expenses											
	Net income											

Solutions for Chapter 14

Problem I

1. T
2. F
3. F
4. T
5. T

Problem II

1. D
2. A
3. C
4. B

Problem III

2	Classified balance sheet	14	Multiple-step income statement
6	Current assets	9	Operating cycle
7	Current liabilities	10	Periodic inventory system
13	General and administrative expenses	3	Reversing entries
5	Intangible assets	12	Selling expenses
1	Long-term investments	11	Single-step income statement
8	Long-term liabilities	4	Unclassified balance sheet

Problem IV

1. debited, credited

2. (a) Is the item a debit or a credit?

   (b) On which statement does it appear?

3. credited, debited

4. Unadjusted Trial Balance columns; adjustments; adjusted trial balance

5. zero

6. zero, zero

Problem V

VALENTINE VARIETY STORE
Income Statement
For the Year Ended December 31, 2010

Revenue:				
Sales			$80,000	
Less: Sales returns and allowances			600	
Net sales				$79,400
Cost of goods sold:				
Merchandise inventory, December 31, 2009			$13,000	
Purchases		$48,500		
Less: Purchases returns and allowances	$400			
Purchase discounts	900	1,300		
Net purchases		47,200		
Add: Transportation-in		2,500		
Cost of goods purchased			49,700	
Goods available for sale			62,700	
Merchandise inventory, December 31, 2010			15,000	
Cost of goods sold				47,700
Gross profit from sales				31,700
Operating expenses:				
General and administrative expenses			8,000	
Selling expenses			13,000	
Total operating expenses				21,000
Net income				$10,700

Part Two: Working Papers

Part Two:
Working Papers

(a) and (b)
  GAAP:
  Importance: _____

_____

_____

  SEC:
  Importance: _____

_____

_____

_____

  FASB:
  Importance: _____

_____

_____

  IASB:
  Importance: _____

_____

_____

_____

Quick Study 1-2

(a) _____	**(g)** _____
(b) _____	**(h)** _____
(c) _____	**(i)** _____
(d) _____	**(j)** _____
(e) _____	**(k)** _____
(f) _____	**(l)** _____

Quick Study 1-3

_____

_____

_____

_____

Three Main Areas of Accounting Opportunities

(1) _____

_____

(2) _____

_____

_____

(3) _____

_____

_____

Quick Study 1-5

_____

_____

_____

_____

_____

_____

Field	Salary Estimate
Controller/treasurer	
Private accounting (senior)	
Payroll manager	
Public accounting (manager)	

Quick Study 1-7

(1) Relevant
(2) Reliable
(3) Comparable

Quick Study 1-8

Three Major Legal Forms and Description:

(1) _____

(2) _____

(3) _____

(4) _____

(5) _____

(6) _____

(7) _____

(8) _____

Exercise 1-2

External User:	
External User:	
External User:	

Exercise 1-3

(a) _____

_____

_____

(b) _____

_____

_____

(c) _____

_____

_____

(d) _____

_____

_____

(1) _____

(2) _____

(3) _____

(4) _____

(5) _____

(6) _____

(7) _____

Exercise 1-5

Sole proprietorship, partnership, or corporation?

(a) _____

(b) _____

(c) _____

(d) _____

(e) _____

(f) _____

(g) _____

Exercise 1-6

Full Name of Professional Certifications

(a) CMA _____

(b) CPA _____

(c) CFE _____

(d) CB _____

(e) PFS _____

(f) CIA _____

(g) CPP _____

Chapter 1   **Problem 1-1A or 1-1B**   *Name* _____

(1) _____   (4) _____
(2) _____   (5) _____
(3) _____   (6) _____

Problem 1-2A or 1-2B

(1) _____   (5) _____
(2) _____   (6) _____
(3) _____   (7) _____
(4) _____   (8) _____

(1)

_____
_____
_____

(2)

_____
_____
_____

(3)

_____
_____
_____

(4)

_____
_____
_____

(5)

_____
_____
_____

Three Users of Best Buy Information and How They Would Use Them:

a. _____

_____

b. _____

_____

c. _____

_____

_____

Ethics Challenge—BTN 1-2

(1) Attach IMA Statement to This Page
_____

(2) Four Overarching Principles Underlining IMA's Statement
_____

_____

_____

(3) Actions to Resolve Ethical Conflicts
_____

_____

_____

_____

_____
_____
_____
_____
_____
_____
_____
_____
_____
_____
_____

Taking it to the Net—BTN 1-4

1. Date: _____

2. Titles of the Financial Statements include:

   a. _____

   b. _____

   c. _____

   d. _____

Teamwork in Action—BTN 1-5

Team Member Names	Phone #	Email

1. **External users of LoveSac's financial information would include:**

(1) _____
    _____
    _____
    _____

(2) _____
    _____
    _____
    _____

(3) _____
    _____
    _____

2. **Loan Officer Information**

_____
_____
_____
_____

You Call It—BTN 1-7

_____
_____
_____
_____
_____
_____
_____

	Assets	=	Liabilities	+		Equity
(a)	$700,000		(a)		(a)	$420,000
(b)	$500,000		(b)		(b)	

Quick Study 2-2

	Assets	=		Liabilities	+		Equity
	$75,000		(a)	_____			$40,000
(b)	_____			$25,000			$70,000
	$85,000			$20,000		(c)	_____

Quick Study 2-3

(a)	_____	(d)	_____	(g)	_____
(b)	_____	(e)	_____		
(c)	_____	(f)	_____		

Quick Study 2-4

Assets: _____

Liabilities: _____

Equity: _____

Accounting Equation Verification: _____

(a) _____

_____

(b) _____

_____

Quick Study 2-6

(a) _____

_____

(b) _____

_____

Quick Study 2-7

(a) _____

_____

(b) _____

_____

Quick Study 2-8

(a) _____

_____

(b) _____

_____

	Assets	=	Liabilities	+	Equity
(a)	(a)		$20,000		$45,000
(b)	$100,000		$34,000		(b)
(c)	$154,000		(c)		$40,000

Exercise 2-2

(1) _____

(2) _____

(3) _____

(4) _____

(5) _____

(6) _____

(7) _____

Exercise 2-3

a. _____

b. _____

c. _____

d. _____

e. _____

f. _____

g. _____

Exercise 2-4

	Assets	=	Liabilities	+	Equity
a.					
b.					
c.					

	Assets			Liabilities		Equity			
Cash	+ Accounts Receivable	+ Equipment	=	Accounts Payable	+ Holden, Capital	− Holden, Withdrawals	+ Revenues	− Expenses
(a)								
(b)								
(c)								
(d)								
(e)								
(f)								
(g)								
(h)								
(i)								
(j)								

Exercise 2-6

(a) _____

(b) _____

(c) _____

(d) _____

(e) _____

Income Statement

Exercise 2-8

Statement of Owner's Equity

Balance Sheet

Exercise 2-10

Income Statement

Exercise 2-11

Balance Sheet

Statement of Owner's Equity

Exercise 2-13

Statement of Owner's Equity

	Assets				Liabilities		Equity		
Cash	+	Accounts Receivable	+	Office Supplies	Office Equipment =	Accounts Payable	+	I. Lopez, Capital	
(a)									
(b)									
(c)									
(d)									

1. Net income

_____

_____

2. _____ **Statement of Owner's Equity** _____

===

_____

_____

_____

_____

_____

_____

_____

_____

_____

Balance Sheet

===

_____

_____

_____

_____

_____

_____

_____

_____

_____

Part 1: Company _____

(a) _____

_____

_____

_____

_____

(b) _____

_____

_____

_____

_____

_____

_____

_____

(c) _____

_____

_____

_____

_____

_____

_____

Part 2: Company _____

(a) _____

_____

_____

(b) _____

_____

_____

(c) _____

_____

_____

_____

_____

Part 3: Company _____

_____
_____
_____
_____
_____
_____
_____
_____
_____
_____
_____
_____
_____
_____
_____
_____
_____

Part 4: Company _____

_____
_____
_____
_____
_____
_____
_____
_____
_____
_____
_____
_____
_____
_____
_____
_____
_____

Part 5: Company _____

_____
_____
_____
_____
_____
_____
_____
_____
_____
_____
_____
_____
_____
_____
_____
_____
_____
_____
_____

| | Balance Sheet | | | INCOME Stmt. |
TRANSACTION	TOTAL ASSETS	TOTAL LIABILITIES	TOTAL EQUITY	NET INCOME
1.				
2.				
3.				
4.				
5.				
6.				
7.				

Parts 1 and 2

DATE	ASSETS			=	LIABILITIES +	EQUITY			
	CASH +	ACCOUNTS + RECEIVABLE	EQUIPMENT	=	ACCOUNTS + PAYABLE	Capital	– Withdrawals	+ REVENUES	– EXPENSES

Part 3

Income Statement

Statement of Owner's Equity

Balance Sheet

Name _____

Parts 1 and 2

	ASSETS				= LIABILITIES +	EQUITY			
DATE	CASH +	ACCOUNTS + RECEIVABLE	OFFICE + SUPPLIES	OFFICE EQUIPMENT	= ACCOUNTS + PAYABLE	Capital	– Withdrawals	+ REVENUES	– EXPENSES

Income Statement

Statement of Owner's Equity

Balance Sheet

Serial Problem-SP 2
Success Systems

Name _____

DATE	ASSETS					=	LIABILITIES	+	EQUITY			
	CASH +	ACCOUNTS RECEIVABLE +	COMPUTER SUPPLIES +	COMPUTER EQUIPMENT +	OFFICE EQUIPMENT	=	ACCOUNTS PAYABLE	+	A. Lopez, Capital	− A. Lopez, Withdrawals	+ REVENUES	− EXPENSES
Oct. 1												
3												
Bal.												
6												
Bal.												
8												
Bal.												
12												
Bal.												
15												
Bal.												
17												
Bal.												
20												
Bal.												
22												
Bal.												
28												
Bal.												
31												
Bal.												
31												
Bal.												

(1) Total assets invested _____

_____

_____

(2) Total expense for the year _____

_____

_____

_____

1. a. Accounting for an Expense

	Assets		= Liabilities	+			Equity		
Cash +	Accounts Receivable	+ Equip- ment	= Accounts Payable	+	Holden, Capital	– Holden, With - drawals	+ Revenue	– Expenses

b. Accounting for an Asset

	Assets		= Liabilities	+			Equity		
Cash +	Accounts Receivable	+ Equip- ment	= Accounts Payable	+	Holden, Capital	– Holden, With - drawals	+ Revenue	– Expenses

2.

_____

_____

_____

_____

To: **Sara Blakely**

From: _____

Date: _____

RE: **Financial Statements and SPANX Performance**

Taking It To the Net—BTN 2-4

(in millions)	2007	2006	2005	2004	2003
Revenues					
Net income					

1. _____

_____

_____

_____

_____

_____

2. _____

_____

_____

_____

Chapter 2   Teamwork in Action—BTN 2-5

Name _____

Grid

Trans #	CASH	+	ASSETS +	+	=	LIABILITIES +	+	=	EQUITY +	+	+ ,	, −	−
1													
2													
3													
4													
5													
6													
7													
8													
9													
10													

_____

_____

_____

_____

_____

_____

_____

_____

You Call It—BTN 2-7

_____

_____

_____

_____

_____

_____

_____

(a) _____   (f) _____
(b) _____   (g) _____
(c) _____   (h) _____
(d) _____   (i) _____
(e) _____

Quick Study 3-2

(a) _____   (g) _____
(b) _____   (h) _____
(c) _____   (i) _____
(d) _____   (j) _____
(e) _____   (k) _____
(f) _____   (l) _____

Quick Study 3-3

(a) _____   (f) _____
(b) _____   (g) _____
(c) _____   (h) _____
(d) _____   (i) _____
(e) _____   (j) _____

Quick Study 3-4

(a) _____   (f) _____
(b) _____   (g) _____
(c) _____   (h) _____
(d) _____   (i) _____
(e) _____

Quick Study 3-6

a.	
b.	
c.	
d.	
e.	
f.	
g.	
h.	
i.	
j.	

Quick Study 3-8

Cash	
40,000	15,000
7,800	6,200
1,000	

Name _____

ACCOUNT	TYPE OF ACCOUNT	INCREASE (Dr. or Cr.)	NORMAL BALANCE
a.			
b.			
c.			
d.			
e.			
f.			
g.			
h.			
i.			
j.			
k.			
l.			

Cash	Accounts Payable

A. Amena, Capital

Accounts Receivable	A. Amena, Withdrawals

Office Supplies	Fees Earned

Office Equipment	Rent Expense

Exercise 3-3

_____

	Trial Balance	

GENERAL JOURNAL

Date		Account Titles and Explanation	PR	Debit	Credit

Transactions not creating revenues and the reasons:

_____
_____
_____
_____
_____
_____
_____
_____
_____
_____
_____
_____
_____
_____
_____
_____

GENERAL JOURNAL

Date	Account Titles and Explanation	PR	Debit	Credit

Transactions not creating expenses and the reasons: _____

_____

_____

_____

_____

_____

_____

_____

_____

_____

_____

_____

_____

_____

_____

_____

	(a)	(b)	(c)	(d)

Exercise 3-7

(a) _____

(b) _____

(c) _____

(d) _____

(e) _____

(f) _____

(g) _____

BELLE COMPANY
Balance Sheet
December 31, _____

Assets			Liabilities		
Cash..............................	$ _____		Accounts payable...............	$ _____	
Office supplies...............	_____				
Prepaid Insurance..........	_____				
Equipment.....................	_____		**Equity**		
Automobiles..................	_____		Capital, D. Belle.................		
Total Assets....................	$ _____		Total Liabilities and Equity...	$ _____	

BELLE COMPANY
Statement of Owner's Equity
For Year Ended December 31, _____

Statement of Owner's Equity

Balance Sheet

Exercise 3-10

Income Statement

Income Statement

_____

_____

_____

_____

_____

_____

_____

_____

_____

_____

_____

_____

Exercise 3-12

Statement of Owner's Equity

_____

_____

_____

_____

_____

_____

_____

_____

(a) _____

(b) _____

(c) _____

(d) _____

Exercise 3-14

	(a)	(b)	(c)	(d)

Part 1

Cash	Accounts Payable

Accounts Receivable	_____, Capital

Prepaid Rent	_____, Withdrawals

Prepaid Insurance	Services Revenue

Office Supplies	Utilities Expense

Office Equipment

Part 2

Trial Balance

Part 1

Cash	

Accounts Payable	

Accounts Receivable	

_____, Capital	

Prepaid Rent	

_____, Withdrawals	

Prepaid Insurance	

Services Revenue	

Office Supplies	

Utilities Expense	

Office Equipment	

Part 2

_____

Trial Balance

_____

Part 3

Income Statement

Part 4

Statement of Owner's Equity

Part 5

Balance Sheet

Part 1

Income Statement

_____

Part 2

Statement of Owner's Equity

_____

Part 3

Balance Sheet

_____

Part 1

Cash

Accounts Payable

_____, Capital

Accounts Receivable

_____, Withdrawals

Computer Supplies

Computer Services Revenue

Prepaid Insurance

Wages Expense

Prepaid Rent

Part 2

Office Equipment

Computer Equipment

Mileage Expense

Miscellaneous Expense

Repairs Expense-Computer

Advertising Expense

Trial Balance

(1) _____
_____

(2) _____
_____
_____

Ethics Challenge—BTN 3-2

(1) _____
_____

(2) _____
_____

(3) _____
_____

(4) _____
_____
_____

MEMORANDUM

TO:

FROM:

SUBJECT:

DATE:

(1) _____

_____

_____

_____

_____

_____

(2) _____

_____

_____

_____

_____

_____

Name _____

(1) **Component selected:** _____

_____

(2) **(a)** _____

_____

     (b) _____

_____

     (c) _____

_____

     (d) _____

_____

     (e) _____

_____

(3) **Presentation Notes:** _____

_____

_____

_____

_____

_____

1.

CAKE LOVE
Balance Sheet
December 31,2010

Assets			Liabilities		
Cash.….….…......................	$ _____		Accounts payable.…..……...	$ _____	
Accounts receivable.…..…	_____		Unearned revenues.…..…….	_____	
Prepaid insurance.….….….	_____		Total liabilities.…..…..……..	_____	
Prepaid rent.…...…......……	_____				
Store supplies.…......……..	_____		**Equity**		
Equipment.…..…....……..….	_____		Total equity.…...…..…….…..	_____	
Total Assets.…..……........	$ _____		Total liabilities and equity…	$ _____	

2.

_____
_____
_____
_____
_____
_____
_____
_____
_____
_____
_____

Likely source documents are: _____

_____

_____

_____

_____

Quick Study 4-2

GENERAL JOURNAL

Date	Account Titles and Explanation	PR	Debit	Credit

GENERAL JOURNAL

Date		Account Titles and Explanation	PR	Debit	Credit

Quick Study 4-5

_____
_____
_____
_____
_____
_____
_____
_____
_____

GENERAL JOURNAL

Date	Account Titles and Explanation	PR	Debit	Credit

Quick Study 4-7

GENERAL JOURNAL

Date	Account Titles and Explanation	PR	Debit	Credit

GENERAL LEDGER

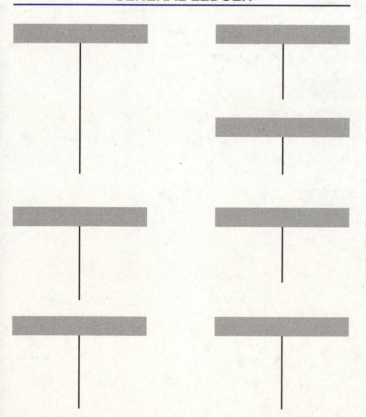

GENERAL JOURNAL

Date	Account Titles and Explanation	PR	Debit	Credit

GENERAL LEDGER

GENERAL JOURNAL

Date	Account Titles and Explanation	PR	Debit	Credit

GENERAL JOURNAL

Date		Account Titles and Explanation	PR	Debit	Credit

Cash		Photography Equipment

		M. Harris, Capital

		Photography Fees Earned

Office Supplies		Utilities Expense

Prepaid Insurance		

Trial Balance

Chapter 4 Exercise 4-3 *Name* ____________________

Income Statement

Exercise 4-4

Statement of Owner's Equity

Balance Sheet

GENERAL JOURNAL

Date	Account Titles and Explanation	PR	Debit	Credit
(a)				
(b)				
(c)				
(d)				
(e)				
(f)				
(g)				

Working Papers 70

GENERAL JOURNAL

Date	Account Titles and Explanation	PR	Debit	Credit

Income Statement

Exercise 4-9

Statement of Owner's Equity

Exercise 4-10

a.
b.
c.
d.
e.
f.

GENERAL JOURNAL

Date	Account Titles and Explanation	PR	Debit	Credit

Income Statement

Exercise 4-13

Statement of Owner's Equity

Part 1

GENERAL JOURNAL

Date	Account Titles and Explanation	PR	Debit	Credit

GENERAL JOURNAL

Date	Account Titles and Explanation	PR	Debit	Credit

Part 2

Cash   No. 101

DATE	PR	Debit	Credit	Balance

Accounts Payable   No. 201

DATE	PR	Debit	Credit	Balance

Notes Payable   No. 250

DATE	PR	Debit	Credit	Balance

_____, Capital   No. 301

DATE	PR	Debit	Credit	Balance

Accounts Receivable   No. 106

DATE	PR	Debit	Credit	Balance

_____, Withdrawals   No. 302

DATE	PR	Debit	Credit	Balance

Prepaid Insurance   No. 108

DATE	PR	Debit	Credit	Balance

_____Fees Earned   No. 402

DATE	PR	Debit	Credit	Balance

Office Equipment   No. 163

DATE	PR	Debit	Credit	Balance

Wages Expense   No. 601

DATE	PR	Debit	Credit	Balance

_____Equipment   No. 164

DATE	PR	Debit	Credit	Balance

_____Rental Expense   No. 602

DATE	PR	Debit	Credit	Balance

Building   No. 170

DATE	PR	Debit	Credit	Balance

Advertising Expense   No. 603

DATE	PR	Debit	Credit	Balance

Land   No. 172

DATE	PR	Debit	Credit	Balance

Repairs Expense   No. 604

DATE	PR	Debit	Credit	Balance

Part 3

Trial Balance

GENERAL JOURNAL

Date		Account Titles and Explanation	PR	Debit	Credit

Date	Account Titles and Explanation	PR	Debit	Credit

GENERAL LEDGER

Cash   ACCOUNT NO. 101

Date	Explanation	PR	DEBIT	CREDIT	BALANCE

Accounts Receivable   ACCOUNT NO. 106

Date	Explanation	PR	DEBIT	CREDIT	BALANCE

Office Supplies   ACCOUNT NO. 124

Date	Explanation	PR	DEBIT	CREDIT	BALANCE

Prepaid Insurance   ACCOUNT NO. 128

Date	Explanation	PR	DEBIT	CREDIT	BALANCE

Prepaid Rent   ACCOUNT NO. 131

Date	Explanation	PR	DEBIT	CREDIT	BALANCE

Office Equipment   ACCOUNT NO. 163

Date	Explanation	PR	DEBIT	CREDIT	BALANCE

Accounts Payable   ACCOUNT NO. 201

Date	Explanation	PR	DEBIT	CREDIT	BALANCE

_____, Capital   ACCOUNT NO. 301

Date	Explanation	PR	DEBIT	CREDIT	BALANCE

_____, Withdrawals   ACCOUNT NO. 302

Date	Explanation	PR	DEBIT	CREDIT	BALANCE

Services Revenue   ACCOUNT NO. 403

Date	Explanation	PR	DEBIT	CREDIT	BALANCE

Utilities Expense   ACCOUNT NO. 690

Date	Explanation	PR	DEBIT	CREDIT	BALANCE

Part 3

_____

_____

Trial Balance

_____

_____

1. _____

Income Statement

2. _____

Statement of Owner's Equity

Balance Sheet

GENERAL JOURNAL

Date	Account Titles and Explanation	PR	Debit	Credit

GENERAL JOURNAL

Date	Account Titles and Explanation	PR	Debit	Credit

Date	Account Titles and Explanation	PR	Debit	Credit

Date	Account Titles and Explanation	PR	Debit	Credit

Part 2

GENERAL LEDGER

Cash   ACCOUNT NO. 101

Date	Explanation	PR	DEBIT	CREDIT	BALANCE

Accounts Receivable   ACCOUNT NO. 106

Date	Explanation	PR	DEBIT	CREDIT	BALANCE

Computer Supplies   ACCOUNT NO. 126

Date	Explanation	PR	DEBIT	CREDIT	BALANCE

Prepaid Insurance   ACCOUNT NO. 128

Date	Explanation	PR	DEBIT	CREDIT	BALANCE

Prepaid Rent   ACCOUNT NO. 131

Date	Explanation	PR	DEBIT	CREDIT	BALANCE

Office Equipment   ACCOUNT NO. 163

Date	Explanation	PR	DEBIT	CREDIT	BALANCE

Computer Equipment   ACCOUNT NO. 167

Date	Explanation	PR	DEBIT	CREDIT	BALANCE

Accounts Payable   ACCOUNT NO. 201

Date	Explanation	PR	DEBIT	CREDIT	BALANCE

A. Lopez, Capital   ACCOUNT NO. 301

Date	Explanation	PR	DEBIT	CREDIT	BALANCE

A. Lopez, Withdrawals   ACCOUNT NO. 302

Date	Explanation	PR	DEBIT	CREDIT	BALANCE

Computer Services Revenue   ACCOUNT NO. 403

Date	Explanation	PR	DEBIT	CREDIT	BALANCE

Wages Expense — ACCOUNT NO. 623

Date	Explanation	PR	DEBIT	CREDIT	BALANCE

Advertising Expense — ACCOUNT NO. 655

Date	Explanation	PR	DEBIT	CREDIT	BALANCE

Mileage Expense — ACCOUNT NO. 676

Date	Explanation	PR	DEBIT	CREDIT	BALANCE

Miscellaneous Expense — ACCOUNT NO. 677

Date	Explanation	PR	DEBIT	CREDIT	BALANCE

Repairs Expense-Computer — ACCOUNT NO. 684

Date	Explanation	PR	DEBIT	CREDIT	BALANCE

Part 3

Trial Balance

(1) _____

_____

(2) _____

_____

(3) _____

_____

_____

(4) _____

_____

_____

Ethics Challenge—BTN 4-2

_____

_____

_____

_____

_____

_____

_____

_____

_____

_____

_____

TO: Mark Ellingson
FROM: _____
SUBJECT: _____
DATE: _____

_____
_____
_____
_____
_____
_____
_____
_____
_____
_____
_____
_____
_____
_____

(1) _____
_____
_____
_____
_____
_____

(2) _____
_____
_____
_____
_____

Entrepreneurs in Business—BTN 4-5

_____
_____
_____
_____
_____
_____
_____
_____
_____
_____

Accrual Basis   **Cash Basis**

_____
_____
_____
_____
_____
_____
_____
_____

Quick Study 5-2

_____
_____
_____

Quick Study 5-3

Account debited   **Account credited**

_____
a. _____
b. _____
c. _____
_____

GENERAL JOURNAL

Date	Account Titles and Explanation	PR	Debit	Credit
(a)				
(b)				

Quick Study 5-5

GENERAL JOURNAL

Date	Account Titles and Explanation	PR	Debit	Credit
(a)				

(b)   Book value: _____

Quick Study 5-6

GENERAL JOURNAL

Date	Account Titles and Explanation	PR	Debit	Credit

Explanation:
_____
_____
_____
_____
_____
_____
_____
_____
_____
_____
_____
_____
_____

Quick Study 5-8

1. _____
2. _____
3. _____

Chapter 5   Exercise 5-1   Name _____

| | Prepaid Insurance Asset Using | | Insurance Expense Using | |
	Accrual Basis	Cash Basis	Accrual Basis	Cash Basis
Dec. 31, 2009				
Dec. 31, 2010				
Dec. 31, 2011				
Dec. 31, 2012				
Total (Expense)				

GENERAL JOURNAL

Date	Account Titles and Explanation	PR	Debit	Credit
(a)				
(b)				
(c)				
(d)				
(e)				

Notes: _____

_____

_____

GENERAL JOURNAL

Date	Account Titles and Explanation	PR	Debit	Credit
(a)				
(b)				
(c)				
(d)				

Notes: _____

_____

_____

_____

GENERAL JOURNAL

Date	Account Titles and Explanation	PR	Debit	Credit
Adjusting Entry:				
Payday Entry:				

Exercise 5-5

	a.	b.	c.	d.

Exercise 5-6

GENERAL JOURNAL

Date	Account Titles and Explanation	PR	Debit	Credit
Adjusting Entry:				
Payday Entry:				

GENERAL JOURNAL

Date		Account Titles and Explanation	PR	Debit	Credit

Exercise 5-8

GENERAL JOURNAL

Date		Account Titles and Explanation	PR	Debit	Credit

Parts 1-4

Work Sheet (partial)
For Year Ended December 31, 2010

ACCOUNT TITLE	Unadjusted Trial Balance		Adjustments		Adjusted Trial Balance	
	Dr.	Cr.	Dr.	Cr.	Dr.	Cr.

Part 5

_____

Income Statement

_____
_____
_____
_____
_____
_____
_____
_____
_____
_____
_____
_____
_____
_____
_____
_____
_____
_____
_____
_____

Statement of Owner's Equity

_____
_____
_____
_____
_____
_____
_____

Balance Sheet

Income Statement

Statement of Owner's Equity

Balance Sheet

Part 1

Journal Entries

GENERAL JOURNAL

Date	Account Titles and Explanation	PR	Debit	Credit

Part 2

Adjusting Entries

GENERAL JOURNAL

Date	Account Titles and Explanation	PR	Debit	Credit

Part 1 & 2

GENERAL LEDGER

Cash   ACCOUNT NO. 101

Date	Explanation	PR	DEBIT	CREDIT	BALANCE
2010 Nov. 30	Balance				68,996

Accounts Receivable   ACCOUNT NO. 106

Date	Explanation	PR	DEBIT	CREDIT	BALANCE
2010 Nov. 30	Balance				15,800

Computer Supplies   ACCOUNT NO. 126

Date	Explanation	PR	DEBIT	CREDIT	BALANCE
2010 Nov. 30	Balance				3,350

Prepaid Insurance   ACCOUNT NO. 128

Date	Explanation	PR	DEBIT	CREDIT	BALANCE
2010 Nov. 30	Balance				2,400

Prepaid Rent   ACCOUNT NO. 131

Date	Explanation	PR	DEBIT	CREDIT	BALANCE
2010 Nov. 30	Balance				3,500

Office Equipment   ACCOUNT NO. 163

Date	Explanation	PR	DEBIT	CREDIT	BALANCE
2010 Nov. 30	Balance				10,000

Accumulated Depreciation—Office Equipment   ACCOUNT NO. 164

Date	Explanation	PR	DEBIT	CREDIT	BALANCE

Computer Equipment   ACCOUNT NO. 167

Date	Explanation	PR	DEBIT	CREDIT	BALANCE
2010 Nov. 30	Balance				25,000

Accumulated Depreciation—Computer Equipment   ACCOUNT NO. 168

Date	Explanation	PR	DEBIT	CREDIT	BALANCE
2010 Nov. 30					0

Accounts Payable   ACCOUNT NO. 201

Date	Explanation	PR	DEBIT	CREDIT	BALANCE
2010 Nov. 30	Balance				0

Wages Payable   ACCOUNT NO. 210

Date	Explanation	PR	DEBIT	CREDIT	BALANCE

Unearned Computer Services Revenue   ACCOUNT NO. 236

Date	Explanation	PR	DEBIT	CREDIT	BALANCE

A. Lopez, Capital   ACCOUNT NO. 301

Date	Explanation	PR	DEBIT	CREDIT	BALANCE
2010 Nov. 30	Balance				110,000

A. Lopez, Withdrawals — ACCOUNT NO. 302

Date	Explanation	PR	DEBIT	CREDIT	BALANCE
2010 Nov. 30	Balance				6,500

Computer Services Revenue — ACCOUNT NO. 403

Date	Explanation	PR	DEBIT	CREDIT	BALANCE
2010 Nov. 30	Balance				32,550

Depreciation Expense—Office Equipment — ACCOUNT NO. 612

Date	Explanation	PR	DEBIT	CREDIT	BALANCE

Depreciation Expense—Computer Equipment — ACCOUNT NO. 613

Date	Explanation	PR	DEBIT	CREDIT	BALANCE

Wages Expense — ACCOUNT NO. 623

Date	Explanation	PR	DEBIT	CREDIT	BALANCE
2010 Nov. 30	Balance				3,150

Insurance Expense — ACCOUNT NO. 637

Date	Explanation	PR	DEBIT	CREDIT	BALANCE

Rent Expense — ACCOUNT NO. 640

Date	Explanation	PR	DEBIT	CREDIT	BALANCE

Computer Supplies Expense — ACCOUNT NO. 652

Date	Explanation	PR	DEBIT	CREDIT	BALANCE

Advertising Expense — ACCOUNT NO. 655

Date	Explanation	PR	DEBIT	CREDIT	BALANCE
2010 Nov. 30	Balance				1,790

Mileage Expense — ACCOUNT NO. 676

Date	Explanation	PR	DEBIT	CREDIT	BALANCE
2010 Nov. 30	Balance				864

Parts 1 & 2   (Continued)

Miscellaneous Expense   ACCOUNT NO. 677

Date	Explanation	PR	DEBIT	CREDIT	BALANCE
2010 Nov. 30	Balance				300

Repairs Expense—Computer   ACCOUNT NO. 684

Date	Explanation	PR	DEBIT	CREDIT	BALANCE
2010 Nov. 30	Balance				900

Income Summary   ACCOUNT NO. 901

Date	Explanation	PR	DEBIT	CREDIT	BALANCE

Part 3

SUCCESS SYSTEMS

Adjusted Trial Balance

December 31, 2010

	Debit	Credit

Part 4

SUCCESS SYSTEMS
Income Statement
For Three Months Ended December 31, 2010

Part 5

SUCCESS SYSTEMS
Statement of Owner's Equity
For Three Months Ended December 31, 2010

Part 6

SUCCESS SYSTEMS
Balance Sheet
December 31, 2010

1. Revenue recognition from the chapter: _____

_____

_____

_____

2. Best Buy's application of the revenue recognition principle: _____

_____

_____

_____

_____

_____

_____

_____

_____

Ethics Challenge—BTN 5-2

_____

_____

_____

_____

_____

_____

_____

Taking It to the Net—BTN 5-3

1. _____

2. _____

3. _____

4. _____

(1) _____

_____

_____

_____

(2) _____

_____

_____

_____

_____

You Call It—BTN 5-6

_____

_____

_____

_____

_____

_____

_____

_____

_____

_____
_____
_____
_____
_____
_____
_____
_____
_____

Quick Study 6-2

Steps

1st	
2nd	
3rd	
4th	
5th	
6th	
7th	
8th	
9th	

Quick Study 6-3

_____
_____
_____
_____
_____
_____
_____

Chapter 6   **Quick Study 6-4**   *Name* _____

(a) _____   (d) _____
(b) _____   (e) _____
(c) _____   (f) _____

Quick Study 6-5

(a) _____   (d) _____
(b) _____   (e) _____
(c) _____

_____ Company

Work Sheet

ACCOUNT TITLE	Unadjusted Trial Balance		Adjustments		Adjusted Trial Balance		Income Statement		Balance Sheet and Statement of Owner's Equity	
	Dr.	Cr.	Dr.	Cr.	Dr.	Cr.	Dr.	Cr.	Dr.	Cr.
Prepaid rent										
Wages expense										
Wages payable										
Rent expense										

GENERAL JOURNAL

Date		Account Titles and Explanation	PR	Debit	Credit

Quick Study 6-8

_____

_____

_____

_____

Closing Entries:

GENERAL JOURNAL

Date	Account Titles and Explanation	PR	Debit	Credit

Working Papers 129

Posted accounts:

M.Muncel, Capital   No. 301

DATE	PR	Debit	Credit	Balance
Dec. 31				40,000

M. Muncel, Withdrawals   No. 302

DATE	PR	Debit	Credit	Balance
Dec. 31				22,000

Services Revenue   No. 401

DATE	PR	Debit	Credit	Balance
Dec. 31				76,000

Depreciation Expense   No. 603

DATE	PR	Debit	Credit	Balance
Dec. 31				15,000

Salaries Expense   No. 622

DATE	PR	Debit	Credit	Balance
Dec. 31				2,0000

Insurance Expense   No. 637

DATE	PR	Debit	Credit	Balance
Dec. 31				4,400

Rent Expense   No. 640

DATE	PR	Debit	Credit	Balance
Dec. 31				8,400

Income Summary   No. 901

DATE	PR	Debit	Credit	Balance

NO.	ACCOUNT TITLE	ADJUSTED TRIAL BALANCE		CLOSING ENTRY INFORMATION		POST-CLOSING TRIAL BALANCE	
		DR	CR	DR	CR	DR	CR

1. Closing

GENERAL JOURNAL

Date		Account Titles and Explanation	PR	Debit	Credit

2. Post-closing Trial Balance

Post-Closing Trial Balance

Income Statement

Statement of Owner's Equity

Balance Sheet

(1)	(5)	(9)	(13)
(2)	(6)	(10)	(14)
(3)	(7)	(11)	
(4)	(8)	(12)	

NO.	ACCOUNT TITLE	ADJUSTED TRIAL BALANCE		INCOME STATEMENT		BALANCE SHEET & STATEMENT OF OWNER'S EQUITY	
		DR	CR	DR	CR	DR	CR

Account Title	Debit	Credit
Rent earned		
Salaries expense		
Insurance expense		
Office Supplies expense		
Bike Repair expense		
Depreciation expense—Bikes		
Totals		
Net Income		
Totals		

GENERAL JOURNAL

Date	Account Titles and Explanation	PR	Debit	Credit

Dylan Delivery Company
Work Sheet
For Year Ended December 31, _____

ACCOUNT TITLE	Unadjusted Trial Balance		Adjustments		Adjusted Trial Balance		Income Statement		Balance Sheet and Statement of Owner's Equity	
	Dr.	Cr.	Dr.	Cr.	Dr.	Cr.	Dr.	Cr.	Dr.	Cr.

Name _____

2. Closing Entries

GENERAL JOURNAL

Date	Account Titles and Explanation	PR	Debit	Credit

Capital on the Balance Sheet: _____

_____

_____

_____

_____

Part 1

_____

Income Statement

_____

Statement of Owner's Equity

Balance Sheet

		Work Sheet					
NO.	ACCOUNT TITLES	ADJUSTED TRIAL BALANCE		CLOSING ENTRY INFORMATION		POST-CLOSING TRIAL BALANCE	
		DR	CR	DR	CR	DR	CR

Part 3

Closing Entries:

GENERAL JOURNAL

Date		Account Titles and Explanation	PR	Debit	Credit

Work Sheet

NO.	Account Title	Unadjusted Trial Balance		Adjustments		Adjusted Trial Balance		Income Statement		Balance Sheet and Statement of Owner's Equity	
		Dr.	Cr.	Dr.	Cr.	Dr.	Cr.	Dr.	Cr.	Dr.	Cr.

Part 5

Closing Entries:

GENERAL JOURNAL

Date	Account Titles and Explanation	PR	Debit	Credit

Income Statement

Statement of Owner's Equity

Balance Sheet

GENERAL LEDGER

Cash — ACCOUNT NO. 101

DATE	EXPLANATION	PR	DEBIT	CREDIT	BALANCE

Accounts Receivable — ACCOUNT NO. 106

DATE	EXPLANATION	PR	DEBIT	CREDIT	BALANCE

Office Supplies — ACCOUNT NO. 124

DATE	EXPLANATION	PR	DEBIT	CREDIT	BALANCE

Prepaid Insurance — ACCOUNT NO. 128

DATE	EXPLANATION	PR	DEBIT	CREDIT	BALANCE

Computer Equipment*   ACCOUNT NO. 167

DATE	EXPLANATION	PR	DEBIT	CREDIT	BALANCE

Accumulated Depreciation-Computer Equipment*   ACCOUNT NO. 168

DATE	EXPLANATION	PR	DEBIT	CREDIT	BALANCE

Buildings**   ACCOUNT NO. 173

DATE	EXPLANATION	PR	DEBIT	CREDIT	BALANCE

Accumulated Depreciation-Buildings**   ACCOUNT NO. 174

DATE	EXPLANATION	PR	DEBIT	CREDIT	BALANCE

Salaries Payable   ACCOUNT NO. 209

DATE	EXPLANATION	PR	DEBIT	CREDIT	BALANCE

_____, Capital   ACCOUNT NO. 301

DATE	EXPLANATION	PR	DEBIT	CREDIT	BALANCE

_____, Withdrawals   ACCOUNT NO. 302

DATE	EXPLANATION	PR	DEBIT	CREDIT	BALANCE

Storage Fees Earned**   ACCOUNT NO. 401

DATE	EXPLANATION	PR	DEBIT	CREDIT	BALANCE

Commissions Earned*   ACCOUNT NO. 405

DATE	EXPLANATION	PR	DEBIT	CREDIT	BALANCE

Depreciation Expense—Buildings**   ACCOUNT NO. 606

DATE	EXPLANATION	PR	DEBIT	CREDIT	BALANCE

Depreciation Expense-Computer Equipment*   ACCOUNT NO. 612

DATE	EXPLANATION	PR	DEBIT	CREDIT	BALANCE

Salaries Expense   ACCOUNT NO. 622

DATE	EXPLANATION	PR	DEBIT	CREDIT	BALANCE

Insurance Expense   ACCOUNT NO. 637

DATE	EXPLANATION	PR	DEBIT	CREDIT	BALANCE

Rent Expense   ACCOUNT NO. 640

DATE	EXPLANATION	PR	DEBIT	CREDIT	BALANCE

Office Supplies Expense   ACCOUNT NO. 650

DATE	EXPLANATION	PR	DEBIT	CREDIT	BALANCE

Repairs Expense   ACCOUNT NO. 684

DATE	EXPLANATION	PR	DEBIT	CREDIT	BALANCE

Telephone Expense   ACCOUNT NO. 688

DATE	EXPLANATION	PR	DEBIT	CREDIT	BALANCE

Income Summary					ACCOUNT NO. 901
DATE	EXPLANATION	PR	DEBIT	CREDIT	BALANCE

GENERAL JOURNAL

Date	Account Titles and Explanation	PR	Debit	Credit

Unadjusted Trial Balance

Part 4

GENERAL JOURNAL

Date	Account Titles and Explanation	PR	Debit	Credit

Part 5

Income Statement

Statement of Owner's Equity

Balance Sheet

Part 6

Closing Entries:

GENERAL JOURNAL

Date		Account Titles and Explanation	PR	Debit	Credit

Part 7

Post-Closing Trial Balance

Part 1

Closing Entries:

GENERAL JOURNAL

Date	Account Titles and Explanation	PR	Debit	Credit

GENERAL LEDGER

Cash   ACCOUNT NO. 101

Date	Explanation	PR	DEBIT	CREDIT	BALANCE
2010 Dec. 31	Balance				80,260

Accounts Receivable   ACCOUNT NO. 106

Date	Explanation	PR	DEBIT	CREDIT	BALANCE
2010 Dec. 31	Balance				5,800

Computer Supplies   ACCOUNT NO. 126

Date	Explanation	PR	DEBIT	CREDIT	BALANCE
2010 Dec. 31	Balance				775

Prepaid Insurance   ACCOUNT NO. 128

Date	Explanation	PR	DEBIT	CREDIT	BALANCE
2010 Dec. 31	Balance				1,800

Prepaid Rent   ACCOUNT NO. 131

Date	Explanation	PR	DEBIT	CREDIT	BALANCE
2010 Dec. 31	Balance				875

Part 1   (Continued)

Office Equipment — ACCOUNT NO. 163

Date	Explanation	PR	DEBIT	CREDIT	BALANCE
2010 Dec. 31	Balance				10,000

Accumulated Depreciation - Office Equipment — ACCOUNT NO. 164

Date	Explanation	PR	DEBIT	CREDIT	BALANCE
2010 Dec. 31	Balance				625

Computer Equipment — ACCOUNT NO. 167

Date	Explanation	PR	DEBIT	CREDIT	BALANCE
2010 Dec. 31	Balance				25,000

Accumulated Depreciation - Computer Equipment — ACCOUNT NO. 168

Date	Explanation	PR	DEBIT	CREDIT	BALANCE
2010 Dec. 31	Balance				1,250

Accounts Payable — ACCOUNT NO. 201

Date	Explanation	PR	DEBIT	CREDIT	BALANCE
2010 Dec. 31	Balance				2,100

Wages Payable — ACCOUNT NO. 210

Date	Explanation	PR	DEBIT	CREDIT	BALANCE
2010 Dec. 31	Balance				600

Part 1   (Continued)

Unearned Computer Services Revenue   ACCOUNT NO. 236

Date	Explanation	PR	DEBIT	CREDIT	BALANCE
2010					
Dec. 31	Balance				2,500

A. Lopez, Capital   ACCOUNT NO. 301

Date	Explanation	PR	DEBIT	CREDIT	BALANCE
2010					
Dec. 31	Balance				117,435

A. Lopez Withdrawals   ACCOUNT NO. 302

Date	Explanation	PR	DEBIT	CREDIT	BALANCE
2010					
Dec. 31	Balance				8,500

Computer Service Revenue   ACCOUNT NO. 403

Date	Explanation	PR	DEBIT	CREDIT	BALANCE
2010					
Dec. 31	Balance				36,170

Depreciation Expense-Office Equipment   ACCOUNT NO. 612

Date	Explanation	PR	DEBIT	CREDIT	BALANCE
2010					
Dec. 31	Balance				625

Depreciation Expense-Computer Equipment   ACCOUNT NO. 613

Date	Explanation	PR	DEBIT	CREDIT	BALANCE
2010					
Dec. 31	Balance				1,250

Wages Expense — ACCOUNT NO. 623

Date	Explanation	PR	DEBIT	CREDIT	BALANCE
2010 Dec. 31	Balance				4,650

Insurance Expense — ACCOUNT NO. 637

Date	Explanation	PR	DEBIT	CREDIT	BALANCE
2010 Dec. 31	Balance				600

Rent Expense — ACCOUNT NO. 640

Date	Explanation	PR	DEBIT	CREDIT	BALANCE
2010 Dec. 31	Balance				2,625

Computer Supplies Expense — ACCOUNT NO. 652

Date	Explanation	PR	DEBIT	CREDIT	BALANCE
2010 Dec. 31	Balance				4,675

Advertising Expense — ACCOUNT NO. 655

Date	Explanation	PR	DEBIT	CREDIT	BALANCE
2010 Dec. 31	Balance				2,990

Mileage Expense — ACCOUNT NO. 676

Date	Explanation	PR	DEBIT	CREDIT	BALANCE
2010 Dec. 31	Balance				1,120

Miscellaneous Expense   ACCOUNT NO. 677

Date	Explanation	PR	DEBIT	CREDIT	BALANCE
2010 Dec. 31	Balance				300

Repairs Expense, Computer   ACCOUNT NO. 684

Date	Explanation	PR	DEBIT	CREDIT	BALANCE
2010 Dec. 31	Balance				1,400

Income Summary   ACCOUNT NO. 901

Date	Explanation	PR	DEBIT	CREDIT	BALANCE

Part 2

SUCCESS SYSTEMS
Post-Closing Trial Balance
December 31, 2010

	Debit	Credit

(1) _____

_____

(2) _____

_____

Ethics Challenge—BTN 6-2

(1) _____

_____

_____

_____

_____

_____

_____

_____

_____

_____

_____

_____

_____

(2) _____

_____

_____

_____

_____

_____

_____

_____

_____

_____

MEMORANDUM

TO:

FROM:

SUBJECT:

DATE:

(1) _____
_____
_____
_____
_____
_____

(2) _____
_____
_____
_____
_____

(3) _____
_____
_____
_____
_____

1. and 2.

Account Title	Trial Balance		Adjustments		Balance Sheet	
	Debit	Credit	Debit	Credit	Debit	Credit
Cash	$16,000					
Supplies	12,000					
Prepaid insurance	3,000					
Equipment	25,000					
Accum. Deprec-Eq.		$7,000				
Accounts payable		3,000				
D.Noseworthy, Cap.		34,000				
D.Noseworthy, With..	6,000					
Investigation fees		33,000				
Rent expense	15,000					
Totals	$77,000	$77,000				

2. Total assets = _____

   Total liabilities = _____

3. Adjusted balances of

   Investigation fees earned = _____

   Rent expense = _____

4.

GENERAL JOURNAL

Date	Account Titles and Explanation	PR	Debit	Credit
	Closing Entries			

(1) _____
_____
_____
_____
_____
_____
_____

(2) _____
_____
_____
_____
_____
_____
_____
_____

You Call It—BTN 6-7
_____
_____
_____
_____
_____
_____

(1) _____

_____

_____

_____

_____

(2) _____

_____

_____

_____

_____

(3) _____

_____

_____

_____

_____

Quick Study 7-2

(1) _____

_____

_____

_____

_____

(2) _____

_____

_____

_____

_____

(3) _____

_____

_____

_____

(1) _____
(2) _____
(3) _____
_____

Quick Study 7-4^A

_____
_____
_____
_____
_____
_____
_____

Quick Study 7-5

_____
_____
_____
_____
_____
_____
_____
_____
_____

Evaluation: _____

_____

_____

Principles Ignored: _____

_____

_____

_____

_____

Exercise 7-2

(1) _____	(6) _____
(2) _____	(7) _____
(3) _____	(8) _____
(4) _____	(9) _____
(5) _____	(10) _____

Exercise 7-3[A]

(1) _____

_____

_____

(2) _____

_____

(3) _____

_____

Exercise 7-4[A]

(1) _____	(3) _____	(5) _____
(2) _____	(4) _____	(6) _____

(1) Principle Violated:
   Recommended

(2) Principle Violated:
   Recommended

(3) Principle Violated:
   Recommended

(4) Principle Violated:
   Recommended

(5) Principle Violated:
   Recommended

(1) Likely Fraud Type:

    Recommended

(2) Likely Fraud Type:

    Recommended

(3) Likely Fraud Type:

    Recommended

(4) Likely Fraud Type:

    Recommended

(5) Likely Fraud Type:

    Recommended

(1) _____

_____

_____

(2) _____

_____

_____

_____

Ethics Challenge—BTN 7-2

_____

_____

_____

_____

Workplace Communication—BTN 7-3

_____

_____

_____

_____

_____

_____

_____

_____

(1) _____
    _____

(2) _____
    _____

(3) _____
    _____

(4) _____
    _____

(5) _____
    _____

(6) _____
    _____

(7) _____
    _____

(8) _____
    _____

(9) _____
    _____

(10) _____
    _____

(1) _____

(2) _____

(3) _____

(4) _____

(5) _____

(6) _____

(7) _____

(8) _____

(9) _____

(10) _____

(1) (a) _____
_____
_____

    (b) _____
_____
_____

    (c) _____
_____
_____

    (d) _____
_____
_____

    (e) _____
_____
_____

    (f) _____
_____
_____

    (g) _____
_____
_____

(2) _____
_____
_____

(1) _____

_____

_____

_____

_____

(2) _____

_____

_____

_____

_____

Quick Study 8-2

(1) (a) _____

(b) _____

(c) _____

(2) _____

(1)

GENERAL JOURNAL

Date	Account Titles and Explanation	PR	Debit	Credit
(a) Establishment of the Fund:				
(b) Reimbursement of the Fund at Period-End:				

(2) _____

_____

_____

_____

Parts 1 and 2

	(1)	(2)
	Bank or Book Effect	**Add or Subtract**	**Journal Entry Required or Not**
(a)		
(b)		
(c)		
(d)		
(e)		
(f)		
(g)		

Quick Study 8-5

1.

2.

3.

4.

Name _____

Use Exhibit 8.4 as a template for a deposit ticket.
Date of Deposit:

Cash

Check

Total

Currency	
Coin	

Total box:

Quick Study 8-7

Use Exhibit 8.6 as a template for a check.

[_____]   **Date** [_____]

Pay to the order of _____ $_____

_____ **Dollars**

Memo: _____   _____

Evaluation: _____

_____

_____

Principles Ignored: _____

_____

_____

_____

_____

Exercise 8-2

(a) Cash Control Problems: _____

_____

_____

_____

_____

_____

_____

(b) Cash Control Recommendations: _____

_____

_____

_____

_____

Exercise 8-3

(1) _____

_____

_____

_____

_____

_____

(2) _____

_____

_____

_____

_____

_____

(1) Establish the Fund

GENERAL JOURNAL

Date	Account Titles and Explanation	PR	Debit	Credit

(2) Reimburse the Fund

GENERAL JOURNAL

Date	Account Titles and Explanation	PR	Debit	Credit

(3) Reimburse and Increase the Fund

GENERAL JOURNAL

Date	Account Titles and Explanation	PR	Debit	Credit

(1) Establish the Fund

GENERAL JOURNAL

Date	Account Titles and Explanation	PR	Debit	Credit

(2) Reimburse the Fund

GENERAL JOURNAL

Date	Account Titles and Explanation	PR	Debit	Credit

(3) Adjust the Fund Balance

GENERAL JOURNAL

Date	Account Titles and Explanation	PR	Debit	Credit

		Bank Balance		Book Balance		Not Shown on the Reconciliation
		Add	Deduct	Add	Deduct	
1.	NSF check from customer returned on Sept. 25 but not recorded by this company.					
2.	Interest earned on the account.					
3.	Deposit made on September 5 and processed by bank on September 6.					
4.	Check written by another depositor but charged against this company's account.					
5.	Bank service charge.					
6.	Checks outstanding on August 31 that cleared the bank in September.					
8.	Checks written and mailed to payees on October 2.					
9.	Checks written by the company and mailed to payees on September 30.					
10.	Deposit made on September 30 after the bank closed.					

Exercise 8-7

Reconciliation Items Requiring Adjusting Entries	Adjustment to Cash Account
1.	
2.	
3.	
4.	

Bank Reconciliation

Exercise 8-9

GENERAL JOURNAL

Date	Account Titles and Explanation	PR	Debit	Credit

(1) Principle Violated:
   Recommended

(2) Principle Violated:
   Recommended

(3) Principle Violated:
   Recommended

(4) Principle Violated:
   Recommended

(5) Principle Violated:
   Recommended

Part 1

GENERAL JOURNAL

Date		Account Titles and Explanation	PR	Debit	Credit

Part 2

_____

_____

Petty Cash Payments Report

_____

_____

_____

_____

_____

_____

_____

_____

_____

_____

_____

_____

_____

_____

_____

_____

_____

Part 3

GENERAL JOURNAL

Date		Account Titles and Explanation	PR	Debit	Credit

Part 1

GENERAL JOURNAL

Date	Account Titles and Explanation	PR	Debit	Credit

Part 2

_____
_____
_____
_____
_____
_____
_____
_____
_____
_____

Part 1

Bank Reconciliation

Part 2

GENERAL JOURNAL

Date	Account Titles and Explanation	PR	Debit	Credit

Part 3

(a) _____

_____

_____

_____

_____

(b) _____

_____

_____

_____

_____

Problem 8-5A or 8-5B

Part 1

_____

_____

Bank Reconciliation

_____

_____

_____

_____

_____

_____

_____

_____

_____

_____

_____

_____

_____

Part 2

GENERAL JOURNAL

Date	Account Titles and Explanation	PR	Debit	Credit

Part 3

(1) _____
_____

(2) _____
_____

(3) _____
_____

(4) _____
_____
_____

Part 1

Bank Reconciliation

Part 2

GENERAL JOURNAL

Date	Account Titles and Explanation	PR	Debit	Credit

Part 1

Account	March 1, 2008		March 3, 2007	
	Balance($)	Cash & Equiv. as % of Balance	Balance($)	Cash & Equiv. as % of Balance

Interpretation:

Part 2

(1) _____
_____
_____
_____

(2) _____
_____
_____
_____

(3) _____
_____
_____
_____
_____
_____

(4) _____
_____
_____
_____
_____
_____
_____

MEMORANDUM

TO:

FROM:

SUBJECT:

DATE:

(1) _____
_____
_____
_____
_____

(2) _____
_____
_____

(3) _____
_____
_____
_____
_____
_____
_____
_____
_____
_____

Entrepreneurs in Business—BTN 8-5

_____
_____
_____
_____
_____
_____
_____

Mura's gross pay: _____

Chavez's gross pay: _____

Quick Study 9-2

Federal Income tax withheld: _____

Quick Study 9-3

Social Security withheld: _____

Medicare withheld: _____

Quick Study 9-4

FICA-Social Security.......... _____

FICA-Medicare.................. _____

Federal income tax............ _____

   Total withheld................ _____

Quick Study 9-5

FICA-Social Security.......... _____

FICA-Medicare.................. _____

Federal income tax............ _____

GENERAL JOURNAL

Date	Account Titles and Explanation	PR	Debit	Credit

Quick Study 9-7

GENERAL JOURNAL

Date	Account Titles and Explanation	PR	Debit	Credit

Quick Study 9-8

FICA-Social Security.......... _____

FICA-Medicare……..………. _____

Total FICA Taxes _____

	Subject to Tax	Rate	Tax
(a)			
FICA-Social Security............	_____	_____	_____
FICA-Medicare....................	_____	_____	_____
Federal Income Tax.............	_____	_____	_____
(b)			
FICA-Social Security............	_____	_____	_____
FICA-Medicare....................	_____	_____	_____
Federal Income Tax.............	_____	_____	_____
(c)			
FICA-Social Security............	_____	_____	_____
FICA-Medicare....................	_____	_____	_____
Federal Income Tax.............	_____	_____	_____

GENERAL JOURNAL

Date	Account Titles and Explanation	PR	Debit	Credit

Exercise 9-3

Federal income tax withholdings:
Keisha...
James...   _____
Tyrell...   _____
Emily...   _____

Exercise 9-5

Exercise 9-6

Exercise 9-7

(1)	(5)	
(2)	(6)	
(3)	(7)	
(4)		

(1) Each Employee's FICA Withholdings for Social Security:

					Total
Maximum base					
Earned through _____					
Amt. subject to tax					
Earned this week					
Subject to tax					
Tax rate					
Social Security tax					

(2) Each Employee's FICA Withholdings for Medicare:

					Total
Earned this week					
Tax rate					
Medicare tax					

(3) Each Employee's Health Insurance Premium Deduction:

					Total
Health ins. prem.					

(4) Each Employee's Other Voluntary Deductions:

					Total
Voluntary deductions					

(5) Each Employee's Net (Take-Home) Pay:

					Total
Gross earnings					
Less:					
FICA Soc. Sec. tax					
FICA Medicare tax					
Withholding taxes					
Health Insurance					
Voluntary deductions					
Take-home pay					

(1)

GENERAL JOURNAL

Date	Account Titles and Explanation	PR	Debit	Credit

(2)

GENERAL JOURNAL

Date	Account Titles and Explanation	PR	Debit	Credit

(1)

		(Partial) Payroll Register								
		Week Ending December 7								
		Income Tax Withholdings		FICA Tax Deductions		Other Deductions				
Employee	Gross Pay	Federal	State	Social Security	Medicare	Medical	Union Dues	United Way	Net Pay
Total										

(2)

GENERAL JOURNAL

Date		Account Titles and Explanation	PR	Debit	Credit

(3)

GENERAL JOURNAL

Date		Account Titles and Explanation	PR	Debit	Credit

Payroll Register

Employee	Cumulative Earnings	Marital Status	Withhold. Allow.	Hourly Wage	# of Hours Worked	Regular Pay	Overtime Pay	Gross Pay
Total								

Employee	Gross Pay	Income Tax Withholdings		FICA Tax Deductions		Net Pay
		Federal	State	Social Security	Medicare	
Total						

Employee Earnings Report
For Month Ended June 29, 2009

Employee
Name   _____
SS No.   _____

Reference	Date	Gross Pay	Federal Income Tax	State Income Tax	FICA-Social Security	FICA-Medicare	Net Pay
				EMPLOYEE DEDUCTIONS			
Beg. Balance							
	6/1/2009						
	6/8/2009						
	6/15/2009						
	6/22/2009						
	6/29/2009						
Total	6/1/2009 thru 6/29/2009						
Year-to-date total	YTDTotal for___, _____						

(1) _____

_____

_____

_____

_____

_____

GENERAL JOURNAL

Date		Account Titles and Explanation	PR	Debit	Credit
(2)					

(1) **Payroll-related liability** _____

_____

(2) **Income Statement Accounts** _____

_____

_____

(3) _____

_____

_____

Ethics Challenge—BTN 9-2

_____

_____

_____

_____

_____

_____

_____

MEMORANDUM

TO:

FROM:

SUBJECT:

DATE:

(1) _____

_____

_____

_____

(2) _____

_____

_____

_____

_____

Teamwork in Action—BTN 9-5

_____

_____

_____

_____

_____

_____

_____

_____

_____

_____

_____

_____

_____

_____

_____

_____

_____

_____

_____

_____

_____

_____

_____

_____

_____

_____

_____

_____

_____

(1) _____	(5) _____
(2) _____	(6) _____
(3) _____	(7) _____
(4) _____	(8) _____

Quick Study 10-2

GENERAL JOURNAL

Date	Account Titles and Explanation	PR	Debit	Credit

Quick Study 10-3

FICA-Social Security.. _____

FICA-Medicare... _____

FUTA.. _____

SUTA.. _____

    Total employer payroll tax expense...

GENERAL JOURNAL

Date	Account Titles and Explanation	PR	Debit	Credit

Quick Study 10-5

	A. Baker	C. Dirkson
W-2 Information:		
Federal Income Tax Withheld.....................................		
Wages, Tips, Other Compensation.............................		
Social Security Tax Withheld....................................		
Social Security Wages...		
Medicare Tax Withheld..		
Medicare Wages..		

Quick Study 10-6

W-3 Information:	
Federal Income Tax Withheld..................................	
Wages, Tips, Other Compensation............................	
Social Security Tax Withheld...................................	
Social Security Wages..	
Medicare Tax Withheld...	
Medicare Wages...	

GENERAL JOURNAL

Date		Account Titles and Explanation	PR	Debit	Credit

Quick Study 10-8

_____

_____

_____

Name _____

	Subject to Tax	Rate	Tax
(a)			
FICA-Social Security............	_____	_____	_____
FICA-Medicare....................	_____	_____	_____
FUTA.................................	_____	_____	_____
SUTA.................................	_____	_____	_____
(b)			
FICA-Social Security............	_____	_____	_____
FICA-Medicare....................	_____	_____	_____
FUTA.................................	_____	_____	_____
SUTA.................................	_____	_____	_____
(c)			
FICA-Social Security............	_____	_____	_____
FICA-Medicare....................	_____	_____	_____
FUTA.................................	_____	_____	_____
SUTA.................................	_____	_____	_____

GENERAL JOURNAL

Date	Account Titles and Explanation	PR	Debit	Credit

Exercise 10-3

GENERAL JOURNAL

Date	Account Titles and Explanation	PR	Debit	Credit

GENERAL JOURNAL

Date		Account Titles and Explanation	PR	Debit	Credit

Exercise 10-5

(1) _____

_____

_____

_____

_____

_____

(2)

GENERAL JOURNAL

Date		Account Titles and Explanation	PR	Debit	Credit

(3)

GENERAL JOURNAL

Date	Account Titles and Explanation	PR	Debit	Credit

(4) _____

_____

_____

Exercise 10-6

(1)

Estimated worker's compensation insurance premium for 2009: _____

   Office workers: _____

   Construction workers: _____

(2)

GENERAL JOURNAL

Date	Account Titles and Explanation	PR	Debit	Credit

GENERAL JOURNAL

Date		Account Titles and Explanation	PR	Debit	Credit

(1) Employer's FICA Taxes for Social Security:

		__	__	__	__	Total

(2) Employer's FICA Taxes for Medicare:

		__	__	__	__	Total

(3) Employer's FUTA Taxes:

	__	__	__	__	Total
Maximum base					
Earned through _____					
Amt. subject to tax					
Earned this week					
Subject to tax					
Tax rate					
FUTA rate					

(4) Employer's SUTA Taxes:

					Total
Subject to tax					
Tax rate					
SUTA tax					

(5) Employer's Total Payroll-Related Expense for Each Employee:

					Total
Gross earnings					
Plus:					
FICA Soc. Sec. tax					
FICA Medicare tax					
FUTA tax					
SUTA tax					
Health Insurance					
Pension contrib.					
Total payroll exp.					

(1)

GENERAL JOURNAL

Date	Account Titles and Explanation	PR	Debit	Credit

(2)

GENERAL JOURNAL

Date	Account Titles and Explanation	PR	Debit	Credit

GENERAL JOURNAL

Date		Account Titles and Explanation	PR	Debit	Credit

Work Space:

GENERAL JOURNAL

Date	Account Titles and Explanation	PR	Debit	Credit
Continued from prior page				

Work Space:

FOR ILLUSTRATION ONLY NOT A REAL FORM

Part 1

**Month Tax
Year Ends** →

AMOUNT OF DEPOSIT (Do NOT type, please print)

DOLLARS   CENTS

EMPLOYER IDENTIFICATION NUMBER

Bank Name/
Date Stamp

Name

Address

City

State   Zip

Telephone number ( )

**Darken only one
TYPE OF TAX**

o ▼ 941   o ▼ 945
o ▼ 1120   o ▼ 1042
o ▼ 943   o ▼ 990-T
o ▼ 720   o ▼ 990-PF
o ▼ CT-1 o ▼ 944
o ▼ 940

**Darken only one
TAX PERIOD**

o ▼ 1st Quarter
o ▼ 2nd Quarter
o ▼ 3rd Quarter
o ▼ 4th Quarter

86

FOR BANK USE IN MICR ENCODING

**Federal Tax Deposit Coupon
Form 8109-B (Rev. 12-2005)**

FOR ILLUSTRATION ONLY NOT A REAL FORM

Form 941 for 2009: Employer's QUARTERLY Federal Tax Return

Department of the Treasury-Internal Revenue Service

Report for this Quarter-- (check one)

(EIN)

Employer identification number

Name (not your trade name)

Trade name (if any)

Address

| Number | Street | Suite or room number |

City   State   Zip code

1. January, February, March

2. April, May, June

3. July, August, September

4. Oct., Nov., Dec.

Read the separate instructions before you fill out this form. Please type or print within the boxes

Part 1: Answer these questions for this quarter.

1. Number of employees who received wages, tips, or other compensation for the pay period including: Mar. 12 (Quarter 1), June 12 (Quarter 2), Sept. 12 (Quarter 3), Dec. 12 (Quarter 4) **1**

2. Wages tips, and other compensation... **2**

3. Total income tax withheld from wages, tips and other compensation..................... **3**

4. If no wages, tips, and other compensation are subject to social security or Medicare tax   Check and go to line 6.

5. Taxable social security and Medicare wages and tips:

Column 1   Column 2

5a. Taxable social security wages   x .124 =

5b. Taxable social security tips   x .124 =

5c. Taxable Medicare wages & Tips   x .124 =

5d. Total social security and Medicare taxes (Column 2, lines 5a +5b+5c=line 5d) **5d**

6. Total taxes before adjustments (lines 3+5d = line 6) **6**

7. TAX ADJUSTMENTS (Read the instructions for line 7 before completing lines 7a through 7h):

7a. Current quarter's fracti...

7b. Current quarter's sick pay..

7c. Current quarter's adjustments for tips and group-term life insurance...........

7d. Current year's income tax withholding (attach Form 941c)...................

7e. Prior quarters' social security and Medicare taxes (attach Form 941c)........

7f. Special additions to federal income tax (attach Form 941c)...................

7g. Special additions to social security and Medicare (attach Form 941c)........

7h. TOTAL ADJUSTMENTS (Combine all amounts: lines 7a through 7g)........... **7h**

8. Total taxes after adjustments (Combine lines 6 and 7h)................ **8**

9. Advance earned income credit (EIC) payments made to employees............ **9**

10. Total taxes after adjustments for advance EIC (line 8-line9= line 10)............ **10**

11. Total deposits for this quarter, including overpayment applied from a prior quarter......... **11**

12. Balance due (If line 10 is more than line 11, write the difference here)............ **12**

13. Overpayment (If line 11 is more than line 10, write the difference here.)....... check one Apply to next return   Send a refund

▶ You **MUST** fill out both pages of this form and **SIGN** it

FOR ILLUSTRATION ONLY

Name (not your trade name)	Employer identification number (EIN)

Part 2: Tell us about your deposit schedule and tax liability for this quarter.

If you are unsure about whether you are a monthly schedule depositor or a semiweekly schedule depositor, see Pub. 15 (Circular E), section 11.

14. ☐ ☐   Write the state abbreviation for the state where you made your deposits OR write "MU" if you made your deposits in multiple states.

15. check one   ☐ Line 10 is less than $25,000. Go to Part 3.

☐ You were a monthly schedule depositor for the entire quarter. Fill out your tax liability for each month. Then go to Part 3.

Tax Liability: Month 1 [.   ]

Month 2 [.   ]

Month 3 [.   ]

Total liability for quarter [.   ]   Total must equal line 10.

☐ You were a semiweekly schedule depositor for any part of this quarter. Fill out Schedule B (Form 941): Report of Tax Liability for Semiweekly Schedule Depositors, and attach it to this form.

Part 3: Tell us about your business. If a question does NOT apply to your business, leave it blank.

16. If your business has closed or you stopped pay wages   ☐ check here, and

enter the final date you paid wages   [/   /   ]

17. If you are a seasonal employer and you do not have to file a return for every quarter of the year   ☐ Check here

Part 4: May we speak with your third-party designee?

Do you want to allow an employee, a paid tax preparer, or another person to discuss this return with the IRS?

See the instructions for details

☐   Yes. Designee's name [   ]

Phone (___) ___ - ___   Personal Identification Number (PIN) [ ][ ][ ][ ][ ]

☐   No.

Part 5: Sign here. You MUST fill out both sides of this form and SIGN IT

Under penalties of perjury. I declare that I have examined this return, including accompanying schedules and statements, and to the best of my knowledge and belief, it is true, correct, and complete.

X   Sign your name here [   ]

Print name and title [   ]

Date [/   /   ]   Phone (___) ___ - ___

Part 6: For PAID preparers only (optional)

Paid Preparer's Signature		
Firm's name		
Address		EIN
		Zip Code
Date [/ /] Phone ( ) -		SSN/PTN

(1)
Quarter ended March 31
SUTA:
FUTA:

Quarter ended June 30
SUTA:
FUTA:

Quarter ended September 30
SUTA:
FUTA:

Quarter ended December 31
SUTA:
FUTA:

(2)

GENERAL JOURNAL

Date	Account Titles and Explanation	PR	Debit	Credit

(3)

GENERAL JOURNAL

Date	Account Titles and Explanation	PR	Debit	Credit

FOR ILLUSTRATION ONLY NOT A REAL FORM

form **940-EZ**	**Employer's Annual Federal**	OMB No. 1545-1110
Department of the Treasury Internal Revenue Service	**Unemployment (FUTA) Tax Return** ▶ See the separate instructions for Form 940-EZ for information on completing this form.	**2008**

		T	
		FF	
You must	Name (as distinguished from trade name)	Calendar year	FD
complete this	Trade name, if any	Employer identification Number (EIN)	FP
section▶			I
	Address (number and street)	City, state, and ZIP code	T

Answer the questions under **Who May Use Form 940-EZ** on page 2. If you cannot use Form 940-EZ, you must use Form 940

A Enter the amount of contributions paid to your state unemployment fund (See the separate instructions)..........................▶ $ _ _ _ _ _ _ _ _ _ _ |

B (1) Enter the name of the state where you have to pay contributions...▶ _ _ _ _ _ _ _ _ _ _ _

    (2) Enter your state reporting number as shown on your state unemployment tax return ▶

If you will not have to file returns in the future, check here *see Who Must File in separate instructions) and complete and sign the return................................▶

If this is an Amended Return, check here (see Amended Returns in the separate instructions)..

Part I	Taxable Wages and FUTA Tax

1. Total payments (including payments shown on lines 2 and 3) during the calendar year for services of employees		1	
2. Exempt payments. (Explain all exempt payments, attaching additional sheets if necessary			
3 Payments of more than $7,000 for services. Enter only amounts over the first $7,000 paid to each employee (see the separate instructions)................................			
4. Add lines 2 and 3................................	4		
5. Total taxable wages (subtract line 4 from line 1)................................	5		
6. FUTA tax, Multiply the wages on line 5 by .008 and enter here. (If the result if over $500, also complete Part II.)	6		
7. Total FUTA tax deposited for the year, including any overpayment applied from a prior year.....................	7		
8. Balance due (subtract line 7 from line 6). Pay to the "United States Treasury".............................. If you owe more than $500, see **Depositing FUTA tax** in separate instructions.	8		
9. Overpayment (subtract line 6 from line 7). Check if it is to be: ☐ Applied to next return or ☐ Refunded ▶	9		

Part II	Record of Quarterly Federal Unemployment Tax Liability (Do not include state liability.) Complete only if line 6 is over $500.

	6.5	First (Jan. 1- Mar. 31)	Second (Apr. 1- June 30)	Third (July 1- Sept.30)	Fourth (Oct 1. Dec 31)	Total for year
Liability for Quarter						

Third-Party **Designee**	Do you want to allow another person to discuss this return with the IRS (see the separate instructions)?		☐ Yes. Complete the following ☐ No
	Designee's name ▶	Phone no. ▶ ( )	Personal identification number (PIN)▶

Under penalties of perjury, I declare that I have examined this return, including accompanying schedules and statements, and, to the best of my knowledge and belief, it is true, correct, and complete, and that no part of any payment made to a state unemployment fund claimed as a credit was, or is to be, deducted from the payments to employees.

Signature ▶ _____   Title (Owener, etc.) ▶ _____   Date ▶ _____

For Privacy Act and Paperwork Reduction Act Notices, see the separate instructio ▼DETACH HERE ▼   Cat. N0. 10983G   Form **940-EZ** (2005)

- -

form **940-V(EZ)**	**Payment Voucher**	OMB NO. 1545-1110
Department of the Treasury Internal Revenue Service	Use this voucher only when making a payment with your return.	**2008**

Complete boxes 1, 2, and 3. Do not send cash, and do not staple your payment to this voucher. Make your check or money order payable to the "United States Treasury". Be sure to enter your employer identification number (EIN), "Form 940 E-Z" and "2005" on your payment.

			Dollars	Cents
1. Enter your employer identification number (EIN). I	2. Enter the amount of your payment. ▶			
	3. Enter your business name (individual name for sole proprietors).			
	Enter your address.			
	Enter your city, state, and ZIP code.			

GENERAL JOURNAL

Date	Account Titles and Explanation	PR	Debit	Credit

GENERAL JOURNAL

Date		Account Titles and Explanation	PR	Debit	Credit

Name _____

(1) _____
_____
_____

(2) _____
_____
_____

(3) _____
_____
_____
_____

Ethics Challenge BTN 10-2

(1) _____
_____
_____
_____

MEMORANDUM

TO:

FROM:

SUBJECT:

DATE:

_____

_____

_____

_____

_____

_____

_____

_____

_____

_____

_____

_____

_____

_____

_____

_____

_____

_____

_____

_____

_____

_____

_____

_____

_____

_____

_____

_____

_____

_____

_____

_____

_____

(1) _____
_____
_____

(2) _____
_____
_____

(3) _____
_____
_____
_____

Teamwork in Action—BTN 10-5

	(1) Estimated	(2) Actual
FICA-Medicare		
FICA-Social Security		
SUTA		
FUTA		
Worker's compensation:		
Office workers		
Stone installers		
(3) Total		

(4) Discussion: _____
_____
_____
_____
_____

MEMORANDUM

TO:

FROM:

SUBJECT:

DATE:

GENERAL JOURNAL

Date	Account Titles and Explanation	PR	Debit	Credit

a. _____

_____

b. _____

_____

c. _____

_____

d. _____

_____

1. _____	5. _____
2. _____	6. _____
3. _____	7. _____
4. _____	8. _____

Quick Study 11-4

Sales Journal						Page 3
Date	Account Debited	Post Ref.		Accounts Receivable Dr.	Sales Tax Payable Cr.	Sales Cr.

Quick Study 11-5

Sales	$ _____
Less: Sales Discounts	_____
Less: Sales Returns and Allowances	_____
Net Sales	$ _____

GENERAL JOURNAL

Date	Account Titles and Explanation	PR	Debit	Credit

Quick Study 11-7

Cash Receipts Journal

Date	Account Credited	Post Ref.	Cash Dr.	Sales Discount Cr.	Accounts Receivable	Sales Cr.

GENERAL JOURNAL

Date	Account Titles and Explanation	PR	Debit	Credit
Entries for Sale of Merchandise:				
Entries for (a):				
Entries for (b):				
Entries for (c):				

1. _____

_____

_____

_____

_____

_____

2. _____

_____

_____

_____

_____

_____

_____

Exercise 11-3

(a) _____

(b) _____

(c) _____

(d) _____

(e) _____

(f) _____

(g) _____

(h) _____

Part 1

ACCOUNTS RECEIVABLE SUBSIDIARY LEDGER

Anna Page	Sara Reed	Aaron Reckers

Part 2

GENERAL LEDGER

Accounts Receivable	Sales	Sales Returns and Allowances

Part 3

_____

_____

Schedule of Accounts Receivable

_____
_____
_____
_____
_____
_____
_____
_____
_____

Accounts Receivable Controlling Account

_____
_____
_____
_____

Part 1

ACCOUNTS RECEIVABLE LEDGER

Eric Horner	**Hong Jiang**

Joe Mack	**Tess Cox**

Part 2

GENERAL LEDGER

Accounts Receivable	**Sales**

Part 3

Schedule of Accounts Receivable

Cash Receipts Journal

Date	Account Credited	Explanation	PR	Cash Dr.	Sales Cr.	Other Accounts Cr.

Exercise 11-7

Cash Receipts Journal

Date	Account Credited	Post Ref.	Cash Dr.	Sales Discount	Accounts Receivable	Sales Cr.	Other Accounts

Part 1

Sales Journal							Page 3
Date	Account Debited	Post Ref.		Accounts Receivable Dr.		Sales Tax Payable Cr.	Sales Cr.

Cash Receipts Journal							
Date	Account Credited	Post Ref.	Cash Dr.	Sales Discount Cr.	Accounts Receivable Cr.	Sales Cr.	Other Accounts Cr.

Part 2

Schedule of Accounts Receivable

Part 1

Sales Journal   Page **3**

Date	Account Debited	Invoice Number	PR	Accounts Receivable Dr.	Sales Cr.	Sales Tax Payable Cr.

Part 2

GENERAL LEDGER

Accounts Receivable

Date	Explanation	PR	Debit	Credit	Balance

Sales

Date	Explanation	PR	Debit	Credit	Balance

Sales Tax Payable

Date	Explanation	PR	Debit	Credit	Balance

ACCOUNTS RECEIVABLE LEDGER

Date	Explanation	PR	Debit	Credit	Balance

Date	Explanation	PR	Debit	Credit	Balance

Date	Explanation	PR	Debit	Credit	Balance

_____COMPANY
Schedule of Accounts Receivable
_____ 30

_____ .... _____

_____ .... _____

_____ .... _____

Total accounts receivable..

Parts 1 and 2

Sales Journal						Page 2
Date	Account Debited	Invoice Number	PR	Accounts Receivable Dr.	Sales Cr.	Sales Tax Payable Cr.

Part 3

GENERAL LEDGER

Accounts Receivable

Date	Explanation	PR	Debit	Credit	Balance

Sales

Date	Explanation	PR	Debit	Credit	Balance

Sales Tax Payable

Date	Explanation	PR	Debit	Credit	Balance

ACCOUNTS RECEIVABLE LEDGER

Date	Explanation	PR	Debit	Credit	Balance

Date	Explanation	PR	Debit	Credit	Balance

Date	Explanation	PR	Debit	Credit	Balance

Part 4

_____ COMPANY		
Schedule of Accounts Receivable		
_____ 30		

_____	....	_____
_____	....	_____
_____	....	_____
Total accounts receivable	....	_____

GENERAL JOURNAL

Date		Account Titles and Explanation	PR	Debit	Credit

Parts 1 and 2

Sales Journal   Page 3

Date	Account Debited	Post Ref.		Accounts Receivable Dr.		Sales Tax Payable Cr.	Sales Cr.

Cash Receipts Journal

Date	Account Credited	Post Ref.	Cash Dr.	Sales Discount Cr.	Accounts Receivable Cr.	Sales Cr.	Other Accounts Cr.

Part 3

GENERAL LEDGER

Cash

Date	Explanation	PR	Debit	Credit	Balance

Accounts Receivable

Date	Explanation	PR	Debit	Credit	Balance

Inventory

Date	Explanation	PR	Debit	Credit	Balance

Long-term Notes Payable

Date	Explanation	PR	Debit	Credit	Balance

Sales

Date	Explanation	PR	Debit	Credit	Balance

Sales Discounts

Date	Explanation	PR	Debit	Credit	Balance

Part 4.

Wiset Company - Trial Balance, April 30

Accounts	Debit	Credit

Totals

_____COMPANY
Schedule of Accounts Receivable
_____ 30

_____..   _____

_____..   _____

_____..   _____

Total accounts receivable...   _____

Name _____

1

	Fiscal 2007	Fiscal 2008
Merchandise Inventory	$ _____	$ _____
Total Current Assets	_____	_____
Total Inventory as a % of Current Assets	_____	_____

2

_____

_____

_____

_____

_____

_____

Part 1

_____
_____
_____
_____
_____
_____
_____
_____
_____
_____
_____

Part 2

_____
_____
_____
_____
_____
_____
_____
_____

Part 3

_____
_____
_____
_____
_____
_____
_____
_____

MEMORANDUM

TO:

FROM:

SUBJECT:

DATE:

_____
_____
_____
_____
_____
_____
_____
_____
_____
_____
_____
_____
_____
_____
_____
_____
_____
_____
_____
_____
_____
_____
_____
_____
_____
_____
_____
_____

GENERAL JOURNAL

Date	Account Titles and Explanation	PR	Debit	Credit

					Sales Journal				
Date	Account Debited	Invoice Number	PR	Accounts Receivable Dr.	Sales Cr.	Sales Tax Payable Cr.

Analysis of Advantages and Disadvantages of General Journal and Sales Journal Entries:

_____
_____
_____
_____
_____
_____
_____
_____

1. _____

_____

_____

_____

_____

_____

_____

2. _____

_____

_____

_____

_____

_____

You Call It—BTN 11-6

_____

_____

_____

_____

_____

GENERAL JOURNAL

Date	Account Titles and Explanation	PR	Debit	Credit

Quick Study 12-2

a. _____

b. _____

c. _____

d. _____

Quick Study 12-3

a. _____

b. _____

c. _____

d. _____

Purchases Journal

Page xx

Date	Invoice Date	Account	Terms	Post Ref.		Accounts Payable Credit	Purchases Debit	Transportation-In Debit

Quick Study 12-5

Purchases Journal

Page xx

Date	Invoice Date	Account	Terms	Post Ref.		Accounts Payable Credit	Purchases Debit	Transportation-In Debit

Cash Disbursements Journal

Date	Check No.	Payee	Account Debited	PR	Cash Cr.	Purchase Discounts Cr.	Accounts Payable Dr.	Other Accounts Dr.

Quick Study 12-7

Cash Disbursements Journal

Date	Check No.	Payee	Account Debited	PR	Cash Cr.	Purchase Discounts Cr.	Accounts Payable Dr.	Other Accounts Dr.

GENERAL JOURNAL

Date	Account Titles and Explanation	PR	Debit	Credit

BUYER

GENERAL JOURNAL

Date		Account Titles and Explanation	PR	Debit	Credit

(1) _____   (6) _____

(2) _____   (7) _____

(3) _____   (8) _____

(4) _____   (9) _____

(5) _____

Exercise 12-4

GENERAL JOURNAL

Date	Account Titles and Explanation	PR	Debit	Credit
Entries for Purchase of Merchandise:				
Entries for (a):				
Entries for (b):				
Entries for (c):				

(1) BUYER

GENERAL JOURNAL

Date		Account Titles and Explanation	PR	Debit	Credit

Name _____

(2) SELLER

GENERAL JOURNAL

Date	Account Titles and Explanation	PR	Debit	Credit

Name _____

GENERAL JOURNAL

Date	Account Titles and Explanation	PR	Debit	Credit

Working Papers 275

Cash Disbursements Journal

Date	Check No.	Payee	Account Debited	PR	Cash Cr.	Purchase Discounts Cr.	Accounts Payable Dr.	Other Accounts Dr.

Exercise 12-8

Cash Disbursements Journal

Date	Check No.	Payee	Account Debited	PR	Cash Cr.	Purchase Discounts Cr.	Accounts Payable Dr.	Other Accounts Dr.

Name _____

Part a.

Purchases Journal

Page xx

Date	√	I n	Account	Terms	Post Ref.	Accounts Payable Credit	Purch. Debit	Trans-In Debit

Cash Disbursements Journal

Date	Check No.	Payee	Account Debited	PR	Cash Cr.	Purchase Discounts Cr.	Accounts Payable Dr.	Other Accounts Dr.

Part b.

Williams Company
Schedule of Accounts Payable
31-May

_____   _____

_____   _____

Total Accounts Payable _____

GENERAL JOURNAL

Date	Account Titles and Explanation	PR	Debit	Credit

GENERAL JOURNAL

Date	Account Titles and Explanation	PR	Debit	Credit

1. Account for these Purchases in a Purchase Journal

Purchases Journal

Page 4

Date	Invoice Date	Account	Terms	Post Ref.		Accounts Payable Credit	Purchases Debit	Transportation-In Debit

2. Post these Accounts to the General Ledger

Purchases Journal

Page 4

Date	Invoice Date	Account	Terms	Post Ref.		Accounts Payable Credit	Purchases Debit	Transportation-In Debit

General Ledger

Account: Accounts Payable			Account No. 207	
Date	Post Ref.	Debit	Credit	Balance

Part 2

Account: Purchases				Account No. 502
Date	Post Ref.	Debit	Credit	Balance

Account: Transportation-In				Account No. 503
Date	Post Ref.	Debit	Credit	Balance

3. Post these Accounts to the Accounts Payable Subsidiary Ledger

_____ Inc.				
Date	Post Ref.	Debit	Credit	Balance

_____ Inc.				
Date	Post Ref.	Debit	Credit	Balance

_____ Inc.				
Date	Post Ref.	Debit	Credit	Balance

_____ Inc.				
Date	Post Ref.	Debit	Credit	Balance

Part 1

Journal Entries

GENERAL JOURNAL

Date	Account Titles and Explanation	P. R.	Debit	Credit

Part 1   (Continued)

Journal Entries

Date		Account Titles and Explanation	PR	Debit	Credit

Part 1   (Continued)

Journal Entries

Date	Account Titles and Explanation	PR	Debit	Credit

Journal Entries

Date		Account Titles and Explanation	PR	Debit	Credit

GENERAL LEDGER

Cash ACCOUNT NO. 101

Date	Explanation	PR	DEBIT	CREDIT	BALANCE
2010 Dec. 31	Balance				80,260

Accounts Receivable - Alex's Engineering Co.   ACCOUNT NO. 106.1

Date	Explanation	PR	DEBIT	CREDIT	BALANCE
2010 Dec. 31	Balance				0

Accounts Receivable - Wildcat Services   ACCOUNT NO. 106.2

Date	Explanation	PR	DEBIT	CREDIT	BALANCE
2010 Dec. 31	Balance				0

Accounts Receivable - Easy Leasing   ACCOUNT NO. 106.3

Date	Explanation	PR	DEBIT	CREDIT	BALANCE
2010 Dec. 31	Balance				0

Accounts Receivable - Clark Co.   ACCOUNT NO. 106.4

Date	Explanation	PR	DEBIT	CREDIT	BALANCE
2010 Dec. 31	Balance				2,300

Accounts Receivable - Chang Corporation   ACCOUNT NO. 106.5

Date	Explanation	PR	DEBIT	CREDIT	BALANCE
2010 Dec. 31	Balance				0

Accounts Receivable - Gomez Co.   ACCOUNT NO. 106.6

Date	Explanation	PR	DEBIT	CREDIT	BALANCE
2010 Dec. 31	Balance				3,500

Accounts Receivable - Delta Co.   ACCOUNT NO. 106.7

Date	Explanation	PR	DEBIT	CREDIT	BALANCE
2010 Dec. 31	Balance				0

Accounts Receivable - KC, Inc.   ACCOUNT NO. 106.8

Date	Explanation	PR	DEBIT	CREDIT	BALANCE
2010 Dec. 31	Balance				0

Accounts Receivable - Dream, Inc.   ACCOUNT NO. 106.9

Date	Explanation	PR	DEBIT	CREDIT	BALANCE
2010 Dec. 31	Balance				0

Accounts Receivable - Bob's Building Co.   ACCOUNT NO. 106.10

Date	Explanation	PR	DEBIT	CREDIT	BALANCE
2010 Dec. 31	Balance				0

Merchandise Inventory   ACCOUNT NO. 119

Date	Explanation	PR	DEBIT	CREDIT	BALANCE
2010 Dec. 31	Balance				0

Computer Supplies   ACCOUNT NO. 126

Date	Explanation	PR	DEBIT	CREDIT	BALANCE
2010 Dec. 31	Balance				775

Prepaid Insurance   ACCOUNT NO. 128

Date	Explanation	PR	DEBIT	CREDIT	BALANCE
2010 Dec. 31	Balance				1,800

Part 2   (Continued)

	Prepaid Rent				ACCOUNT NO. 131
Date	Explanation	PR	DEBIT	CREDIT	BALANCE
2010 Dec. 31	Balance				875

	Office Equipment				ACCOUNT NO. 163
Date	Explanation	PR	DEBIT	CREDIT	BALANCE
2010 Dec. 31	Balance				10,000

	Accumulated Depreciation - Office Equipment				ACCOUNT NO. 164
Date	Explanation	PR	DEBIT	CREDIT	BALANCE
2010 Dec. 31	Balance				625

	Computer Equipment				ACCOUNT NO. 167
Date	Explanation	PR	DEBIT	CREDIT	BALANCE
2010 Dec. 31	Balance				25,000

	Accumulated Depreciation - Computer Equipment				ACCOUNT NO. 168
Date	Explanation	PR	DEBIT	CREDIT	BALANCE
2010 Dec. 31	Balance				1,250

Accounts Payable   ACCOUNT NO. 201

Date	Explanation	PR	DEBIT	CREDIT	BALANCE
2010 Dec. 31	Balance				2,100

Wages Payable   ACCOUNT NO. 210

Date	Explanation	PR	DEBIT	CREDIT	BALANCE
2010 Dec. 31	Balance				600

Unearned Computer Services Revenue   ACCOUNT NO. 236

Date	Explanation	PR	DEBIT	CREDIT	BALANCE
2010 Dec. 31	Balance				2,500

A. Lopez, Capital   ACCOUNT NO. 301

Date	Explanation	PR	DEBIT	CREDIT	BALANCE
2010 Dec. 31	Balance				117,435

A. Lopez, Withdrawals   ACCOUNT NO. 302

Date	Explanation	PR	DEBIT	CREDIT	BALANCE
2010 Dec. 31	Balance				0

		Computer Services Revenue			ACCOUNT NO. 403	
Date	Explanation	PR	DEBIT	CREDIT	BALANCE

		Sales			ACCOUNT NO. 413	
Date	Explanation	PR	DEBIT	CREDIT	BALANCE

		Sales Returns and Allowances			ACCOUNT NO. 414	
Date	Explanation	PR	DEBIT	CREDIT	BALANCE

Sales Discounts   ACCOUNT NO. 415

Date	Explanation	PR	DEBIT	CREDIT	BALANCE

Cost of Goods Sold   ACCOUNT NO. 502

Date	Explanation	PR	DEBIT	CREDIT	BALANCE

Depreciation Expense-Office Equipment   ACCOUNT NO. 612

Date	Explanation	PR	DEBIT	CREDIT	BALANCE

Depreciation Expense-Computer Equipment   ACCOUNT NO. 613

Date	Explanation	PR	DEBIT	CREDIT	BALANCE

Wages Expense   ACCOUNT NO. 623

Date	Explanation	PR	DEBIT	CREDIT	BALANCE

Insurance Expense					ACCOUNT NO. 637	
Date	Explanation	PR	DEBIT	CREDIT	BALANCE	

Rent Expense					ACCOUNT NO. 640	
Date	Explanation	PR	DEBIT	CREDIT	BALANCE	

Computer Supplies Expense					ACCOUNT NO. 652	
Date	Explanation	PR	DEBIT	CREDIT	BALANCE	

Advertising Expense					ACCOUNT NO. 655	
Date	Explanation	PR	DEBIT	CREDIT	BALANCE	

Mileage Expense					ACCOUNT NO. 676	
Date	Explanation	PR	DEBIT	CREDIT	BALANCE	

Miscellaneous Expense					ACCOUNT NO. 677	
Date	Explanation	PR	DEBIT	CREDIT	BALANCE	

Repairs Expense - Computer					ACCOUNT NO. 684	
Date	Explanation	PR	DEBIT	CREDIT	BALANCE	

Part 3

SUCCESS SYSTEMS
Partial Work Sheet
March 31, 2010

Acct. No.	ACCOUNT TITLES	UNADJUSTED TRIAL BALANCE	
		Dr.	Cr.

_____

_____

_____

_____

_____

_____

_____

_____

_____

_____

Ethics Challenge—BTN 12-2

_____

_____

_____

_____

_____

_____

_____

_____

_____

_____

_____

_____

Taking it to the Net—BTN 12-3

_____

_____

_____

_____

_____

_____

TO: _____
FROM: _____
DATE: _____
RE: _____
_____
_____
_____
_____
_____
_____
_____
_____
_____
_____
_____
_____

Name _____

_____
_____
_____
_____

Quick Study 13-2

_____
_____
_____
_____
_____
_____
_____
_____
_____

Quick Study 13-3

GENERAL JOURNAL

Date	Account Titles and Explanation	PR	Debit	Credit

Quick Study 13-4

_____
_____
_____
_____

GENERAL JOURNAL

Date		Account Titles and Explanation	PR	Debit	Credit

Quick Study 13-6

GENERAL JOURNAL

Date		Account Titles and Explanation	PR	Debit	Credit

Quick Study 13-7

GENERAL JOURNAL

Date		Account Titles and Explanation	PR	Debit	Credit

Quick Study 13-8

GENERAL JOURNAL

Date		Account Titles and Explanation	PR	Debit	Credit

Adjusting entry	Debit	Credit
1. Accrue salaries expense		
2. Adjust the Unearned Services Revenue account		
to recognize earned revenue		
3. Record the earnings of services revenue for which		
cash will be received the following period		

Answer is _____

Explanation: _____

_____

_____

_____

_____

Quick Study 13-11

Answer is _____

Explanation: _____

_____

_____

_____

_____

Quick Study 13-12[A]

Answer is _____

Supporting work: _____

_____

_____

_____

Name _____

	(a)	(b)	(c)
Sales................................	$550,000	$38,700	$255,700
Sales discounts...........................			
Sales returns and allowances........			
Net sales....................................			
Cost of goods sold......................			
Gross profit................................			

Exercise 13-2

	(a)	(b)	(c)
Purchases...............................			
Less: Purchase discounts..........			
Purchase returns..............			
Net purchases...........................			
Plus: Beginning inventory...........			
Cost of goods available for sale...			
Less: Ending inventory................			
Cost of goods sold......................			
Sales.......................................			
Gross profit...............................			

GENERAL JOURNAL

Date	Account Titles and Explanation	PR	Debit	Credit
(a)				
(b)				
(c)				

Exercise 13-4

1. _____
2. _____
3. _____
4. _____
5. _____

GENERAL JOURNAL

Date	Account Titles and Explanation	PR	Debit	Credit
Adjusting entry:				
Payday entry:				

Exercise 13-6

GENERAL JOURNAL

Date	Account Titles and Explanation	PR	Debit	Credit

a. Cost of goods available for sale:

_____

_____

b. Sales:

_____

_____

c. Cost of goods sold:

_____

_____

d. Ending inventory:

_____

_____

e. Beginning inventory:

_____

_____

Exercise 13-8

GENERAL JOURNAL

Date		Account Titles and Explanation	PR	Debit	Credit
(a)					
(b)					
(c)					
(d)					

GENERAL JOURNAL

Date	Account Titles and Explanation	PR	Debit	Credit

GENERAL JOURNAL

Date	Account Titles and Explanation	PR	Debit	Credit

Parts 1 and 2

ACCOUNT TITLES	UNADJUSTED TRIAL BALANCE		ADJUSTMENTS		ADJUSTED TRIAL BALANCE	
	DR	CR	DR	CR	DR	CR

3. Net sales

_____

_____

_____

_____

4. Net purchases

_____

_____

_____

_____

_____

5. Cost of good sold

_____

_____

_____

_____

_____

6. Gross profit

_____

_____

_____

Problem 13-2A or 13-2B

1.	6.	11.
2.	7.	
3.	8.	
4.	9.	
5.	10.	

GENERAL JOURNAL

Date	Account Titles and Explanation	PR	Debit	Credit

Part 2

GENERAL JOURNAL

Date	Account Titles and Explanation	PR	Debit	Credit

Name _____

ACCOUNT TITLES	UNADJUSTED TRIAL BALANCE		ADJUSTMENTS		ADJUSTED TRIAL BALANCE	
	DR	CR	DR	CR	DR	CR

Net sales

_____
_____
_____
_____
_____

Net purchases

_____
_____
_____
_____
_____
_____

Cost of good sold

_____
_____
_____
_____
_____
_____
_____

Gross profit

_____
_____
_____

(1) _____

_____

_____

_____

(2) _____

_____

_____

_____

Ethics Challenge—BTN 13-2

(1) _____

_____

_____

_____

(2) _____

_____

_____

_____

Taking It to the Net—BTN 13-3

(1) _____

_____

_____

(2) _____

_____

_____

(3) _____

_____

_____

_____

_____

_____

_____

_____

_____

_____

_____

_____

_____

_____

_____

_____

_____

_____

_____

_____

_____

_____

_____

_____

_____

_____

_____

_____

_____

_____

_____

_____

_____

_____

_____

_____

(1) _____

_____

_____

(2) _____

_____

_____

You Call It—BTN 13-6

(1) _____

_____

_____

(2) _____

_____

_____

(1) _____   (5) _____
(2) _____   (6) _____
(3) _____   (7) _____
(4) _____   (8) _____

Quick Study 14-2

(a) _____   (d) _____
(b) _____   (e) _____
(c) _____

Quick Study 14-3

(1) _____   (6) _____
(2) _____   (7) _____
(3) _____   (8) _____
(4) _____   (9) _____
(5) _____   (10) _____

Quick Study 14-4

(1) _____   (4) _____
(2) _____   (5) _____
(3) _____

Income Statement (Net sales section)

Quick Study 14-6

Income Statement (Cost of goods sold section)

Quick Study 14-7

Statement of Owner's Equity

Accounts on Post-Closing Trial Balance:

_____
_____
_____
_____
_____
_____
_____

Quick Study 14-9

GENERAL JOURNAL

Date	Account Titles and Explanation	PR	Debit	Credit

Quick Study 14-10

GENERAL JOURNAL

Date	Account Titles and Explanation	PR	Debit	Credit

Statement of Owner's Equity

Exercise 14-2

Balance Sheet

Account	Permanent (P) or Temporary (T)	Income Statement (IS) or Balance Sheet (BS)	Closed (C) or Not Closed (NC)	Closed with a Debit (Dr) or Credit (Cr)
a. Accounts payable............................	P	BS	NC	—
b. Accounts receivable.........................				
c. Accumulated depreciation-Equipment...				
d. Advertising expense...........................				
e. Cash..				
f. Depreciation expense-Equipment.........				
g. Equipment...				
h. Insurance expense.............................				
i. Interest expense...............................				
j. Merch. Inventory (ending)...................				
k. Notes payable..................................				
l. Office supplies..................................				
m. Office supplies expense.....................				
n. Purchases..				
o. Purchase returns...............................				
p. Owner, capital..................................				
q. Owner, withdrawals............................				
r. Salaries expense..............................				
s. Sales..				
t. Sales discounts................................				
u. Transportation-in..............................				

Balance Sheet

Income Statement

Income Statement

Exercise 14-7

Statement of Owner's Equity

Balance Sheet

Post-Closing Trial Balance

Exercise 14-10[A]

GENERAL JOURNAL

Date	Account Titles and Explanation	PR	Debit	Credit

(1) _____   (6) _____   (11) _____   (16) _____
(2) _____   (7) _____   (12) _____   (17) _____
(3) _____   (8) _____   (13) _____   (18) _____
(4) _____   (9) _____   (14) _____   (19) _____
(5) _____   (10) _____ (15) _____   (20) _____

Problem 14-2A or 14-2B

Part 1

_____
_____
_____
_____
_____
_____
_____
_____
_____
_____

Part 2

_____
_____
_____
_____
_____
_____
_____
_____
_____

Part 3

_____

Income Statement

_____
_____
_____
_____
_____
_____
_____
_____
_____
_____
_____
_____
_____
_____
_____
_____
_____
_____
_____
_____
_____
_____
_____
_____
_____
_____
_____

Part 4

_____

Income Statement

_____
_____
_____
_____
_____
_____
_____
_____
_____

GENERAL JOURNAL

Date	Account Titles and Explanation	PR	Debit	Credit

GENERAL JOURNAL

Date	Account Titles and Explanation	PR	Debit	Credit

GENERAL JOURNAL

Date	Account Titles and Explanation	PR	Debit	Credit

GENERAL JOURNAL

Date	Account Titles and Explanation	PR	Debit	Credit

SUCCESS SYSTEMS
Income Statement
For Three Months Ended March 31, 2008

SUCCESS SYSTEMS
Income Statement
For Three Months Ended March 31, 2011

SUCCESS SYSTEMS
Statement of Owner's Equity
For Three Months Ended March 31, 2011

Part 1   (Continued)

SUCCESS SYSTEMS
Balance Sheet
March 31, 2011

(1) _____
_____
_____
_____
_____

Taking It to the Net—BTN 14-2

	Current Year	1 Year Prior	2 Years Prior
Revenues			
Cost of goods sold			
Gross profit			

_____
_____
_____
_____
_____

Entrepreneurs in Business—BTN 14-3

(1) _____
_____
_____
_____
_____
_____
_____
_____
_____

You Call It—BTN 14-4

_____
_____
_____
_____
_____
_____

Appendix B   Quick Study B-1   *Name* _____

(1) _____
(2) _____
(3) _____
(4) _____
(5) _____
(6) _____

Quick Study B-2

(1) _____
(2) _____
(3) _____
(4) _____

Quick Study B-3

(1) _____
(2) _____
(3) _____
(4) _____

Quick Study B-4

(1) _____
(2) _____
(3) _____
(4) _____

Quick Study B-5

(1) _____
(2) _____
(3) _____

a. _____
b. _____
c. _____

Exercise B-2

a. _____   e. _____
b. _____   f. _____
c. _____   g. _____
d. _____

Exercise B-3

(1) _____
(2) _____
(3) _____
(4) _____

Exercise B-4

(1) _____
(2) _____
(3) _____
(4) _____

Exercise B-5

(1) _____
(2) _____
(3) _____
(4) _____
(5) _____

Appendix B **Exercise B-6** Name _____

(1) _____

(2) _____

(3) _____

(4) _____

Exercise B-7

(1) _____

(2) _____

(3) _____

Exercise B-8

(1) _____

(2) _____

(3) _____

(4) _____

Exercise B-9

(1) _____

_____

_____

_____

_____

(2) _____

_____

_____

_____

_____

(3) _____

_____

_____

_____

_____

Appendix B   Problem B-1A or B-1B

Name _____

(1) _____   (4) _____

(2) _____   (5) _____

(3) _____   (6) _____

Problem B-2A or B-2B

(1) _____   (4) _____

(2) _____   (5) _____

(3) _____

(1) Identification of Preferred Investment _____

_____

_____

(2) Explanation of Why Investment B might be Preferred to Investment A

_____

_____

_____

_____

_____

_____

_____

_____

Quick Study C-2

Payback Period _____

_____

_____

_____

_____

_____

_____

Quick Study C-3

Net Present Value _____

_____

_____

_____

_____

_____

_____

_____

_____

_____

Accounting Rate of Return

_____
_____
_____
_____
_____
_____

Quick Study C-5

Year	Cash Flows	Present Value of 1 at 10%	Present value of cash flows	Cumulative present value of cash flows
0				
1				
2				
3				
4				
5				

Break-Even Time

_____
_____
_____
_____
_____

Appendix C   Exercise C-1

Name _____

(a) **Payback Period**

_____
_____
_____
_____
_____
_____
_____
_____

(b) **Payback Period**

_____
_____
_____
_____
_____
_____
_____
_____
_____

Name _____

	Annual Net Cash flows	Cumulative Cash Flows
Year 1		
Year 2		
Year 3		
Year 4		
Year 5		

Payback Period

_____
_____
_____
_____

Exercise C-3

	Net Income	Depreciation	Net Cash Flow	Cumulative Cash Flow
Year 1				
Year 2				
Year 3				
Year 4				
Year 5				

Payback Period

_____
_____
_____
_____
_____
_____
_____
_____

Accounting Rate of Return

_____
_____
_____
_____
_____
_____
_____
_____

Exercise C-5

	Net Income	Cash Flows
Sales		
Materials, labor & overhead		
Depreciation		
Selling and administrative		
Pretax income		
Income taxes		
Net income		
Net cash flows		

(1) Payback Period

_____
_____
_____
_____
_____
_____
_____
_____

(2) Accounting Rate of Return

_____
_____
_____
_____
_____
_____
_____
_____
_____

Name _____

	Annual Net Cash Flows	Present Value of Annuity at 8%	Present Value of Net Cash Flows
Years 1 through 6			
Amount invested			
Net present value of investment			

Acceptability of Investment

_____

_____

_____

Exercise C-7

1.

Project C1

	Net Cash Flows	Present Value of 1 at 12%	Present Value of Net Cash Flows
Year 1			
Year 2			
Year 3			
Totals			
Amount invested			
Net present value			

Project C2

	Net Cash Flows	Present Value of 1 at 12%	Present Value of Net Cash Flows
Year 1			
Year 2			
Year 3			
Totals			
Amount invested			
Net present value			

1.   (Continued)
Project C3

	Net Cash Flows	Present Value of 1 at 12%	Present Value of Net Cash Flows
Year 1			
Year 2			
Year 3			
Totals			
Amount invested			
Net present value			

Analysis and interpretation:

_____

_____

_____

_____

2. Internal Rate of Return vs. 12% Net Present Value

_____

_____

_____

_____

3. Internal Rate of Return for C2

_____

_____

_____

_____

_____

Appendix C   Exercise C-8   *Name* _____

(1) Recovery time for:

     Payback Period

_____

_____

_____

     Break-even Time

_____

_____

_____

_____

(2) Advantages of Break-Even time

_____

_____

_____

_____

(3) Conditions Yielding Similar Results for Payback Period and Break-Even Time

_____

_____

_____

_____

_____

Part 1

Annual Straight-Line Depreciation _____

_____

_____

_____

_____

_____

Part 2

	Net Income	Net Cash Flow
Expected annual sales of new product		
Expected annual costs of new product		
Direct materials		
Direct labor		
Overhead excluding depr. on new asset		
Depreciation on new asset		
Selling and administrative expenses		
Income before taxes		
Income taxes		
Net income		
Net cash flow		

Computations: _____

_____

_____

_____

Part 3

Payback period _____

_____

_____

_____

_____

_____

Part 4

Accounting rate of return _____

_____

_____

_____

_____

_____

_____

_____

_____

_____

Part 5

	Net Cash Flows	Present Value of 1 at ____ %	Present Value of Net Cash Flows
Year 1			
Year 2			
Year 3			
Year 4*			
Totals			
Amount invested			
Net present value			

* Includes the salvage value impact.

_____

_____

_____

_____

_____

Part 1

Project _____ Net Cash Flow _____

_____

_____

_____

_____

_____

_____

Project _____ Net Cash Flow _____

_____

_____

_____

_____

_____

_____

Part 2

Project _____ Payback Period _____

_____

_____

_____

_____

_____

_____

Project _____ Payback Period _____

_____

_____

_____

_____

_____

_____

Part 3

Project _____ **Accounting Rate of Return**
_____
_____
_____
_____
_____
_____

Project _____ **Accounting Rate of Return**
_____
_____
_____
_____
_____
_____

Part 4

Project _____ **Present Value of Net Cash Flows**

	Net Cash Flows	Present Value of Annuity of 1 at ____ %	Present Value of Net Cash Flows

Project _____ **Present Value of Net Cash Flows**

	Net Cash Flows	Present Value of Annuity of 1 at ____ %	Present Value of Net Cash Flows

Part 5

Management Recommendation: _____

_____

_____

_____

_____

_____

_____

_____

_____

Problem C-3A or C-3B

Part 1

Results Using Straight-Line

	(a) Income Before Deprec.	(b) Straight-Line Deprec.	(c) Taxable Income (a) - (b)	(d) __% Income Taxes	(e) Net Cash Flows (a) - (d)
Year 1					
Year 2					
Year 3					
Year 4					
Year 5					
Year 6					

Part 2

Results Using MACRS

	(a) Income Before Deprec.	(b) MACRS Deprec.	(c) Taxable Income (a) - (b)	(d) __% Income Taxes	(e) Net Cash Flows (a) - (d)
Year 1					
Year 2					
Year 3					
Year 4					
Year 5					
Year 6					

Part 3

NPV Using Straight-Line

	Net Cash Flows	Present Value of 1 at ____ %	Present Value of Net Cash Flows
Year 1			
Year 2			
Year 3			
Year 4			
Year 5			
Year 6			
Totals			
Amount invested			
Net present value			

Part 4

NPV Using MACRS

	Net Cash Flows	Present Value of 1 at ____ %	Present Value of Net Cash Flows
Year 1			
Year 2			
Year 3			
Year 4			
Year 5			
Year 6			
Totals			
Amount invested			
Net present value			

Part 5

Explanation of MACRS Implications for NPV

_____
_____
_____
_____
_____
_____
_____
_____

COMPUTING NET CASH FLOWS FROM NET INCOME

	Net income	Cash flows
Sales..	$ 300,000	$
Materials, labor, & overhead............................	(160,000)	
Depreciation...	(40,000)	
Selling and administrative...............................	(30,000)	
Pretax income..	70,000	
Income taxes (30%)..	(21,000)	
Net income...	$ 49,000	
Net cash flows..		$

1. Payback period _____

_____

_____

_____

_____

_____

_____

_____

2. Accounting rate of return _____

_____

_____

_____

_____

_____

_____

Part 1

_____
_____
_____
_____
_____
_____
_____
_____
_____
_____
_____
_____

Part 2—Fast Forward

_____
_____
_____
_____
_____
_____
_____
_____

Part 1

Present Value Computation

_____
_____
_____
_____
_____
_____
_____
_____
_____

Part 2

Estimation Errors and Investment Project Evaluation

_____
_____
_____
_____
_____
_____
_____
_____
_____
_____
_____

MEMORANDUM

TO:

FROM:

DATE:

SUBJECT: Evaluating Capital Investment Opportunities

Name _____

Project Identification

_____
_____
_____
_____
_____
_____
_____

Qualitative Factors in Management's Decision

_____
_____
_____
_____
_____
_____
_____
_____
_____
_____
_____
_____
_____
_____
_____
_____

(1) _____

(2) _____

(3) _____

(4) _____

Quick Study D-2

Annual Rate of Interest

_____

_____

_____

_____

Quick Study D-3

Years of Investment

_____

_____

_____

_____

Quick Study D-4

Value of Investment

_____

_____

_____

_____

Quick Study D-5

Cash Proceeds at Liquidation

_____

_____

_____

_____

Quick Study D-6

Amount Willing to Pay for Project

_____

_____

_____

_____

Future Value of Retirement Program

_____
_____
_____

Exercise D-1

Years Until Payment

_____
_____
_____

Exercise D-2

Rate of Interest to be Earned

_____
_____
_____

Exercise D-3

Rate of Interest to be Earned

_____
_____
_____

Exercise D-4

Number of Annual Payments to be Received

_____
_____
_____

Exercise D-5

Rate of Interest to be Earned

_____
_____
_____

Number of Annual Investments

_____
_____
_____

Exercise D-7

Cost (Present Value) of Automobile

_____
_____
_____
_____
_____

Exercise D-8

Cash Proceeds from Bond

_____
_____
_____
_____
_____
_____

Exercise D-9

Present Value of Investment

_____
_____
_____

(1) _____
_____
_____

(2) _____
_____
_____

Exercise D-11

Amount Borrowed _____
_____
_____
_____
_____

Exercise D-12

	Single Future Payment	*Number of Periods*	*Interest Rate*	*Table B.1 Value*	*Amount Borrowed*
(a)					
(b)					
(c)					
(d)					
(e)					
(f)					

(1) First Annuity:

_____
_____
_____
_____
_____
_____
_____
_____

Second Annuity:

_____
_____
_____
_____
_____
_____
_____
_____

(2) First Annuity:

_____
_____
_____
_____

Second Annuity:

_____
_____
_____
_____
_____

Exercise D-14

(1) Present Value of Annuity

_____
_____
_____

(2) Present Value of Annuity

_____
_____
_____

(3) Present Value of Annuity

_____
_____
_____
_____

Total Accumulated in the Account _____

_____

_____

_____

_____

_____

Exercise D-16

Total Accumulated in the Account _____

_____

_____

_____

_____

_____

Exercise D-17

Future Value of the Fund _____

_____

_____

_____

Exercise D-18

Future Value of Investment _____

_____

_____

_____

Exercise D-19

	Present or Future Value	Single Amount or Annuity	Relevant Table	Interest Rate	Number of Periods
(a)					
(b)					
(c)					
(d)					